# Oxford KS3 Science

# Activate
*Question • Progress • Succeed*

## Physics

## Teacher Handbook

Nicky Thomas

**Assessment Editor**
Dr Andrew Chandler-Grevatt

OXFORD
UNIVERSITY PRESS

# Contents

| | |
|---|---|
| Introduction | IV |
| Assessment and progress | VI |
| Differentiation and skills | VIII |
| Kerboodle | X |

## Working Scientifically

| | | | | | |
|---|---|---|---|---|---|
| 1.1 | Asking scientific questions | 2 | 1.4 | Analysing data | 8 |
| 1.2 | Planning investigations | 4 | 1.5 | Evaluating data | 10 |
| 1.3 | Recording data | 6 | | | |

## Physics P1

**Physics P1 Unit Opener** — 12

### Chapter 1: Forces

| | | | | | |
|---|---|---|---|---|---|
| 1.1 | Introduction to forces | 14 | 1.4 | Forces at a distance | 20 |
| 1.2 | Squashing and stretching | 16 | 1.5 | Balanced and unbalanced | 22 |
| 1.3 | Drag forces and friction | 18 | 1.6 | P1 Chapter 1 Checkpoint | 24 |

### Chapter 2: Sound

| | | | | | |
|---|---|---|---|---|---|
| 2.1 | Waves | 26 | 2.4 | Detecting sound | 32 |
| 2.2 | Sound and energy transfer | 28 | 2.5 | Echoes and ultrasound | 34 |
| 2.3 | Loudness and pitch | 30 | 2.6 | P1 Chapter 2 Checkpoint | 36 |

### Chapter 3: Light

| | | | | | |
|---|---|---|---|---|---|
| 3.1 | Light | 38 | 3.4 | The eye and the camera | 44 |
| 3.2 | Reflection | 40 | 3.5 | Colour | 46 |
| 3.3 | Refraction | 42 | 3.6 | P1 Chapter 3 Checkpoint | 48 |

### Chapter 4: Space

| | | | | | |
|---|---|---|---|---|---|
| 4.1 | The night sky | 50 | 4.4 | The Moon | 56 |
| 4.2 | The Solar System | 52 | 4.5 | P1 Chapter 4 Checkpoint | 58 |
| 4.3 | The Earth | 54 | | | |

## Physics P2

**Physics P2 Unit Opener** — 60

### Chapter 1: Electricity and magnetism

| | | | | | |
|---|---|---|---|---|---|
| 1.1 | Charging up | 62 | 1.6 | Magnets and magnetic fields | 72 |
| 1.2 | Circuits and current | 64 | 1.7 | Electromagnets | 74 |
| 1.3 | Potential difference | 66 | 1.8 | Using electromagnets | 76 |
| 1.4 | Series and parallel | 68 | 1.9 | P2 Chapter 1 Checkpoint | 78 |
| 1.5 | Resistance | 70 | | | |

### Chapter 2: Energy

| | | | | | |
|---|---|---|---|---|---|
| 2.1 | Food and fuels | 80 | 2.6 | Energy resources | 90 |
| 2.2 | Energy adds up | 82 | 2.7 | Energy and power | 92 |
| 2.3 | Energy and temperature | 84 | 2.8 | Work, energy, and machines | 94 |
| 2.4 | Energy transfer: particles | 86 | 2.9 | P2 Chapter 2 Checkpoint | 96 |
| 2.5 | Energy transfer: radiation | 88 | | | |

### Chapter 3: Motion and pressure

| | | | | | |
|---|---|---|---|---|---|
| 3.1 | Speed | 98 | 3.5 | Pressure on solids | 106 |
| 3.2 | Motion graphs | 100 | 3.6 | Turning forces | 108 |
| 3.3 | Pressure in gases | 102 | 3.7 | P2 Chapter 3 Checkpoint | 110 |
| 3.4 | Pressure in liquids | 104 | | | |

## Physics P3

**Physics P3 Unit Opener** — **112**

### Chapter 1: New technology

| | | | | | |
|---|---|---|---|---|---|
| 1.1 | Your phone | 114 | 1.5 | Your sports | 122 |
| 1.2 | Your house | 116 | 1.6 | Your planet | 124 |
| 1.3 | Your hospital – intensive care | 118 | 1.7 | P3 Chapter 1 Checkpoint | 126 |
| 1.4 | Your hospital – seeing inside | 120 | | | |

### Chapter 2: Turning points in physics

| | | | | | |
|---|---|---|---|---|---|
| 2.1 | Discovering the Universe 1 | 128 | 2.6 | Radioactivity 1 | 138 |
| 2.2 | Discovering the Universe 2 | 130 | 2.7 | Radioactivity 2 | 140 |
| 2.3 | The Big Bang | 132 | 2.8 | Electromagnetism 1 | 142 |
| 2.4 | Spacecraft and satellites | 134 | 2.9 | Electromagnetism 2 | 144 |
| 2.5 | Mission to the Moon | 136 | 2.10 | P3 Chapter 2 Checkpoint | 146 |

### Chapter 3: Detection

| | | | | | |
|---|---|---|---|---|---|
| 3.1 | Detecting planets | 148 | 3.4 | Detecting messages | 154 |
| 3.2 | Detecting alien life | 150 | 3.5 | Detecting particles | 156 |
| 3.3 | Detecting position | 152 | 3.6 | P3 Chapter 3 Checkpoint | 158 |

Index — 160

# Introduction

## About the series

*Activate* is designed to match the 2014 Key Stage 3 Programme of Study and to help prepare your students for success in the new Key Stage 4 Physics and equivalent qualifications. Across the Student Books, Teacher Handbooks, and Kerboodle courses *Activate* allows you to track your students' progress through Key Stage 3 using innovative and reliable assessment and learning resources.

*Activate* is also flexible to suit your preferred route through Key Stage 3. The Programme of Study for physics is covered in the P1 and P2 units, making it a perfect match for a two-year course. If you're continuing Key Stage 3 into Year 9, the P3 unit offers consolidation and extension of core concepts through engaging contexts, with plenty of practice in the skills needed for success at Key Stage 4 Physics.

All of the content in the *Activate* series has been written and reviewed by our expert author and editor teams, all of whom have significant teaching experience, and our Assessment Editor is a school-assessment expert. You can be confident that *Activate* provides the best support for the new curriculum.

## Your Teacher Handbook

This Teacher Handbook aims to save you time and effort by offering lesson plans, differentiation suggestions, and assessment guidance on a page-by-page basis that is a direct match to the Student Book.

You can use the Unit Openers to see the prior knowledge required of students for each topic at a glance. You can also use the Checkpoint Lessons at the end of each chapter to support students who have yet to grasp a secure knowledge of the outcomes covered in each chapter. Lesson plans are written for 55-minute lessons but are flexible and fully adaptable so you can choose the activities that suit your classes best.

## Unit Opener

### Overview
The Unit Opener provides an overview of the unit and how it links to Key Stage 2, Key Stage 3, and Key Stage 4 Physics.

### Curriculum links
This table provides an overview of the chapters in this unit, and the Key Stage 3 topics they link to.

### Preparing for Triple Science success
This table provides an overview of the Key Stage 4 skills and underpinning knowledge that are covered in the unit. It also provides details of where Triple Science style assessment questions can be found throughout the unit.

### Key Stage 2 and *Activate* catch-up
This table outlines the Key Stage 2 knowledge that is a pre-requisite for this unit. In the case of the P3 Unit Opener, this section refers to previous knowledge covered in P1 and P2. This can be assessed using the automarked Unit Pre-test on Kerboodle.

For each statement, a suggestion for how you can help students to catch up is provided, as well as an index of which topic each statement links to.

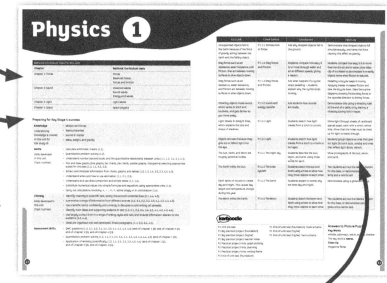

# Lesson

### Curriculum links
This indicates the area of the 2014 Programme of Study this lesson covers. A Working Scientifically link is also given for most lessons. This indicates the main Working Scientifically focus of the lesson.

### Differentiated outcomes
This table summarises the possible lesson outcomes. They are ramped and divided into three ability bands. Levels for each outcome are given in brackets. The three ability bands are explained on the following page.

An indication of where each outcome is covered is given in the checkpoint column, helping you to monitor progress through the lesson.

### Maths and Literacy
These boxes provide suggestions of how Maths and Literacy skills can be developed in the lesson. They also indicate when a Maths or Literacy activity is given in the Student Book.

Maths and Literacy skills are ramped through *Activate*. A Progression Grid and Progress Tasks are supplied on Kerboodle.

### Assessing Pupil Progress (APP)
Opportunities for integration of APP (based on the 2009 APP framework) are included in the APP box.

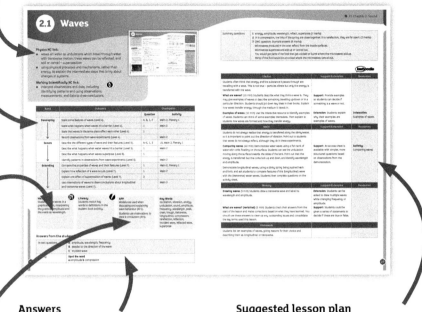

### Answers
Answers to the Student Book activities and questions can be found here. For Quality of Written Communication (QWC) questions, only the correct scientific points for marking are given. When marking these questions, attention needs to be given to the quality of the writing in the answer.

### Suggested lesson plan
A suggested route through the lesson is provided, including ideas for support, extension, and homework. The right-hand column indicates where Kerboodle resources are available.

Each lesson plan is supported by an editable Lesson Plan and Presentation on Kerboodle.

# Checkpoint Lesson

### Overview
The Checkpoint Lesson is a suggested follow-up lesson after students have completed the automarked Checkpoint Assessment on Kerboodle. There are two routes through the lesson, with the route for each student being determined by their mark in the assessment. Route A helps students to consolidate what they have learnt through the chapter, whilst Route B offers extension for students who have already grasped the key concepts.

### Checkpoint routes
A summary of the two suggested routes through the lesson.

### Progression table
This table summarises the outcomes covered in the Revision Lesson, and provides guidance for how students can make progress to achieve each outcome.

The tasks outlined in the table, resources for the Extension Lesson, and detailed Teacher Notes are all available on Kerboodle.

### Answers
Answers to the End-of-Chapter questions in the Student Book.

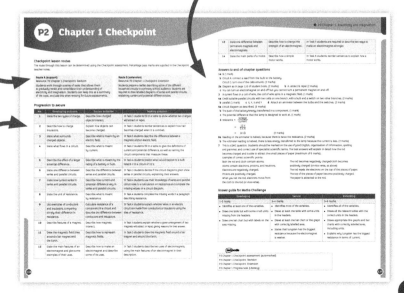

# Assessment and progress

**About the Assessment Editor**

Dr Andrew Chandler-Grevatt has a doctorate in school assessment, and has a real passion for science teaching and learning. Having worked as a science teacher for ten years, of which five was spent as an AST, Andy has a real understanding of the pressures and joys of teaching in the classroom. This stays at the forefront of his mind during all of his work in education.

Alongside his national and international research in school assessment, Andy is a teaching fellow on the PGCE course at the University of Sussex, and is a successful published assessment author.

## Welcome
### from the Assessment Editor

Welcome to your *Activate Physics* Teacher Handbook. The Teacher Handbooks, together with Kerboodle, and the Student Books, provide comprehensive assessment support for the new curriculum.

The new Key Stage 3 curriculum has no prescribed assessment framework. Our assessment model will help your school monitor progress and attainment against the new curriculum, whether you want to continue using levels, or adopt a new model based on curriculum statements. Throughout *Activate*, formative assessment has been made easy, and we have followed a set of guiding assessment principles.

### *Activate* assessment principles

Assessment in *Activate* aims to:

- inform teaching and/or learning directly (have a formative function)
- assess agreed and shared objectives
- provide opportunities for peer- and self-assessment
- provide opportunities for specific feedback to be given to and acted upon by individual students
- provide usable data or information that informs teachers of progress of classes and individuals.

I have been working closely with our expert author teams across all components of *Activate* to ensure consistency in the assessment material, meaning you can be confident when using *Activate* to monitor your students' progress.

## Assessing the new curriculum

The current system of levels will be removed from the National Curriculum. Schools are expected to set their own methods of tracking progress, whilst ensuring students gain a secure level of understanding of each block of content.

The *Activate* assessment model is based on bands; the middle band indicates that students have a *secure* grasp of the content or skills specified in the Programme of Study.

The band working towards *secure* is *developing*, and the band moving past *secure* is *extending*. The bands have been matched to levels and grades, meaning you can adopt a system that works for your school.

| Activate bands | Developing | | Secure | | Extending | |
|---|---|---|---|---|---|---|
| Level equivalent | 3 | 4 | 5 | 6 | 7 | 8 |
| Grade indicator | To ensure grade indicators are up-to-date with KS4 qualifications, this information is stored on Kerboodle. | | | | | |
| Bloom's Taxonomy links | Remembering & Understanding | | Application & Analysing | | Evaluation & Creating | |

# Flexible assessment that works for you

Assessment in *Activate* is designed to be flexible, formative, and summative, allowing you to choose what best suits your students and school. All paper assessments are fully editable for you to adapt to your chosen approach.

All automarked assessments have the option of providing either formative feedback (where students receive feedback on each question and additional attempts) or summative feedback (with one attempt at each question and feedback at the end).

| Bands | Levels | Grades | Comment only |
|---|---|---|---|
| All outcomes are banded throughout this book and in progress tasks. Use this model to assess students on their grasp of curriculum statements and set improvement targets, with a focus on ensuring students are always aiming for a *secure* band or higher. | All outcomes are matched to levels in this book and in progress tasks. This means you can continue using levels with *Activate* content, as well as integrating content you already have with *Activate*. This enables progress to be monitored and targets to be set. | Grade indicators are provided on Kerboodle. This enables progress to be monitored with reference to KS4 qualifications. | Some schools have adopted the 'no grades or marks' approach to assessment, opting for comment-only feedback. Interactive assessments provide comments and feedback to facilitate progression, and all paper assessments are fully editable, so banding and levelling can be removed. |

## The Checkpoint system

At the end of each chapter, there is an automarked online assessment. It will help you to determine if your students have a *secure* understanding of the chapter.

Activities for a follow-up Checkpoint Lesson are provided on Kerboodle. There are two recommended routes through the lesson for students, depending on the percentage they achieve in the assessment. Revision and Extension routes can be followed in the same lesson, allowing students to either consolidate their understanding or attempt an extension task.

Each lesson also includes informal checkpoints to track progress through a lesson.

## Follow assessment with learning

*Activate* includes a Checkpoint assessment system.

1. Use the automarked Checkpoint Assessment at the end of each chapter to determine next steps.
2. Use the Checkpoint Lesson and resources to support and extend your students as needed.

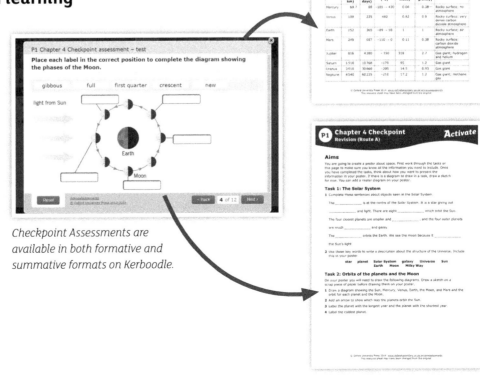

*Checkpoint Assessments are available in both formative and summative formats on Kerboodle.*

# Differentiation and skills

## Maths skills

Maths skills have always been important for physics but with the introduction of the new GCSEs, competence in maths in scientific contexts will be vital for success.

Key Maths skills for physics include quantitative problem solving, use of scientific formulae, and the calculation of arithmetic means. Each skill has been integrated across components in *Activate*, with progress in each skill mapped out. You can view the Progression Grid for Maths on Kerboodle.

The **Student Books** contain maths activities and hints to support and develop Maths skills as students work from their books. There are also Maths Challenges at the end of some chapters, focusing on quantitative problem-solving skills.

On **Kerboodle**, you will find maths Skills Interactives that are automarked and provide formative feedback. Maths questions are also incorporated into other assessments where appropriate, and designated Progress Tasks for Maths will help you track progress.

In this **Teacher Handbook**, you will find maths suggestions for most lessons, linking to the Student Book where relevant. By using *Activate* resources, students will gain plenty of experience in a range of Maths skills that have been identified as vital for success at Triple Science.

## Literacy skills

Literacy skills enable students to effectively communicate their ideas about physics, and access the information they need. Since the introduction of extended writing and QWC at GCSE, Literacy skills are now more important than ever.

Literacy skills are vital for success in any subject but key Literacy skills for physics include understanding meaning of scientific texts and identifying supporting ideas and evidence, adapting writing styles to suit audience and purpose, and the organisation of ideas and information.

The **Student books** contain literacy activities and hints to support and develop Literacy skills as students work from their books. There are also Big Writes at the end of some chapters, focusing on extended writing skills. QWC questions are provided on most spreads, and Key Words and a Glossary help students get to grips with scientific terms.

On **Kerboodle** you will find Skills Interactives and Progress Quizzes that will help assess Literacy skills, including spelling of key words. Question-led Lessons offer an alternative approach to one lesson in each chapter, focusing on the Literacy skills needed to answer a Big Question, and Progress Tasks for Literacy will help you track progress in key skill areas throughout the key stage. You can view the Progression Grid for Literacy on Kerboodle.

In this **Teacher Handbook**, you will find Literacy suggestions for most lessons, linking to the Student Book where relevant. By using *Activate* resources, students will gain plenty of experience in a range of Literacy skills that have been identified as vital for success at Triple Science.

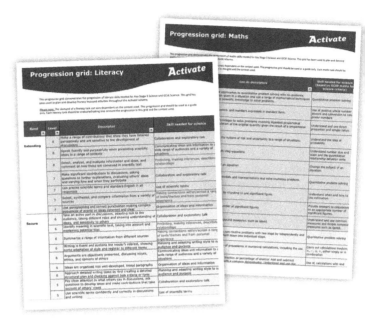

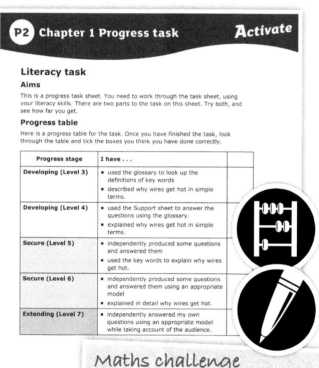

# Working Scientifically

Working Scientifically is new to the 2014 Key Stage 3 Programme of Study and the new GCSE criteria. It is divided into four areas, and is integrated into the teaching and learning of physics. The four areas are:

**Scientific attitudes**, in which students need to be aware of accuracy, precision, repeatability, and reproducibility, and demonstrate understanding of scientific methods and the scientific process.

**Experimental skills and investigations**, in which students ask scientific questions based on observations, make predictions using scientific knowledge and understanding, carry out investigations to test predictions, make and record measurements, and evaluate methods.

**Analysis and evaluation**, in which students apply mathematical concepts and calculate results, present and interpret data using tables and graphs, draw conclusions, and evaluate data.

**Measurement**, in which students calculate results using scientific formulae, using basic data analysis, SI units, and IUPAC chemical nomenclature where appropriate.

Working Scientifically is integrated throughout the **Student Book**, and it also contains activities and hints to help students build their investigative skills and understand the process of working scientifically. A dedicated Working Scientifically chapter is provided at the beginning of this book, and there are also Case Studies at the end of some chapters, focusing on the application of Working Scientifically in different contexts..

On **Kerboodle** you will find Practicals and Activities, most with their own Working Scientifically objectives, as well as Interactive Investigations, Skills Interactives, Skill Sheets and Progress Tasks.

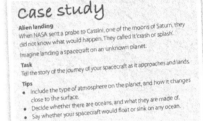

The **Teacher Handbook** lessons often have one Working Scientifically focus in mind for the activities of that lesson. Working Scientifically outcomes are ramped and included as part of the lesson outcomes.

# Differentiation

*Activate* will help you to support students of every ability through Key Stage 3. A variety of support is available, combining opt-in differentiation, ramped questions and tasks, and differentiation by task, as appropriate for each type of activity.

### Differentiation using the Checkpoint system

- The end-of-chapter Checkpoint lessons will help you to progress students of every ability.
- The revision tasks are designed to be used with students in need of support. Teacher input will help them grasp important concepts from the chapter, in order to move from *developing* to *secure*.
- The extension tasks provide an opportunity to stretch *extending* students who require an extra challenge. These students can work independently through tasks provided.

### Teacher Handbook
Lesson outcomes are differentiated, including Working Scientifically. Suggestions for activities throughout lesson plans are also accompanied by support and extension opportunities.

### Student Book
The Summary Questions and End-of-Chapter Questions in the Student Book are ramped. The level of demand of each question is indicated by the number of conical flasks depicted at the beginning of the question.

### Practicals and Activities
Each Practical or Activity includes an extension task. Support Sheets or Access Sheets are available as an extra resource for most Practicals and Activities. Support Sheets offer opt-in differentiation, providing additional support with a difficult area of the task. Access Sheets offer alternative lesson activities where the main Practical or Activity is not accessible by some students.

Skill Sheets may also be used in tandem with Practicals and Activities to provide extra support. These can be found in Additional support on Kerboodle.

### Interactive Assessments
Interactive Assessments are ramped in difficulty and support is provided in the feedback.

### Written assessments
- End-of-Unit Tests and Big Practical Projects have Foundation and Higher versions.
- Progress Tasks each contain two tasks and a progress ladder to cater for all abilities.

# Kerboodle

*Activate* **Kerboodle** is packed full of guided support and ideas for running and creating effective Key Stage 3 Physics lessons, and assessing and facilitating students' progress. It's intuitive to use, customisable, and can be accessed online.

**Activate Kerboodle consists of:**
- *Activate* Lessons, Resources, and Assessment (includes teacher access to the accompanying Kerboodle Book)
- *Activate* Kerboodle Books.

## Lessons, Resources, and Assessment

*Activate* **Kerboodle – Lessons, Resources,** and **Assessment** provides hundreds of engaging lesson resources as well as a comprehensive assessment package. Kerboodle offers flexibility and comprehensive support for both the *Activate* course and your own scheme of work.

You can **adapt** many of the resources to suit your students' needs, with all non-interactive activities available as editable Word documents. You can also **upload** your existing resources so that everything can be accessed from one location.

Kerboodle is online, allowing you and your students to access the course anytime, anywhere. Set homework and assessments through the Assessment system, and **track** progress using the Markbook.

Lessons, Resources, and Assessment provide:
- Lessons
- Resources
- Assessment and Markbook
- Teacher access to the Kerboodle Book.

### Lessons

Click on the **Lessons tab** to access the *Activate* Lesson Plan and Presentations (with accompanying notes).

**Ready-to-play Lesson Plan and Presentations** complement every spread in the Teacher Handbook and Student Book. Each lesson presentation is easy to launch and features lesson objectives, settlers, starters, activity guidance, key diagrams, plenaries, and homework suggestions. You can further **personalise** the lessons by adding in your own resources and notes. This means that the Lesson Presentations and accompanying notes sections are 100% customisable. Your lessons and notes can be accessed by your whole department and they are ideal for use in cover lessons.

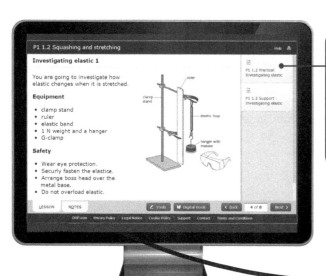

Resources are built into each lesson presentation so that associated interactive content, practical, or activity worksheets are ready to launch.

Every lesson is accompanied by teacher notes that provide additional support and extension opportunities, to fully support lesson delivery.

**Investigating elastic (35 min)**

Students investigate how changing the mass suspended from an elastic band affects its length (and extension). Students record their results and display these on an appropriate graph.

A Support Sheet is available with a results table for students to fill in.

Fully editable resources and Teacher and Technician Notes (offering further guidance on this practical and answers to the questions on the Practical Sheet) are available from the Resources tab on Kerboodle, under Activate Physics > Physics 1 > P1, 1 Forces.

## Resources

Click on the **Resources tab** to access the full list of *Activate* lesson resources.

Fully customisable content to cater all your classes. Resources can be created using the create button.

Existing resources can be uploaded onto the platform using the upload button.

Page navigator shows resources matching to particular pages in the Student Book and Kerboodle Book.

Navigation panel and search bar allow for easy navigation between resources by book, unit, and chapter.

Resources matching every lesson in the *Activate* series are shown here.

The resource section contains:

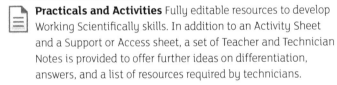
**Practicals and Activities** Fully editable resources to develop Working Scientifically skills. In addition to an Activity Sheet and a Support or Access sheet, a set of Teacher and Technician Notes is provided to offer further ideas on differentiation, answers, and a list of resources required by technicians.

**Interactive Screens** Starters and plenaries to accompany each lesson, as an interactive alternative to maximise student participation.

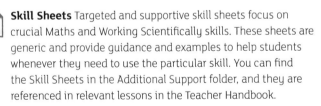
**Skill Sheets** Targeted and supportive skill sheets focus on crucial Maths and Working Scientifically skills. These sheets are generic and provide guidance and examples to help students whenever they need to use the particular skill. You can find the Skill Sheets in the Additional Support folder, and they are referenced in relevant lessons in the Teacher Handbook.

**Animations** Animations focus on explaining difficult concepts using real-life contexts, engaging visuals, and narration. They are structured to clearly support a set of learning objectives and are followed by an Interactive Screen to help consolidate key points.

**Videos** Videos help students to visualise difficult concepts using engaging visuals and narration. They are structured to clearly address a set of learning objectives.

**Skills Interactives** Automarked interactive activities with formative feedback that focus on key Maths, Literacy, and Working Scientifically skills. You can use these activities in class to help consolidate key skills relevant to the lesson. They can also be set as homework by accessing them through the Assessment tab.

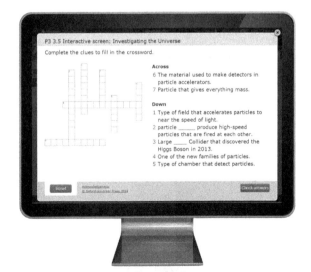

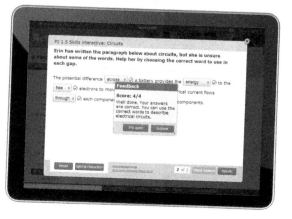

# Kerboodle

## Assessment and Markbook

All of the Assessment material on Kerboodle has been quality assured by our expert Assessment Editor. Click on the **Assessment tab** to find a wide range of assessment materials to help you deliver a varied, motivating, and effective assessment programme.

It's easy to import class registers and create user accounts for your students. Once your classes are set up, you can assign them assessments to do at home, individually, or as a group.

A **Markbook** with reporting function helps you to keep track of your students' results. This includes both automarked assessments and work that needs to be marked by you.

A Markbook and reporting function help you track your students' progress.

Assign assessments with 'practice' in this column if you want your students to get formative feedback on each answer before having another go.

Assign assessments with 'test' in this column if you want your students to have summative feedback, with only one attempt at each question.

## Practice or test?

Each automarked assessment in *Activate* is available in formative or summative versions.

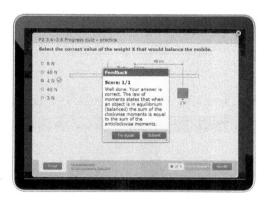

Practice versions of the assessment provide screen-by-screen feedback, focusing on misconceptions, and provide hints for the students to help them revise their answer. Students are given the opportunity to try again. Marks are reported to the Markbook.

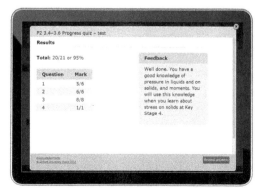

Test versions of the assessment provide feedback on performance at the end of the test. Students are only given one attempt at each screen but can review them and see which answers they got wrong after completing the activity. Marks are reported to the Markbook.

The Assessment section provides ample opportunity for student assessment before, during, and after studying a unit.

## Before each unit

 **Unit Pre-tests** These automarked tests revise and assess students' prior knowledge. Students are given feedback on their answers to help them correct gaps and misconceptions.

## Through each chapter

 **Progress Quizzes** These automarked assessments focus on content midway through a chapter to help you keep track of students as they move through the course.

 **Skills Interactives** These automarked interactives focus specifically on Maths, Literacy, and Working Scientifically skills.

 **Interactive Investigations** These automarked assessments are set in the context of an investigation. Each screen assesses a different Working Scientifically skill.

 **Progress Tasks** These written task-based assessments focus on progress in Maths, Literacy, and Working Scientifically skills. Each task uses a real-life scenario and comes with a progress ladder for students to self- or peer-assess their work.

 **Checkpoint Assessments** These automarked assessments determine whether students have a *secure* grasp of concepts from the chapter. These assessments are ramped in difficulty and can be followed up by the Checkpoint Lesson revision and extension activities.

 **End-of-Chapter Tests** These paper-based tests mimic examination-style questions, and can be used in conjunction with the End-of-Chapter Summary questions in the Student Book to give a comprehensive offline alternative to end-of-chapter assessments.

## After each unit

 **End-of-Unit Revision Quizzes** These automarked assessments are ramped and focus on revising content from the unit. They can be assigned to students as homework revision ahead of formal end-of-unit testing.

 **End-of-Unit Tests** These written assessments mimic examination-style questions. They include QWC, Working Scientifically, and quantitative problem-solving questions and are available in two tiers. The Foundation paper contains *developing* and *secure* questions. The Higher paper has a full range of questions, stretching to *extending*. You can use the Raw Score Converter, available on Kerboodle, to convert scores to levels, bands, or grades.

**Big Practical Projects** These written assessments focus on Working Scientifically and Literacy skills. Students plan and complete an investigation based on a given scenario. The Foundation paper contains *developing* and *secure* questions. The Higher paper has a full range of questions, stretching to *extending*.

## Kerboodle Book

The *Activate* Kerboodle Book provides a digital version of the Student Book for you to use on your students at the front of the classroom.

Teacher access to the Kerboodle Book is automatically available as part of the Lessons, Resources, and Assessment package. You can also purchase additional access for your students.

A set of tools is available with the Kerboodle Book so you can personalise your book and make notes.

Like all other resources offered on Kerboodle, the Kerboodle Book can also be accessed using a range of devices.

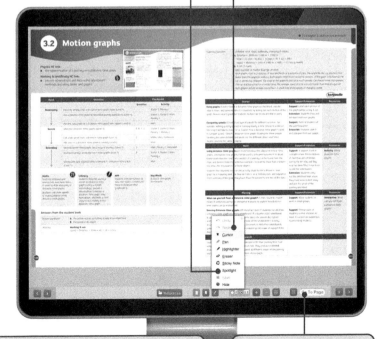

Zoom in and spotlight any part of the text.

Use different tools such as sticky notes, bookmarks, and pen features to personalise each page.

Every teacher and student has their own digital notebook for use within their Kerboodle Book. You can even choose to share some of your notes with your students, or hide them from view – all student notes are accessible to themselves only.

Navigate around the book quickly with the contents menu, key-word search, or page-number search.

# 1.1 Asking scientific questions

## Working Scientifically NC link:
- ask questions and develop a line of enquiry based on observations of the real world, alongside prior knowledge and experience
- select, plan, and carry out the most appropriate types of scientific enquiries to test predictions, including identifying independent, dependent, and control variables, where appropriate.

| Band | Outcome | Checkpoint | |
|---|---|---|---|
| | | Question | Activity |
| **Developing** | State some questions that can be investigated (Level 4). | | Starter 2, Main 1 |
| | Name things that can vary in an investigation (Level 4). | | Starter 1, Main 1 |
| | State that some questions cannot be investigated (Level 4). | | Starter 2 |
| **Secure** | Describe how scientists develop an idea into a question that can be investigated (Level 5). | 2 | Starter 2, Main 1 |
| | Identify independent, dependent, and control variables (Level 5). | A, B | Main 1 |
| | Explain that some questions can be investigated and others cannot (Level 6). | 3 | Starter 2, Main 1 |
| **Extending** | Explain why some questions cannot be investigated (Level 7). | 3 | Main 1 |
| | Suggest examples of independent, dependent, and control variables in an unfamiliar situation (Level 7). | | Main 1, Plenary 1 |
| | Explain in detail why a specific question cannot be investigated, suggesting alternative questions that can be investigated (Level 8). | | Main 1 |

### Literacy
Use of scientific terms when asking questions.

### APP
Students find questions to investigate, and recognise scientific questions that do not yet have definitive answers (AF1).

Students recognise a range of variables from investigations (AF4).

### Key Words
observation, investigation, data, variable, independent variable, dependent variable, control variable, prediction

## Answers from the student book

| In-text questions | **A** independent, dependent<br>**B** control |
|---|---|
| Activity | **Name those variables**<br>**a** dependent: how high the ball bounces, independent: the size of the ball<br>**b** controls: surface the ball is dropped on, height it is dropped from, type of ball |

# Chapter 1: Working Scientifically

| Summary questions | 1 idea, question, questions, data, observations, variables, some (7 marks) <br> 2a For example, how does the temperature of the water affect how long it takes the ice cube to melt? (1 mark) <br>   b It is a question that you can collect data for by measuring the temperature and the time. (2 marks) <br> 3 QWC question (6 marks). Example answers: <br> What is the energy content each food? <br> Because you could measure the energy content to answer it. <br> What is the vitamin content of different foods? <br> Because you could measure the vitamin content to answer it. <br> What type of foods do different animals eat? <br> Because you could watch different animals to answer it. <br> What is the best food? <br> Because it depends on what you mean by best – you cannot collect data. <br> Why do different people like different food? <br> Because you could not collect data to answer it – it is a matter of opinion. <br> Is there enough food to feed everyone in the future? <br> Because you could not collect data to answer it. |

| Starter | Support/Extension | Resources |
| --- | --- | --- |
| **What varies?** (5–10 min) Students make a list of things that could change in an investigation. The investigation could be one they have done or are planning to do, for example, 'How quickly does a drink cool?'. <br><br> **Asking questions** (10 min) Students make lists of questions they could ask if they were given something to investigate, for example, 'Melting ice-cream' or 'Floating or sinking'. Pick out examples of questions that can be investigated and examples that cannot. | **Support**: Provide a list of different things connected with an investigation for students to choose from. | |

| Main | Support/Extension | Resources |
| --- | --- | --- |
| **Asking scientific questions** (35 min) Introduce the idea that investigations need to answer questions, using examples from the starter. For each example, introduce the independent variable, dependent variable, and control variable. Explain that the type of variable something belongs to depends on the question and how it is asked. Work though the activity sheet and encourage students to share their ideas. | **Support**: A support sheet is available where students focus on the ideas, questions, and variables of two stations, instead of four. Try to decrease the number of technical terms used. For example, teachers can ensure students understand that you can choose the values of some variables, rather than stressing the term independent variable. | **Activity**: Asking scientific questions |

| Plenary | Support/Extension | Resources |
| --- | --- | --- |
| **Identifying variables** (5–10 min) Students are given a hypothetical investigation for which they must categorise variables as independent, dependent, and control using the interactive resource. <br><br> **Grouping variables** (5–10 min) Provide a list of 12 variables and a scientific question. Students identify which variables are independent, dependent, and control. | **Extension**: Students make up their own questions based on variables given. | **Interactive**: Identifying variables |

| Homework | | |
| --- | --- | --- |
| Students write down variables linked to things they can investigate in everyday life, for example, boiling a kettle, kicking a football, or getting a seat on the tube. | | |

# 1.2 Planning investigations

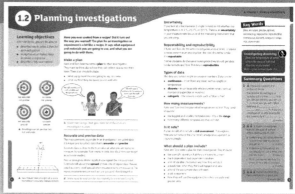

**Working Scientifically NC link:**
- select, plan, and carry out the most appropriate types of scientific enquiries to test predictions, including identifying independent, dependent, and control variables, where appropriate
- use appropriate techniques, apparatus, and materials during fieldwork and laboratory work, paying attention to health and safety.

| Band | Outcome | Checkpoint | |
|---|---|---|---|
| | | Question | Activity |
| **Developing** | State what should be included in the plan for an investigation (Level 3). | A, 1 | Main 1 |
| | Identify data as accurate or precise (Level 4). | | Main 1 |
| | State what is meant by a risk assessment (Level 4). | 1 | |
| **Secure** | Describe how to write a plan for an investigation (Level 5). | 1 | WS |
| | Recognise what makes data accurate and precise (Level 6). | 2 | Main 1 |
| | Describe a risk assessment (Level 5). | C | Main 1 |
| **Extending** | Write a detailed plan for a hypothetical investigation (Level 7). | | WS, Main 1 |
| | Explain the difference between accurate and precise data (Level 7). | 3 | Main 1 |
| | Identify risks in an experiment and write an appropriate risk assessment for an investigation (Level 7). | C | WS, Main 1 |

**Literacy**
Students adopt the appropriate writing style when writing a plan for an investigation; presenting ideas in structured sentences, and in a coherent manner.

**APP**
Students apply scientific knowledge and understanding in the planning of investigations, identifying significant variables, and recognising which are independent and which are dependent (AF4).

**Key Words**
plan, accurate, precise, spread, uncertainty, repeatable, reproducible, continuous, discrete, categoric, range, risk assessment

## Answers from the student book

| In-text questions | A What equipment and method you are going to use and why.<br>B Align the object for measurement with the zero mark on the ruler. Ensure the ruler is straight. Read the scale on the ruler by looking straight at it. |
|---|---|
| Activity | **Investigating dissolving**<br>Independent: temperature of the water<br>Dependent: mass of salt that dissolves<br>Control: volume of water, time allowed for salt to dissolve, type of beaker, stirring or not stirring<br>Plan to include: method of changing temperature, method of measuring mass of salt, variables to control, range of temperature, need to repeat measurements, risk assessment |

# Chapter 1: Working scientifically

| Summary questions | |
|---|---|
| | 1 equipment, accurate, precise, repeatable, reproducible, risk assessment (6 marks) |
| | 2a To get an accurate reading of the height and avoid parallax error. (2 marks) |
| |   b There is an uncertainty in all measurements that produces a spread of results. (2 marks) |
| |   c All experiments require a risk assessment for safety, for example, to reduce the chance of someone falling because of a rolling ball on the floor. (2 marks) |
| | 3 QWC question (6 marks). Example answers: |
| |     The scientific question that they are trying to answer. |
| |     The independent and dependent variables. |
| |     A list of all the variables that they need to control and how they will do it. |
| |     A prediction: what they think will happen and why. |
| |     A list of the equipment they will need. |
| |     A risk assessment. |
| |     How they will use the equipment to collect precise, accurate, and repeatable data. |

| Starter | Support/Extension | Resources |
|---|---|---|
| **Planning** (5 min) Remind students of occasions they had to plan, for example, packing their bags for school. Students state what they need to plan, consequences of not planning, and how they can tell their plan was good enough. | **Support**: Help students by asking questions, for example, 'What did you do next?' or 'What happens if you forget to bring something?'. | |
| **Risks** (10 min) Students state different risks they took that day, for example, crossing the road or jumping the queue at lunch. Ask them to classify the consequences as minor and severe, and the likelihood as likely or unlikely. Discuss whether a severe but unlikely risk is worth taking. | **Extension**: Students discuss why people are more worried about unfamiliar risks, for example, flying compared with familiar risks, for example, driving. | |

| Main | Support/Extension | Resources |
|---|---|---|
| **Planning investigations** (40 min) The activity sheet leads students through structured questions so they come across the main ideas and terminology used when planning. It is important to keep circulating around the groups to ask them why they are carrying out an activity in a certain way. You can help them compare their method or equipment at the time they carry out the activity. | **Support**: The support sheet includes a suggested table of results. The emphasis of the teacher should be to help students understand the ideas rather than worrying about remembering terminology. | **Activity**: Planning investigations<br>**Skill sheet**: Accuracy and precision<br>**Skill sheet**: Recording results |

| Plenary | Support/Extension | Resources |
|---|---|---|
| **Accurate or precise?** (10 min) Students are presented with four sets of data on the interactive resource and must decide whether each set of data is accurate, precise, or neither. Students can then suggest why these uncertainties have occurred and suggest ways to improve data collection. | | **Interactive**: Accurate or precise? |
| **Planning revisited** (5 min) Students look again at their plans and suggest improvements based on what they have covered in the lesson. | **Support**: Demonstrate several ways to collect data, for example, measuring the volume of water using a beaker or a measuring cylinder. Students decide if the data is precise, accurate, or neither. | |

| Homework | | |
|---|---|---|
| Students write a plan including a risk assessment for a simple activity, for example, preparing a meal or measuring how quickly a hot drink cools in different containers. | | |

# 1.3 Recording data

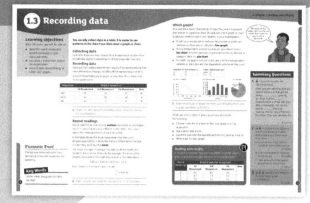

**Working Scientifically NC link:**
- use appropriate techniques, apparatus, and materials during fieldwork and laboratory work, paying attention to health and safety
- present observations and data using appropriate methods, including tables and graphs.

| Band | Outcome | Checkpoint | |
|---|---|---|---|
| | | Question | Activity |
| **Developing** | State an example of how data can be recorded (Level 4). | A | Starter 2 |
| | With help, calculate a mean of two values (Level 4). | | Maths, Main 1, Plenary 2 |
| | Add data to a graph or chart (Level 4). | | Main 1 |
| **Secure** | Describe how to make and record observations and measurements (Level 5). | 1, 2 | Starter 1, Starter 2, Main 1, Plenary 1 |
| | Calculate a mean from three repeat measurements (Level 6). | | Maths, Main 1, Plenary 2 |
| | Present data appropriately as tables and graphs (Level 5). | | Main 1 |
| **Extending** | Explain how to collect and record accurate and precise data (Level 7). | 3 | Main 1, Plenary 1 |
| | Calculate a mean for repeat readings in a range of situations (Level 7). | | Maths, Main 1, Plenary 2 |
| | Design an appropriate table or graph (Level 7). | | Main 1 |

**Maths**
In the student-book activity students calculate arithmetic means based on data given from an experiment.

**Literacy**
Students are required to summarise what they have learnt in their approach to collecting and presenting data to a range of audiences.

**APP**
Students choose the best method to obtain precise and accurate data in their experiment (AF4).
Experimental data obtained are presented in the appropriate graph or chart (AF3).

**Key Words**
outlier, mean, line graph, bar chart, pie chart

## Answers from the student book

| In-text questions | A In a table with clearly labelled headings with units. |
| | B Add them all together and divide by the number of numbers. |
| | C bar chart (or sometimes pie chart) |
| Activity | **Dealing with results** |
| | 3.5, 4.85, 5.3 |

● Chapter 1: Working scientifically

| Summary questions | 1 measuring, instruments, repeat, outliers, mean (5 marks) |
| --- | --- |
| | 2a repeat his reading, use the thermometer correctly (2 marks) |
| | b (2 marks) |

| Temperature of water (°C) | Time to dissolve (s) | | | |
| --- | --- | --- | --- | --- |
| | 1st measurement | 2nd measurement | 3rd measurement | Mean |
| | | | | |

c A line graph, both the variables are continuous. (2 marks)

3 Example answers (6 marks):
The seven elements of a plan from the corresponding student-book spread.
Draw a table for your results.
Include columns for your repeat readings.
Include a column for the mean.

**kerboodle**

| Starter | Support/Extension | Resources |
| --- | --- | --- |
| **Equipment** (5 min) Students describe how to use equipment to collect precise and accurate data. This reinforces the work in the previous lesson, for example, measuring volumes accurately using a measuring cylinder.<br><br>**Using tables** (5 min) Draw a table showing results from a mock investigation. Include incomplete headings. Ask students to identify what is missing and why the missing data is important, for example, missing units. | **Extension**: Students suggest the advantages of using different equipment, for example, ease of use and precision of reading.<br><br>**Support**: Give students missing items to choose from.<br>**Extension**: Give students a context and ask them to draw a results table from scratch. | |

| Main | Support/Extension | Resources |
| --- | --- | --- |
| **Collecting and presenting data** (40 min) Remind students of the terminology (independent, dependent, and control variables).<br>It is important at this stage to introduce ways to display data – line graphs for continuous data and bar charts or pie charts if data is discrete or categoric. Students carry out a straight forward experiment dropping different types of ball onto the floor from a vertical height of 1 metre. Students then measure how high the balls bounce. They prepare a suitable table to record the data and draw a graph to display their results. | **Support**: An access sheet is available with simplified questions. Tables and graph grids have also been partially filled in to help students with complex skills.<br>**Extension**: Students can see if they can spot a pattern, attempt a conclusion, and explain why it is important to display data as graphs/charts (to display patterns). | **Practical**: Collecting and presenting data<br>**Skill sheet**: Calculating means<br>**Skill sheet**: Choosing scales<br>**Skill sheet**: Recording results<br>**Skill sheet**: Drawing graphs |

| Plenary | Support/Extension | Resources |
| --- | --- | --- |
| **'Good' data** (10 min) Use examples from real-life to discuss issues raised by 'bad' use of data, for example, to compare different medical approaches including alternative medicine. The website www.badscience.net is a rich source of examples of misused data.<br><br>**Calculating means** (10 min) Example data sets are provided in the interactive resource for students to calculate arithmetic means, given multiple choice answers. | **Extension**: Students take a question, for example, 'Should doctors prescribe homeopathic medicine?' to suggest what data is needed to answer this question. | **Interactive**: Calculating means |

| Homework | | |
| --- | --- | --- |
| Students collect data at home, for example, timing how long they take to do certain activities. They record the data in a suitable table for discussion in the next lesson. | | |

# 1.4 Analysing data

**Working Scientifically NC link:**
- interpret observations and data, including identifying patterns and using observations, measurements, and data to draw conclusions
- present observations and data using appropriate methods, including tables and graphs.

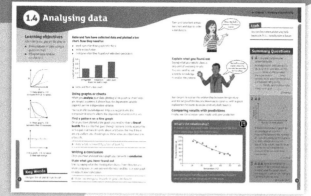

| Band | Outcome | Checkpoint | |
|---|---|---|---|
| | | Question | Activity |
| **Developing** ↓ | State what is meant by a line of best fit (Level 4). | A | Plenary 1 |
| | List what should be included in a conclusion (Level 4). | B, 1 | Main 1 |
| **Secure** ↓ | Find a pattern in data using a graph or chart (Level 5). | 3 | WS, Main 1 |
| | Interpret data to draw conclusions (Level 5). | 3 | WS, Main 1 |
| **Extending** ↓ | Plot data on a graph and draw the line of best fit (Level 7). | | Main 1, Plenary 1 |
| | Analyse data from an investigation to draw up a detailed conclusion, giving quantitative examples in data (Level 8). | 3 | WS, Main 1, Plenary 1 |

**Maths**
Students construct and interpret graphs to find a relationship between data.

**Literacy**
Students select and analyse information, presenting conclusions using scientific terms.

**APP**
Students interpret data in a variety of formats, spotting inconsistencies such as outliers (AF5).

Identify relationships between variables to draw conclusions (AF5).

**Key Words**
analyse, line of best fit, scatter plot, scatter graph, correlation, conclusion

## Answers from the student book

| In-text questions | **A** A line that goes through most of the points and has the same number of points above and below the line. <br> **B** What you have found out, why you think this has happened. |
|---|---|
| Activity | **What's the relationship?** <br> If you double the temperature of the water, the time it takes to dissolve does not halve, it is more than half. |
| Summary questions | **1** relationship, conclusion, scientific, knowledge, prediction (5 marks) <br> **2** Draw a line of best fit, find the pattern on the graph, state what you have found out, explain what you have found out. (4 marks) <br> **3** QWC question (6 marks). Example answers: <br> The graph shows the relationship between shark attacks and ice cream sales. <br> There is an outlier when approximately 65 ice creams are sold. <br> The line shows that if there are more ice creams sold there are more shark attacks. <br> If you double the sales of ice creams, the number of shark attacks approximately doubles. <br> Conclusion: There is a correlation between the sales of ice cream and the number of shark attacks. <br> There is no scientific reason to suggest why this is the case. <br> The shark attacks don't depend on ice cream sales. <br> There is a third variable – the temperature. <br> Both ice cream sales and shark attacks increase in the summer. |

# Chapter 1: Working scientifically

| Starter | Support/Extension | Resources |
|---|---|---|
| **Is there a relationship?** (10 min) Students are presented with a range of statements on the interactive resource, for which they must decide whether the relationship in the statement is likely or unlikely. | | **Interactive**: Is there a relationship? |
| **What stages?** (10 min) Show students data, for example, from a previous experiment stretching springs. Students will find it hard to state a relationship simply. Ask students to suggest the missing stages needed to analyse data. | **Support**: Provide a list of stages of analysis for students to put in order. | |

| Main | Support/Extension | Resources |
|---|---|---|
| **Analysing data** (35 min) Use the activity sheet to plot graphs showing different relationships. Part of this skill is choosing correct scales and drawing the axes. This is a written task, but students could use results from their own experiments. This will increase relevance and engagement for the students. Alternatively, graph axes could be drawn on the floor in chalk and students can demonstrate the shapes of their graphs by walking over the graph area. | **Support**: A support sheet is available where students are given pre-labelled graph grids to plot their data. An alternative source of support is to use the skill sheet for choosing scales instead of the accompanying support sheet.  **Extension**: Encourage students to give numerical examples when describing patterns in graphs. Non-linear graphs are discussed in the extension. | **Activity**: Analysing data  **Skill sheet**: Choosing scales  **Skill sheet**: Drawing graphs |

| Plenary | Support/Extension | Resources |
|---|---|---|
| **Line of best fit** (10 min) Draw a graph with data plotted on it. Ask one student to draw a line of best fit. Other students decide if this is good enough or draw an improved line. | **Extension**: Describe the relationship shown by the graph in detail, encouraging students to give quantitative relationships. | |
| **What does the graph show?** (10 min) Show different graphs and ask students to suggest suitable variables to go on the axes (e.g., height of student and their age or speed of runner and distance travelled). | | |

| Homework | | |
|---|---|---|
| Provide students with further data to practise drawing graphs and ask students to describe different relationships. | | |

# 1.5 Evaluating data (extending)

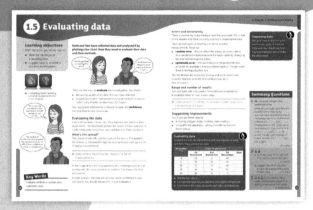

The content of this spread is aimed at extending students.

## Working Scientifically NC link:
- evaluate data, showing awareness of potential sources of random and systematic error
- evaluate the reliability of methods and suggest possible improvements.

| Band | Outcome | Checkpoint | |
|---|---|---|---|
| | | Question | Activity |
| **Developing** ↓ | State how to evaluate data (Level 4). | 1 | |
| | Suggest one improvement to an investigation (Level 4). | 2 | Main 1 |
| **Secure** ↓ | Describe the stages in evaluating the data (Level 5). | 1 | Main 1 |
| | Suggest ways of improving a practical investigation (Level 5). | B, 2 | Main 1 |
| **Extending** ↓ | Compare and contrast data, suggesting reasons why the data may be different (Level 7). | 3 | Main 1 |
| | Explain ways of improving data in a practical investigation (Level 7). | 4 | Main 1 |

### Maths
Extract and interpret information from charts, graphs, and tables to evaluate the data.

### Literacy
Students describe stages in evaluating data using scientific terminology and summarise information from scientific methods.

### APP
Students evaluate information and evidence from different sources, comparing the two data sets and explaining their limitations (AF3).

Students make valid comments on the quality of data and evaluate working methods, suggesting different ways to improve results (AF5).

### Key Words
evaluate, confidence, random error, systematic error, valid

## Answers from the student book

| In-text questions | A The difference between the highest and lowest value of the repeat measurements.<br>B wide range |
|---|---|
| Activity | **How good is that?**<br>a 3rd measurement for -4, 2nd measurement for 60<br>b 0.26, 0.27, 0.50, 0.58, 0.68<br>c The spreads overlap for all the readings, the spreads are large. |

# Chapter 1: Working scientifically

| Summary questions | |
|---|---|
| | **1** outliers, highest, lowest, range, number, data (6 marks) |
| | **2a** Any two of the following: |
| | measure temperature using a thermometer, include a bigger range, take more readings, or use different apparatus to give smaller spread and fewer outliers. |
| | **b** Ask other people to do the experiment using their method to see if their results are reproducible. (3 marks) |
| | **3** QWC question (6 marks). Example answers: |
| | A video camera takes lots of photographs in a short time period. |
| | If they put a ruler against the wall while they were bouncing the ball they could measure height. |
| | They could pause the video at exactly the point where the ball reached the highest point of the bounce. |
| | They could take accurate readings (it is the height of the bounce). |
| | Repeat readings would have a much smaller spread that makes the data more precise. |
| | High-quality data is more precise than low-quality data. |

**kerboodle**

| Starter | Support/Extension | Resources |
|---|---|---|
| **Do you believe it?** (10 min) Provide students with examples of statistics, for example, 9 out of 10 cats prefer a certain brand of cat food. Encourage students to ask questions to judge whether to believe the data or not, for example, who prepared the data or how many cats were tested. | | |
| **Improving data** (10 min) Students look at data from previous experiments, or on the activity sheet Analysing data. They suggest ways to improve the quality of the data, for example, repeat experiments or measure a bigger range of the independent variable. | **Support**: Provide cloze suggestions for students to complete, for example, take fewer/more results, show data on a graph/in a table, take one/two sets of readings. | |

| Main | Support/Extension | Resources |
|---|---|---|
| **Evaluating data** (35 min) Students consider the collected data when they all measure one event, for example, you dropping a ball. Then complete the activity sheet to compare two different experiments and identify differences that make one experiment better than another. Suggest how to evaluate data and the importance of evaluating data carefully. | **Support**: The support sheet offers students a simplified text to summarise when considering differences between two experiments. | **Activity**: Evaluating data |

| Plenary | Support/Extension | Resources |
|---|---|---|
| **What if?** (10 min) Students consider problems if data is not evaluated correctly using real-life examples. For example, ask if a cough sweet will really stop students coughing? Students suggest why it is important that we know if medicines really work and what the side effects are. | **Extension**: This is a rich topic for in-depth discussion, for example, do placebos and alternative medicines work? Is global warming really happening? Does following the five-a-day principle really reduce cancer risk? | |
| **Patrick's claim** (10 min) In the interactive resource, students decide what scientists would want to know from a list of possible options in order to decide whether to trust a claim made by a fertiliser company. | | **Interactive**: Patrick's claim |

| Homework | | |
|---|---|---|
| Write a paragraph explaining ways to evaluate food data information correctly or stating reasons why this is important. For example, nutritional content from a food label; horse-meat scandal; why Mars changed their slogan from 'A mars a day helps you work rest and play' to 'Work rest play your part for England'. | | |

# Physics 1

| National curriculum links for this unit | |
|---|---|
| **Chapter** | **National Curriculum topic** |
| Chapter 1: Forces | Forces<br>Balanced forces<br>Forces and motion |
| Chapter 2: Sound | Observed waves<br>Sound waves<br>Energy and waves |
| Chapter 3: Light | Light waves |
| Chapter 4: Space | Space physics |

## Preparing for Key Stage 4 success

| | |
|---|---|
| **Knowledge**<br>Underpinning knowledge is covered in this unit for KS4 study of: | • Motion and forces<br>• Wave properties<br>• Sound in matter<br>• Mass, weight, and gravity |
| **Maths**<br>Skills developed in this unit (Topic number). | • Calculate arithmetic means (3.1).<br>• Quantitative problem solving (1.2).<br>• Understand number size and scale, and the quantitative relationship between units (1.1, 1.2, 1.4, 2.1, 3.1).<br>• Plot and draw graphs (line graphs, bar charts, pie charts, scatter graphs, histograms) selecting appropriate scales for the axes (1.2, 1.3, 2.2, 2.3).<br>• Extract and interpret information from charts, graphs, and tables (1.2, 1.3, 1.4, 2.2, 2.3, 4.2, 4.3).<br>• Understand when and how to use estimation (1.1, 2.1, 2.3).<br>• Understand and use direct proportion and simple ratios (1.1, 1.4).<br>• Substitute numerical values into simple formulae and equations using appropriate units (1.4).<br>• Carry out calculations involving $+$, $-$, $\times$, $\div$, either singly or in combination (1.4). |
| **Literacy**<br>Skills developed in this unit (Topic number). | • Identify meaning in scientific text, taking into account potential bias (2.1, 4.4, 4.5).<br>• Summarise a range of information from different sources (1.2, 2.1, 2.2, 2.3, 3.5, 4.1, 4.2, 4.3, 4.5).<br>• Use scientific terms confidently and correctly in discussions and writing (all spreads).<br>• Identify main ideas and supporting evidence in text (1.3, 2.1, 2.3, 2.4, 3.4, 3.5, 4.1, 4.2, 4.3, 4.4).<br>• Use largely correct form in a range of writing styles and text, and include information relevant to the audience (3.2, 4.4).<br>• Ideas are organised into well-developed, linked paragraphs. (1.1, 2.3, 2.4, 4.1). |
| **Assessment Skills** | • QWC questions (1.2, 2.1, 2.2, 2.3, 3.4, 3.5, 4.1, 4.2, 4.3, 4.4) (end-of-chapter 1 Q6, end-of-chapter 2 Q9, end-of-chapter 3 Q9, end-of-chapter 4 Q3).<br>• Quantitative problem solving (1.2, 1.4, 2.1, 2.3, 2.4, 3.1, 3.2, 4.2, 4.3, 4.4, 4.5) (end-of-chapter 1 Q5).<br>• Application of Working Scientifically (1.2, 1.3, 2.3, 3.2, 3.5, 4.2, 4.4) (end-of-chapter 1 Q3, end-of-chapter 2 Q8, end-of-chapter 3 Q4). |

| KS2 Link | Check before | Checkpoint | Catch-up |
|---|---|---|---|
| Unsupported objects fall to the Earth because of the force of gravity acting between the Earth and the falling object. | P1 1.1 Introduction to forces | Ask why dropped objects fall to the ground. | Demonstrate that dropped objects fall simultaneously, and name the force causing this effect as gravity. |
| Drag forces such as air resistance, water resistance, and friction, that act between moving surfaces to slow objects down. | P1 1.3 Drag forces and friction | Students compare how easy it is to move through water and air at different speeds, giving a reason. | Students compare how easy it is to move their hand in air and in water. Show video clip of ice skater to demonstrate how easily objects move when friction is reduced. |
| Drag forces such as air resistance, water resistance, and friction act between moving surfaces to slow objects down. | P1 1.3 Drag forces and friction | Ask what happens if a cyclist stops pedalling – students explain why the cyclist stops moving. | Pedalling a bicycle keeps it moving. Applying brakes increases friction and slow the bicycle down. Draw force arrow diagrams showing friction/drag forces in the opposite direction to driving forces. |
| Vibrating objects make sound, which varies in pitch and loudness, and gets fainter as you move away. | P1 2.2 Sound and energy transfer | Ask students how sounds are made. | Demonstrate this using a vibrating ruler at the end of a table, or by placing a vibrating tuning fork in water. |
| Light travels in straight lines, which explains the size and shape of shadows. | P1 3.1 Light | Students sketch how light travels from a torch to a book. | Shine light through sheets of cardboard spaced apart, each with a small central hole. Show that the holes must be lined up for light to travel through. |
| Objects are seen because they give out or reflect light into the eye. | P1 3.1 Light | Students sketch how light travels from a torch to a book to our eyes. | Students group objects as ones that give out light (lit torch bulb, candle) and ones that reflect light (book, mirror). |
| The Sun, Earth, and Moon are roughly spherical bodies. | P1 4.1 The night sky | Students describe the Sun, Moon, and Earth using three words for each. | Show photographs of the Sun, Moon, and Earth. |
| The Earth orbits the Sun. | P1 4.2 The Solar System | Students sketch the Sun and Earth using arrows to show how they move relative to each other. | Two students act out the relative motion for the class, or demonstrate using a lamp and a tennis ball. |
| Earth spins on its axis to create day and night. This causes day length and temperature change during the year. | P1 4.3 The Earth | Students explain in words why we have day and night. | Demonstrate using a globe and lamp. |
| The Moon orbits the Earth. | P1 4.4 The Moon | Students sketch the Moon and Earth using arrows to show how they move relative to each other. | Two students act out the relative motion for the class, or demonstrate using a globe and a tennis ball. |

# kerboodle

- P1 Unit pre-test
- P1 Big practical project (foundation)
- P1 Big practical project (higher)
- P1 Big practical project teacher notes
- P1 Practical project hints: graph plotting
- P1 Practical project hints: planning
- P1 Practical project hints: writing frame
- P1 End-of-unit test (foundation)
- P1 End-of-unit test (foundation) mark scheme
- P1 End-of-unit test (higher)
- P1 End-of-unit test (higher) mark scheme

## Answers to Picture Puzzler
**Key Words**
whistle, astronaut, velcro, eclipse, shadow
The key word is **waves**.
**Close Up**
magazine fibres

# 1.1 Introduction to forces

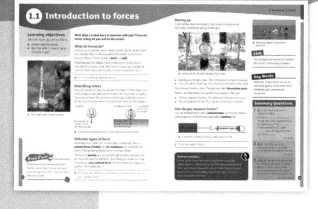

**Physics NC link:**
- forces as pushes or pulls, arising from the interaction between two objects
- using force arrows in diagrams, adding forces in one dimension
- forces measured in newtons, measurements of stretch or compression as force is changed
- opposing forces and equilibrium: weight supported on a compressed surface.

**Working Scientifically NC link:**
- make predictions using scientific knowledge and understanding.

| Band | Outcome | Checkpoint | |
|---|---|---|---|
| | | Question | Activity |
| **Developing** | Identify some forces acting on objects in everyday situations (Level 4). | | Starter 1, Plenary 1 |
| | Identify an interaction pair (Level 3). | 2 | Main 1 |
| | Use a newtonmeter to make predictions about sizes of forces (Level 4). | | Main 1 |
| **Secure** | Explain what forces do (Level 5). | A | Main 2 |
| | Describe what is meant by an interaction pair (Level 6). | 2 | Starter 2 |
| | Make predictions about forces in familiar situations (Level 5). | | Main 2, Plenary 1 |
| **Extending** | Explain the differences between contact and non-contact forces (Level 6). | | Starter 1 |
| | Explain which pairs of forces are acting on an object (Level 7). | 3 | Main 2 |
| | Make predictions about pairs of forces acting in unfamiliar situations (Level 7). | | Main 2 |

**Maths**
In the student-book activity students use units for force.

Students can use size and scale and the quantitative relationship between units in the practical.

**Literacy**
In the student-book activity students use scientific terms confidently and correctly in writing about forces.

Students can make clear descriptions of forces when using newtonmeters.

**APP**
Students can use abstract models to explain forces (AF1).

Students can select appropriate formats to present data (AF3).

**Key Words**
push, pull, contact force, friction, air resistance, gravity, non-contact force, interaction pair, newtonmeter, newton (N)

## Answers from the student book

| In-text questions | A Forces change the shape, speed, or direction of motion. |
|---|---|
| | B For a contact force to act the objects have to be touching (e.g., the air and a car for air resistance) but non-contact forces act at a distance. |
| | C newtons |

# P1 Chapter 1: Forces

| Summary questions | 1 push, pull, arrows, interaction, newtonmeter (5 marks) |
|---|---|
| | 2 The force of the Earth on the apple AND the force of the apple on the Earth OR the force of the tree on the apple AND the force of the apple on the tree. (2 marks) |
| | 3 QWC question. Example answers (6 marks): |
| | The Earth exerts a force on you. |
| | You exert a force on the Earth. |
| | The chair exerts a force on you. |
| | You exert a force on the chair. |
| | These are two interaction pairs. |
| | The two forces acting on you are from two different interaction pairs. |
| | This means one can be bigger than the other. |

| Starter | Support/Extension | Resources |
|---|---|---|
| **What's the force?** (10 min) Students recap on what forces are (from KS2), and individually name as many forces as possible. | **Support**: Show a picture as a prompt for listing forces, for example, forces acting on a cyclist. | |
| **Who pulls harder?** (10 min) Give groups of students a pair of newtonmeters, linking the hooks together. Ask them to predict the readings on each newtonmeter if one student holds their newtonmeter and the other student pulls theirs away. | | |

| Main | Support/Extension | Resources |
|---|---|---|
| At this point it is important that students are clear on the effects and names of forces, as well as what interactive pairs are. | | |
| **Measuring forces** (20 min) Introduce students to the idea of a newtonmeter and measuring forces in newtons. | **Support**: Make sure the forces are straightforward to measure. For example, objects with hooks or straps. | **Practical**: Measuring forces |
| Students measure the force needed to carry out different activities (e.g., to lift a pencil case) and record these in a table. Students should compare readings with each other, explaining differences. For accurate readings, the newtonmeter hook should be in line with its spring. | **Extension**: Students prepare their own table to record results. Students identify several forces acting on one object and explain why they chose these groups, for example, as pairs of interaction forces. | |
| **Force arrows** (15 min) Introduce students to force diagrams and force arrows. Give students three arrows of different lengths cut out of card. Students choose an arrow each time they measure a force, showing the direction of the force and comparing its size. | | |

| Plenary | Support/Extension | Resources |
|---|---|---|
| **Comparing the size of forces** (10 min) Students list at least six situations involving forces and put these in order, ranked by size. This can be done using the list from the interactive resource or non-interactively on the board. | **Support**: Supply a list and ask students to rank these forces by size. | **Interactive**: Comparing the size of forces |
| | **Extension**: Ask students to estimate the size of different forces in newtons. | |
| **What's the difference?** (10 min) If students have measured the same thing during the practical (for example, lifting a book) ask them to compare results. Students suggest reasons for any different results, for example, linked to technique. | | |

| Homework | Support/Extension | |
|---|---|---|
| Provide students with a strong rubber band stapled to the top of a piece of stiff card, and tie one side of the top of a small sandwich plastic bag to the other end of the rubber band. Attach a piece of paper to the elastic band as a pointer. Students use this to measure forces at home calibrating the scale using their own units, depending on what is available to measure, by placing items in the plastic bag. | **Support**: Calibrate the newtonmeter in the classroom and ask students to use it to measure forces at home. | |
| | **Extension**: Ask students to make their own newtonmeter using their own design. | |

# 1.2 Squashing and stretching

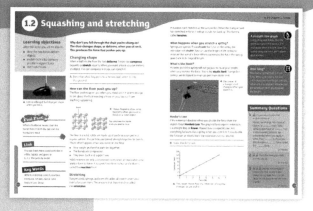

**Physics NC link:**
- forces: associated with deforming objects; stretching and squashing – springs
- force–extension linear relation; Hooke's Law as a special case
- opposing forces and equilibrium: weight held by a stretched spring
- energy changes on deformation.

**Working Scientifically NC link:**
- present observations and data using appropriate methods, including tables and graphs.

| Band | Outcome | Checkpoint | |
|---|---|---|---|
| | | Question | Activity |
| **Developing** | State an example of a force deforming an object (Level 4). | A, B | Starter 1 |
| | Recognise a support force (Level 4). | 1 | Starter 2 |
| | Use Hooke's Law to identify proportional stretching (Level 4). | | Main 1 |
| | Present data in a line graph and identify a pattern (Level 4). | | Main 1 |
| **Secure** | Describe how forces deform objects (Level 5). | A, B | Starter 1 |
| | Explain how solid surfaces provide a support force (Level 5). | 1–3 | Starter 2 |
| | Use Hooke's Law to predict the extension of a spring (Level 6). | | Maths, Main 1 |
| | Present data on a graph, and identify a quantitative relationship in the pattern (Level 5). | | Main 1 |
| **Extending** | Explain how forces deform objects in a range of situations (Level 7). | A, B | Starter 2, Main 1 |
| | Explain how solid surfaces provide a support force, using scientific terminology and bonding (Level 7). | 2, 3 | |
| | Apply Hooke's Law to make quantitative predictions with unfamiliar materials (Level 7). | | Maths, Main 1 |
| | Present data in a graph and recognise quantitative patterns and errors (Level 7). | | Main 1 |

**Maths**
In the student book students complete a maths task using direct proportion, measuring extension for a given force.
In the practical students can plot data on a line graph, or interpret data from a line graph of extension and force.

**Literacy**
Students read and summarise information about applications of Hooke's Law such as toys or bungee jumping.
Students can use their ideas to explain how a newtonmeter works.

**APP**
Plan and carry out Hooke's Law experiment (AF4).
Interpret data, conclusion, and evaluation (AF3).

**Key Words**
deform, compress, stress, reaction, extension, tension, elastic limit, Hooke's Law, linear

## Answers from the student book

| In-text questions | A  The shape of the tennis ball changes/is deformed. |
|---|---|
| | B  Hooke's Law says that if you double the force the extension will double. |

# P1 Chapter 1: Forces

| Activity | **A straight-line graph** |
|---|---|
| | When the force is 3 N the extension is 6 cm and when the force is 6 N the extension is 12 cm. This shows that if you double the force the extension doubles. The spring obeys Hooke's Law. |
| | **How long** |
| | The extension = 6 cm − 4 cm = 2 cm |
| | If you doubled the force the extension would be 4 cm. |
| Summary questions | **1** deform, bonds, support, push, reaction (5 marks) |
| | **2** The bonds between the particles in the solid behave like springs |
| | When they are compressed they push you back up (2 marks) |
| | **3** Example answers (6 marks): |
| | Use a range of springs that stretch differently. |
| | Some springs would not stretch so much/be stiffer. |
| | You would bounce less. |
| | Some springs would stretch more. |
| | You would bounce more. |
| | Different areas of the trampoline could have different springs. |
| | You would bounce differently depending on where you were. |
| | Would be more fun because the bounce would vary. |

| Starter | Support/Extension | Resources |
|---|---|---|
| An alternative question-led lesson is also available. **Changing shape** (10 min) Hand round a selection of objects, for example, sponge, springs to stretch or squash, plasticine, rubber band, balloon. Students explain what happens when a force is applied and when the force is removed. Introduce the idea of the reaction force, how this is formed, and the energy transfers associated with deformation of material. **Why don't you fall through the floor?** (10 min) Place a heavy ball on the table, on a sponge, and in a beaker of water. Identify similarities and differences (weight acts down – table provides support but not the sponge or water). Explain that some support forces seem invisible but are present. Support forces vary in size. Introduce the idea of the reaction force and how this is formed. | **Support**: Students describe what happens; the teacher explains why in terms of forces. **Extension**: Students identify elastic and non-elastic objects and how to distinguish between them. | **Question-led lesson**: Squashing and stretching |

| Main | Support/Extension | Resources |
|---|---|---|
| **Investigating elastic (35 min)** Make two marks 10 cm apart in the middle of the elastic. Loop one end of the elastic from the boss head of the clamp stand. Add the hanger to the loop at the other end of the elastic and measure the new length between the marks. Repeat measurements whilst adding extra masses. Record results in a table and calculate each change in length. Students then plot a line graph of change in length against force, draw a line of best fit, and describe the pattern. This is done as part of the questions on the practical sheet. A partially labelled graph grid may be used to support students and to speed up the process. Introduce Hooke's Law. | **Support**: A support sheet is available with a pre-drawn table. **Extension**: Students understand that extension should be proportional to force and use their graph to predict extension for different masses. | **Practical**: Investigating elastic **Skill sheet**: Choosing scales **Skill sheet**: Calculating means **Skill sheet**: Recording results |

| Plenary | Support/Extension | Resources |
|---|---|---|
| **Bungee jumpers** (10 min) Show a video clip of a bungee jumper. Explain that the rope is elastic. Students explain how to calculate the right length of rope to use, and what happens if you get it wrong. **Stretching experiment** (10 min) Interactive resource that can be used as a recap for the experiment carried out in the lesson. | **Support**: Students describe what happens to the rope in the video and why it helps to keep the jumper safe. **Extension**: Students explain problems caused if the wrong spring or elastic is chosen. | **Interactive**: Stretching experiment |

| Homework | Support/Extension | |
|---|---|---|
| Students research one idea about the application of springs. They must find out why the elastic behaviour is used, how it is controlled, how problems are avoided, and the energy changes that occur on deformation of the spring. | **Support**: Students can be supported by coming up with uses of springs during the lesson. | |

# 1.3 Drag forces and friction

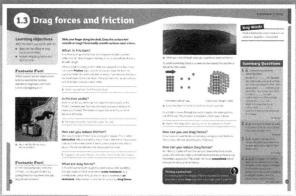

**Physics NC link:**
- forces: associated with rubbing and friction between surfaces, with pushing things out of the way; resistance to motion of air and water.

**Working Scientifically NC link:**
- select, plan, and carry out the most appropriate types of scientific enquiries to test predictions, including identifying independent, dependent, and control variables, where appropriate.

| Band | Outcome | Checkpoint | |
|---|---|---|---|
| | | Question | Activity |
| **Developing** | Identify examples of drag forces and friction (Level 3). | C, 1 | |
| | Describe how drag forces and friction arise (Level 4). | A, B | Starter 1 |
| | Carry out an experiment to test a prediction of friction caused by different surfaces (Level 4). | | Main 1 |
| **Secure** | Describe the effect of drag forces and friction (Level 5). | | Main 2, Homework |
| | Explain why drag forces and friction arise (Level 6). | | Main 1 |
| | Plan and carry out an experiment to investigate friction, selecting suitable equipment (Level 5). | | Main 1 |
| **Extending** | Explain the effect of drag forces and friction in terms of forces (Level 7). | 3, 4 | |
| | Explain why drag forces and friction slow things down in terms of forces (Level 7). | 3, 4 | |
| | Plan and carry out an experiment, stating the independent, dependent, and control variables (Level 7). | | Main 2 |

**Maths**
In the practical students plot and draw graphs selecting appropriate scales for the axes when representing their results.

**Literacy**
In the student-book activity students write up their practical, planning and adapting writing style to suit audience and purpose.

**APP**
In the student-book activity students plan to test a parachute (AF4).

Investigate designs used to reduce drag forces (AF3).

Interpret data, conclusion, and evaluation (AF5).

**Key Words**
friction, lubrication, water resistance, air resistance, drag force, streamlined

## Answers from the student book

| In-text questions | A Friction can stop something moving or it can slow down something that is moving. |
|---|---|
| | B The friction produces the force between your foot and the floor that means that you can walk forwards. |
| | C You need to lubricate surfaces to reduce friction. |
| | D air resistance |
| Activity | **Testing a parachute**<br>Keep these things the same:<br>• the weight of the object beneath the parachute<br>• the area of the parachute<br>• the thickness of the material. |

| Summary questions | 1 friction, rough, force, air resistance, water resistance, air/gas, water (7 marks) |
| --- | --- |
| | 2 Water resistance slows the bird down. (1 mark) |
| | 3 The brake blocks become worn away because of friction between the surfaces. (2 marks) |
| | 4 QWC question. Example answers (6 marks): |
| | Air resistance depends on area. |
| | Bigger area means that more molecules hit the parachute. |
| | The air resistance is bigger with a bigger parachute. |
| | Air resistance depends on speed. |
| | Bigger speed means that more molecules hit the parachute. |
| | The air resistance is bigger with a bigger speed. |
| | The biggest air resistance will act on a large parachute attached to a fast car. |

**kerboodle**

| Starter | Support/Extension | Resources |
| --- | --- | --- |
| **Slipping and sliding** (10 min) Students name surfaces that are slippery/non-slippery and compare them. They list features of the best surfaces to slide on with the idea of reducing friction. | **Support**: Show images of different surfaces (e.g., icy road, wet road, a slide, tarmac). Group these as high/low friction. | |
| **Friction and drag** (10 min) Students list three or four objects (or animals) that move easily through water. The interactive resource can then be used to identify features that change friction and drag. | **Extension**: Students suggest how birds alter their shape to change their speed or stop quickly. | **Interactive**: Friction and drag |

| Main | Support/Extension | Resources |
| --- | --- | --- |
| **Investigating friction** (35 min) Students use newtonmeters to pull a box with masses in it along different surfaces. They record and analyse their results, drawing a graph of their results. | **Support**: An access sheet is available with a given method and results table. | **Practical**: Investigating friction |
| OR | | **Skill sheet**: Choosing scales |
| **Streamlining** (optional practical) Students drop 1 cm$^3$ of plasticine in a column of water. They change its shape and compare how the shape affects the time taken to fall a fixed distance, and link this with forces involved. The plasticine can be retrieved using thread. Students present data in a table. | **Extension**: Students measure the cross-sectional area for each shape. They look for a relationship between area and time, plotting a suitable graph. | **Skill sheet**: Planning investigations |
| | | **Skill sheet**: Recording results |
| Resources have not been provided for this practical. | | **Skill sheet**: Drawing graphs |

| Plenary | Support/Extension | Resources |
| --- | --- | --- |
| **Phonebook friction** (10 min) Interleave the pages of two magazines or phonebooks. Ask students to hold the spines and pull them apart. | **Extension**: Students explain why it is hard to separate the magazines (each page in contact contributes to the total friction to be overcome). | |
| **Shoes for the job** (10 min) Students match features of different sport shoe soles with the surfaces and movement (e.g., football, rugby, ice skating, running, ballet). | **Support**: Students identify if soles of shoes have a large/small surface area, and if they are rough or smooth. Teacher links this to the sport's requirements. | |

| Homework | Support/Extension | |
| --- | --- | --- |
| Students write a short article about how the design of sportswear for athletes, swimmers, and runners helps them move faster. | **Support**: Students list design features of sportswear that increase speed. | |
| | **Extension**: Students link specific features of clothes to how it reduces drag, for example, close fitting or smooth. | |

# 1.4 Forces at a distance

**Physics NC link:**
- non-contact forces: gravity forces acting at a distance on Earth and in space
- gravity force, weight = mass × gravitational field strength (g), on Earth g = 10 N/kg, different on other planets and stars.

**Working Scientifically NC link:**
- present observations and data using appropriate methods, including tables and graphs.

| Band | Outcome | Checkpoint | |
|---|---|---|---|
| | | Question | Activity |
| Developing | Identify gravity as a force that acts at a distance (Level 3). | A | |
| | State that gravity changes with distance (Level 4). | | Starter 1 |
| | With help, draw a table and present results (Level 3). | | Main 1 |
| Secure | Describe the effect of a field (Level 5). | 1 | |
| | Describe the effect of gravitational forces on Earth and in space (Level 5). | 3 | Main 2, Plenary 1 |
| | Present results in a simple table (Level 4). | | Main 1 |
| Extending | Apply the effects of forces at a distance to different fields (Level 7). | | Starter 1, Main 2, Plenary 1 |
| | Explain how the effect of gravity changes moving away from Earth (Level 7). | | Main 1, Main 2 |
| | Present results in a table, ensuring they are reliable (Level 6). | | Main 1 |

**Maths**
In the student book students use number size and scale, and the quantitative relationship between units of mass and weight.

In the practical students extract and interpret information from graphs and tables they have produced.

**Literacy**
Students communicate ideas and information to a wide range of audiences by writing holiday brochures for different planets for homework.

Students collaborate and use exploratory talk when they present ideas for the Olympics in Space.

**APP**
Use an abstract model of forces to explain gravitational force (AF1).

When doing the practical, repeat sets of observations or measurements where appropriate, selecting suitable ranges and intervals (AF4).

Interpret data from the Gravity cups practical, recognising obvious inconsistencies (AF5).

**Key Words**
magnetic force, electrostatic force, field, weight, mass, kilogram (kg), gravitational field strength

## Answers from the student book

| In-text questions | **A** magnetic forces, electrostatic forces, and gravitational forces/gravity |
| | **B** A field is a region where something experiences a force. It doesn't have to be touching the thing to produce the force. |
| | **C** Mass is measured in kg, weight is measured in newtons. |
| Activity | **Units of mass**<br>**a** 2000 g  **b** 3500 g  **c** 400 g  **d** 4.7 kg  **e** 0.25 kg |

P1 Chapter 1: Forces

| Summary questions | 1 mass, electrostatic, magnetic, force, newtons, mass, kilograms (7 marks) |
| --- | --- |
| | 2 The gravitational field on Jupiter is bigger. Weight increases with gravity. Mass does not change. (3 marks) |
| | 3 Gravity gets weaker. (1 mark) |
| | 4 Example answers (6 marks): |
| | Events that involve throwing something a distance would produce new records, javelin/shot put/hammer, Because the gravitational field strength is less, Events that involve lifting things would produce new records, weightlifting, Because the gravitational field strength is less, Objects will travel further before they hit the ground, Events that are affected by air/water resistance would not be affected, cycling/swimming |

| Starter | Support/Extension | Resources |
| --- | --- | --- |
| **The levitating paperclip and spinning pepperoni** (10 min) Students list similarities and differences between a levitating paperclip and a spinning pepperoni sausage, naming forces involved. Tie thread to the paperclip, attach thread to the bench, hold a magnet so the paperclip levitates. Suspend a pepperoni sausage from a clamp stand using thread. Hold an electrostatically charged balloon near the pepperoni sausage – it turns. Although this does not involve gravity, this can show how forces get weaker with distance. | **Support**: Demonstrate the scenarios and ask students which non-contact force was used. **Extension**: Students explain what happens if the other pole of the magnet faces the paperclip, or different materials are moved between the magnet and paperclip. | |
| **Contact and non-contact forces** (10 min) Students group forces given on the interactive resource into contact and non-contact forces as a recap and introduction to this lesson. | | **Interactive**: Contact and non-contact forces |

| Main | Support/Extension | Resources |
| --- | --- | --- |
| **Gravity cups** (25 min) Prepare sealed containers (e.g., drinking chocolate containers) by placing different masses of sand in each to represent different celestial bodies. For example, 100 g for Earth, 17 g for the Moon, 270 g for Jupiter, 38 g for Mars, and 120 g for Saturn. Students weigh the containers, and use $W = mg$ to decide on which planet/Moon the container would weigh that amount. Students present data in a table. It is extremely important at this stage to distinguish between g (gravitational field strength) and g (for grams). | **Support**: A support sheet is available with a pre-drawn table for results, and a step-by-step guide to work out the identity of each station. **Extension**: Students explain why the mass of the container varies. | **Practical**: Gravity cups |
| **A meal on the Moon** (15 min) Provide a graph showing mass ($x$-axis) against weight on the Moon ($y$-axis). Students weigh items of food and use this and the graph to calculate the weight of each food on the Moon. | **Support**: Students explain if an astronaut gains or loses mass if their meal weighs less on the Moon. | |

| Plenary | Support/Extension | Resources |
| --- | --- | --- |
| **Match the weight** (5 min) Provide a list of 5 masses (and 5 equivalent weights) on the Earth and on the Moon. Students link the correct masses and weights. | **Support**: Present data for one mass at a time. **Extension**: Students use the idea of gravity and weight to explain their answer. | |
| **Olympics in space** (5 min) Ask students to compare an astronaut doing sport on the Earth and on the Moon (wearing the same clothes) – long jump, high jump, basketball, and so on. | | |

| Homework | Support/Extension | |
| --- | --- | --- |
| Write a holiday brochure for a trip to another planet. Explain what the conditions would be like, and how to prepare for the trip. | **Support**: Provide summary data about a specific planet (temperature, atmosphere, surface, distance). **Extension**: There is scope for a detailed discussion linking the conditions and preparations needed. | |
| An alternative WebQuest homework activity is also available on Kerboodle where students research the International Space Station. | | **WebQuest**: International Space Station |

# 1.5 Balanced and unbalanced

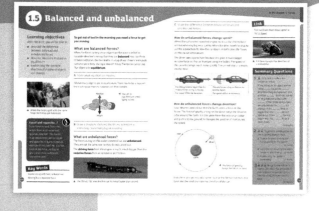

**Physics NC link:**
- using force arrows in diagrams, adding forces in one dimension, balanced and unbalanced forces
- forces being needed to cause objects to stop or start moving, or to change their speed or direction of motion (qualitative only)
- change depending on direction of force and its size
- opposing forces and equilibrium: weight held by a stretched spring or supported on a compressed surface.

**Working Scientifically NC link:**
- present observations and data using appropriate methods, including tables and graphs.

| Band | Outcome | Checkpoint | |
|---|---|---|---|
| | | Question | Activity |
| **Developing** | Identify familiar situations of balanced and unbalanced forces (Level 4). | 1 | |
| | Define equilibrium (Level 4). | A | |
| | Identify when the speed or direction of motion of an object changes (Level 4). | | Main 1, Starter 1 |
| | Present observations in a table with help (Level 3). | | Main 1 |
| **Secure** | Describe the difference between balanced and unbalanced forces (Level 6). | C | Main 1, Plenary 1 |
| | Describe situations that are in equilibrium (Level 5). | B | |
| | Explain why the speed or direction of motion of objects can change (Level 6). | 2 | Starter 2 |
| | Present observations in a table including force arrow drawings (Level 6). | B | Main 1 |
| **Extending** | Explain the difference between balanced and unbalanced forces (Level 7). | 2 | |
| | Describe a range of situations that are in equilibrium (Level 7). | B | Main 1 |
| | Explain why the speed or direction of motion of objects can change using force arrows (Level 7). | | Main 1 |
| | Predict and present changes in observations for unfamiliar situations (Level 7). | | Main 1 |

**Maths**
In the student-book activity students use proportion when estimating force arrows.
In the practical activity students can carry out calculations involving +, −, ×, ÷, either singly or in combination.

**Literacy**
Students make connections within/across a range of texts when reading an account of Newton's work on forces.

**APP**
Use abstract ideas such as force arrows to explain how resultant forces affect motion (AF1).
Plan and use investigative approaches to compare forces (AF4).

**Key Words**
balanced, equilibrium, unbalanced, driving force, resistive forces

# P1 Chapter 1: Forces

## Answers from the student book

| In-text questions | **A** An object is in equilibrium if the forces on it are balanced. |
|---|---|
| | **B** Diagram of mass with arrow pointing up labelled 'tension' and the same size arrow pointing down labelled 'weight'. |
| | **C** Balanced forces cancel out/are equal in size and opposite in direction. Unbalanced forces are not of equal size/direction/do not cancel out. |
| Summary questions | **1** size, opposite/opposing, equilibrium, balanced, speed, driving, resistive, resistive, driving (9 marks) |
| | **2a** Force diagram with an arrow showing that the resistive force is bigger than the driving force. (1 mark) |
| | **b** Arrow pointing backwards labelled resistive, arrow pointing forwards labelled driving. (1 mark) |
| | **c** The forces are unbalanced. (1 mark) |
| | **3** Example answers (6 marks): |
| | An object speeds up or slows down when the forces acting on it are unbalanced. |
| | An object is stationary or moving at a steady speed when the forces acting on it are balanced. |
| | Ride will be exciting if there are lots of sections where the forces are unbalanced. |
| | The force of gravity acts at all times so there will need to be a mechanism for lifting people up. |
| | You can use gravity to accelerate people on different sections of the ride. |
| | People will need restraints so that they are safe when they accelerate/decelerate. |

**kerboodle**

| Starter | Support/Extension | Resources |
|---|---|---|
| **Forces and sport** (10 min) Show a short video of a sports activity. Students list what happens as the motion of a person or object changes, for example, the ball was kicked or the player swung a racket. **Changing speed** (10 min) Students describe their motion on a short car/bus journey, explaining how the driver changed the motion, for example, braked, accelerated, turned the steering wheel. | **Extension**: Students identify the type and direction of forces changing the motion. | |

| Main | Support/Extension | Resources |
|---|---|---|
| **Force circus** (40 min) Students identify forces acting on several experiments in a circus, deciding if they are balanced or not, and describing the different forces acting on the object. As part of the practical sheet, students sketch the force diagram for each experiment showing the size and direction of the forces acting on the object. | **Support**: The support sheet provides a pre-drawn table. **Extension**: Students identify the relative size and direction of unbalanced forces, linking this to the motion. | **Practical**: Force circus **Skill sheet**: Scientific apparatus |

| Plenary | Support/Extension | Resources |
|---|---|---|
| **Riding a bicycle** (5 min) Students describe and act out how to change motion when you ride a bicycle, linking the ideas to the forces. | **Support**: Name the forces and ask students to identify the direction, and if one force is larger or smaller than another. **Extension**: Students estimate the size of the different forces. | |
| **Balanced and unbalanced forces** (5 min) Interactive resource where students sort statements describing the motion of a football being kicked into balanced or unbalanced forces. | | **Interactive**: Balanced and unbalanced forces |

| Homework | Support/Extension | |
|---|---|---|
| Students list different situations at home where forces are balanced or unbalanced. Students name the forces involved in each case, identifying the direction and relative size. | **Support**: Students identify if the forces are balanced or unbalanced. **Extension**: Students name the forces involved and prepare force arrow diagrams. | |

# P1 Chapter 1 Checkpoint

## Checkpoint lesson routes

The route through this lesson can be determined using the Checkpoint assessment. Percentage pass marks are supplied in the Checkpoint teacher notes.

**Route A (support)**
Resource: P1 Chapter 1 Checkpoint: Revision
Students will work through a series of mini experiments and a revision activity that allows them to gradually revisit and consolidate their understanding of forces.

**Route B (extension)**
Resource: P1 Chapter 1 Checkpoint: Extension
Students need to produce a storyboard for a film explaining the forces acting on a car in a car chase (drag/air resistance, friction on the wheels and brakes, thrust from engine). They will need to draw a series of pictures showing how these forces change as the car is moving and changing direction.

## Progression to *secure*

| No. | Developing outcome | Secure outcome | Making progress |
|---|---|---|---|
| 1 | Identify some forces acting on objects in everyday situations. | Explain what forces do. | In Task 1 students should explain what a number of forces do. To help with this, demonstrate objects experiencing the forces listed. Ask students to say what the effect of the named force is. |
| 2 | Identify an interaction pair. | Describe what is meant by an interaction pair. | In Task 2 students consider some basic interaction pairs. Demonstrate examples of interaction pairs and ask students to identify pairs of forces involved. Start with an example of a book, which is the first part of Task 2. |
| 3 | State an example of a force deforming an object. | Describe how forces deform objects. | In Task 3 Experiment 1, students complete sentences using key words to form their descriptions. Demonstrate to students how to deform a rubber band. Allow students to deform sponges. They can complete their own description for this. |
| 4 | Recognise a support force. | Explain how solid surfaces provide a support force. | In Task 3 Experiment 2, students describe situations where objects are supported in the classroom (e.g., a book on a bench) and state what supports the object. |
| 5 | Use Hooke's Law to identify proportional stretching. | Use Hooke's Law to predict the extension of a spring. | In Task 3 Experiment 1, allow students to stretch rubber bands with a newtonmeter. They predict the length when the force is doubled using the support in the sheet. |
| 6 | Identify examples of drag forces and friction. | Describe the effect of drag forces and friction. | Talk with students about the difference between running through water and running on a road. Encourage them to use key words and write a description in Task 3. |
| 7 | Describe how drag forces and friction arise. | Explain why drag forces and friction arise. | To demonstrate this concept to students, you can draw pictures of the particle arrangement of a gas and a liquid. Students are given diagrams in Task 3 to annotate. |
| 8 | Identify gravity as a force that acts at a distance. | Describe the effect of gravity on an unsupported mass. | In Task 3 Experiment 2, provide students with pieces of paper to drop. They should describe what they observe, then describe what happens to an unsupported object using key terms. |
| 9 | Describe how gravity forces affect an unsupported object. | Describe how gravity forces change the weight of an object on different planets. | Before completing Task 3 students should watch a brief video of people dropping objects on the Moon and compare this with people dropping objects on Earth. |
| 10 | Identify familiar situations of balanced and unbalanced forces. | Describe the difference between balanced and unbalanced forces. | In Experiments 2 and 3 you can demonstrate different situations with balanced and unbalanced forces. Examples given are dropping a piece of paper and rolling a ball across a bench. |

# P1 Chapter 1: Forces

| 11 | Define equilibrium. | Describe a range of situations that are in equilibrium. | In Task 4 discuss with students situations that are in equilibrium. Before writing their descriptions students should annotate the diagrams provided. |
|---|---|---|---|
| 12 | Identify when the speed or direction of motion of an object changes. | Explain why the speed or direction of motion of objects can change. | This can be a difficult concept for students to understand and is best demonstrated physically before explanations are produced. Guidance is provided in Task 5. |

## Answers to end-of-chapter questions

1. Contact: friction, air resistance, upthrust. Non-contact: gravitational force, magnetic force, electrostatic force. (6 marks)
2. **a** unbalanced (1 mark) **b** balanced (1 mark) **c** unbalanced (1 mark)
3. **a** surface (1 mark) **b** height of ramp (1 mark) **c** size, material, and shape of block (1 mark) **d** One of the variables (the surface) is categorical, not continuous. (2 marks)
4. **a** Diagram showing a reaction force up and weight down. The force arrows are the same size. (2 marks)
   **b** When the cyclist sits on the seat it deforms and pushes back on her. (2 marks) **c** unbalanced (1 mark)
5. **a** Measure the length of the spring with no force on it. Measure the length with a certain force on it. Subtract the length with no force on it from the length with a force on it to find the extension. (3 marks)
   **b** A mass of 100 g is a measure of how much force it takes to make it move. A weight of 1N is a measure of the gravitational force of the Earth on the mass. (2 marks)
   **c** The graph is a straight line. This means that if you double one thing then the other thing doubles.
   In this case the graph shows that if the force doubles, the extension doubles. This is Hooke's Law. (2 marks)
6. This is a QWC question. Students should be marked on the use of good English, organisation of information, spelling and grammar, and correct use of specialist terms. The best answer will be organised clearly in paragraphs, linking ideas and reasoning correctly to provide a full explanation (maximum of 6 marks).
   Examples of correct scientific points:
   A newtonmeter measures force.
   A bigger force produces a bigger extension.
   An elastic band would get longer.
   The extension of the elastic band would not be proportional (does not obey Hooke's Law).
   So if you doubled the force the extension would not double.
   The extension of a spring is proportional to the force (obeys Hooke's Law).

## Answer guide for Big Write

| Developing | Secure | Extending |
|---|---|---|
| 1–2 marks | 3–4 marks | 5–6 marks |
| • Describes motion but with little explanation or attention to the text type (blog).<br>• Example points made:<br>Rocket takes off because of thrust. There is gravity acting on the rocket. Some forces slow it down. It accelerates at the start, and again as it approaches Mars. | • Explains motion with some indication they have paid attention to the text type.<br>• Example extra points made:<br>There is a gravitational force on the rocket due to the Earth at all times.<br>As the rocket takes off, it accelerates because the forces on it are unbalanced.<br>If the forces on the rocket are balanced it will move at a steady speed.<br>The spacecraft needs fuel to accelerate away from Mars to get home. | • Explains motion in detail, paying attention to the text type.<br>• Example of extra points made:<br>There is an interaction pair between the rocket and the Earth.<br>In space, if the engine stops it will slow down because the force of the Earth is acting on it.<br>As it approaches Mars, the force of gravity due to the interaction between Mars and the rocket will speed it up. |

**kerboodle**

P1 Chapter 1 Checkpoint assessment (automarked)
P1 Chapter 1 Checkpoint: Revision
P1 Chapter 1 Checkpoint: Extension
P1 Chapter 1 Progress task (Handling information)

# 2.1 Waves

**Physics NC link:**
- waves on water as undulations which travel through water with transverse motion; these waves can be reflected, and add or cancel – superposition
- using physical processes and mechanisms, rather than energy, to explain the intermediate steps that bring about changes in systems.

**Working Scientifically NC link:**
- interpret observations and data, including identifying patterns and using observations, measurements, and data to draw conclusions.

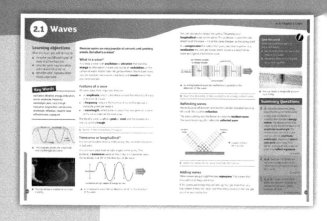

| Band | Outcome | Checkpoint | |
|---|---|---|---|
| | | Question | Activity |
| **Developing** | State some features of waves (Level 4). | A, B, 1, 2 | Main 2, Plenary 1 |
| | State what happens when waves hit a barrier (Level 4). | 1 | Main 2 |
| | State that waves in the same place affect each other (Level 4). | 1 | |
| | Record observations from wave experiments (Level 4). | | Main 2 |
| **Secure** | Describe the different types of wave and their features (Level 5). | A–C, 1, 2 | Lit, Main 2, Plenary 1 |
| | Describe what happens when water waves hit a barrier (Level 5). | 1 | Main 2 |
| | Describe what happens when waves superpose (Level 6). | 1 | |
| | Identify patterns in observations from wave experiments (Level 5). | | Main 2 |
| **Extending** | Compare the properties of waves and their features (Level 7). | 1 | Main 2, Plenary 1 |
| | Explain how reflection of a wave occurs (Level 7). | 1 | Main 2 |
| | Explain one effect of superposition of waves (Level 7). | 3 | |
| | Use observations of waves to draw conclusions about longitudinal and transverse waves (Level 7). | | Main 2 |

**Maths**
Students draw waves in a graphical form, interpreting the $y$-axis as amplitude and the $x$-axis as wavelength.

**Literacy**
Students match key words to definitions in the student-book activity.

**APP**
Models are used when discussing and explaining wave behaviour (AF1).

Students use observations to draw a conclusion (AF5).

**Key Words**
oscillation, vibration, energy, undulation, sound, amplitude, frequency, wavelength, peak, crest, trough, transverse, longitudinal, compression, rarefaction, reflection, incident wave, reflected wave, superpose

## Answers from the student book

| In-text questions | **A** amplitude, wavelength, frequency |
| | **B** parallel to the direction of the wave |
| | **C** incident wave |
| Activity | **Spot the word** |
| | **a** amplitude **b** compression |

| Summary questions | 1 energy, amplitude, wavelength, reflect, superpose (5 marks) |
| --- | --- |
| | 2 In a compression, the links of the spring are close together. In a rarefaction, they are far apart. (2 marks) |
| | 3 QWC question. Example answers (6 marks): |
| | Microwaves produced in the oven reflect from the inside surfaces. |
| | Microwaves superpose and add up or cancel out. |
| | You would get parts of the food that get cooked or burnt where the microwaves add up. |
| | Parts of the food would be uncooked where the microwaves cancel out. |

| Starter | Support/Extension | Resources |
| --- | --- | --- |
| Students often think that energy *and* the substance it passes through are travelling with a wave. This is not true – particles vibrate but only the energy is transferred with the wave. | | |
| **What are waves?** (10 min) Students describe what they think a wave is. They may give examples of waves or describe something travelling up/down or in a particular direction. Students should jot down key ideas in their books. Explain how waves transfer energy through the medium it travels in. | **Support**: Provide examples so students can decide if something is a wave or not. | |
| **Examples of waves** (10 min) Use the interactive resource to identify examples of waves. Students can think of some examples themselves. Then explain to students how waves are formed and how they transfer energy. | **Extension**: Students explain why their examples are examples of waves. | **Interactive**: Examples of waves |

| Main | Support/Extension | Resources |
| --- | --- | --- |
| Students do not always realise that energy is transferred along the slinky/water, so it is important to point out the *direction* of vibration. Point out to students that waves do not always reflect, although they do in these experiments. | | |
| **Comparing waves** (40 min) Demonstrate water waves using a fish tank of water with corks floating on the surface. Students can see the undulation moving along the surface towards the sides of the tank. Point out that the energy is transferred but the corks bob up and down, and identify wavelength and amplitude. | **Support**: An access sheet is available with simpler, more structured questions based on observations from the demonstration. | **Activity**: Comparing waves |
| Demonstrate longitudinal waves, using a slinky spring being pushed back and forth, and ask students to compare features of this (longitudinal) wave with the (transverse) water waves. Students then complete questions on the activity sheet. | | |

| Plenary | Support/Extension | Resources |
| --- | --- | --- |
| **Drawing waves** (5 min) Students draw a transverse wave and label its wavelength and amplitude. | **Extension**: Students can be asked to draw multiple waves while changing frequency or amplitude. | |
| **What are waves? (revisited)** (5 min) Students check their answers from the start of the lesson and make corrections based on what they have learned. You should use these answers to clear up any outstanding issues and consolidate the key terms used this lesson. | **Support**: Students could be given a series of statements to decide if these are true or false. | |

| Homework | | |
| --- | --- | --- |
| Students list ten examples of waves, giving reasons for their choice and describing them as longitudinal or transverse. | | |

# 2.2 Sound and energy transfer

**Physics NC link:**
- sound needs a medium to travel, the speed of sound in air, in water, in solids
- sound produced by vibrations of objects, in loud speakers.

**Working Scientifically NC link:**
- present reasoned explanations, including explaining data in relation to predictions and hypotheses.

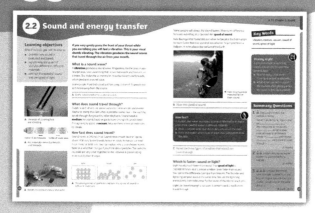

| Band | Outcome | Checkpoint | |
|---|---|---|---|
| | | Question | Activity |
| **Developing** | Name some sources of sound (Level 3). | 1 | Starter 1, Starter 2 |
| | Name materials that sound can travel through (Level 4). | C, 1 | Main |
| | State that sound travels more slowly than light (Level 3). | 1 | Main |
| | Use data to compare the speed of sound in different materials (Level 4). | | Main |
| **Secure** | Describe how sound is produced and travels (Level 5). | 1 | Starter 1, Starter 2, Main |
| | Explain why the speed of sound is different in different media (Level 6). | 1, 2 | Main |
| | Contrast the speed of sound and the speed of light (Level 5). | 1, 3 | Maths |
| | Compare the time for sound to travel in different materials using data given (Level 5). | | Main |
| **Extending** | Explain what is meant by supersonic travel (Level 7). | | Plenary 2, Homework |
| | Describe sound as the transfer of energy through vibrations and explain why sound cannot travel through a vacuum (Level 8). | | Main |
| | Compare the time taken for sound and light to travel the same distance (Level 7). | 3 | Maths |
| | Explain whether sound waves from the Sun can reach the Earth. (Level 7). | | Main |

**Maths**
Students calculate speeds of light and sound using simple calculations of distance and time.

**Literacy**
For homework students write about supersonic travel, linking key concepts and scientific terminology gained from the lesson.

**APP**
Students decide on the best method to present data in the student-book activity (AF3).

Students interpret secondary data to draw conclusions and apply these to questions (AF5).

**Key Words**
vibration, vocal chords, medium, vacuum, speed of sound, speed of light

## Answers from the student book

| In-text questions | **A** vibrations<br>**B** 340 m/s<br>**C** solids, liquids, and gases |
|---|---|
| Activity | **How fast?**<br>**a** Table should have two columns, with headings 'material' and 'speed (m/s)'.<br>**b** A bar chart because one of the variables is categoric.<br><br>**Stormy night**<br>**a** 1.32 km<br>**b** There would be no time difference between seeing the lightning and hearing the thunder. |

| Summary questions | 1 vibrating, vibrate, solids, gases, vacuum (5 marks) |
| --- | --- |
| | 2 The particles in a gas are further apart than the particles in a liquid. The vibration is not passed on so quickly. (2 marks) |
| | 3 Example answers (6 marks): |
| | Light travels much faster than sound. |
| | So the light reaches you first. |
| | It takes about 0.03 seconds for the sound to reach you. |
| | The speed of sound is about 300 m/s. |
| | It would take 0.000 000 03 seconds for light to reach you. |
| | The speed of light is 300 million m/s. |
| | So light is about 1 million times faster than sound. |
| | The time it takes light to reach you is about a millionth of the time it takes sound to reach you. |

| Starter | Support/Extension | Resources |
| --- | --- | --- |
| An alternative question-led lesson is also available. **Sources of sound** (5 min) Students list five sources of sound, explaining how the sounds are caused. They should identify the source of the vibration (which is not always obvious, for example, in the loudspeaker). **Good vibrations** (5–10 min) Students hum with their hand resting on their throat to feel the larynx vibrating. When students are quiet, hit a tuning fork on the bench so it vibrates and produces a sound, then dip the tips of its prongs just under the surface of water to show it is vibrating. Explain that all sounds are caused by vibrations and travel through a medium. | **Extension**: Students describe how the sound can be controlled. **Extension**: Use several tuning forks and ask students for the link with pitch and size, or as a recap on superposition of waves. | **Question-led lesson**: Sound and energy transfer |

| Main | Support/Extension | Resources |
| --- | --- | --- |
| **The speed of sound** (40 min) Explain that sound travels at different speeds in different materials. Students often think (wrongly) that sound travels slowest in solids but in fact it travels slowest in gases. It travels faster in solids due to the proximity of particles making the transfer of vibrations easier. Review the particle arrangement in solids, liquids, and gases. Explain that sound waves transfer energy from particle to particle. You should emphasise the need for particles in sound vibrations (and so sound cannot travel through a vacuum). Students predict whether sound travels fastest in solids, liquids, or gases, then complete the questions on the activity sheet. | **Support**: Sketch diagrams of particle arrangements for students to identify as solid, liquids, or gases. **Extension**: Students make clear links with the arrangement of particles and the transfer of energy by sound waves. | **Activity**: The speed of sound |

| Plenary | Support/Extension | Resources |
| --- | --- | --- |
| **Vibrations and energy** (10 min) The interactive resource involves students linking up sentences to consolidate the ideas of the lesson. **Faster than the speed of sound** (10 min) Explain that *supersonic* means faster than the speed of sound. Show video clips of supersonic objects, for example, Concorde, rockets, Thrust SSC (land speed world record holder), and remind students how fast these objects are travelling (the speed of sound in air is 340 m/s). | **Support**: Pause the video at points where features of supersonic travel can be emphasised. **Extension**: Students can suggest how an observer could tell something was supersonic (the object is ahead of the sound). | **Interactive**: Vibrations and energy |

| Homework | | |
| --- | --- | --- |
| Students explain what is meant by supersonic travel, and how the objects are designed to travel faster than the speed of sound. Students suggest what the implications of supersonic travel are, and present their ideas on the benefits (e.g., being able to travel greater distances or reduce journey time) and drawbacks (e.g., cost) of supersonic travel. | | |

# 2.3 Loudness and pitch

**Physics NC link:**
- auditory range of humans and animals
- frequencies of sound waves, measured in hertz (Hz).

**Working Scientifically NC link:**
- make predictions using scientific knowledge and understanding.

| Band | Outcome | Checkpoint | |
|---|---|---|---|
| | | Question | Activity |
| **Developing** | State the link between loudness and amplitude (Level 4). | A, 1 | Main 1, Plenary 1 |
| | State that frequency is measured in hertz (Level 4). | 1 | Maths |
| | State the range of human hearing (Level 4). | | Maths, Main 1 |
| | Predict how sounds will change in different situations (Level 4). | 3 | Main 1 |
| **Secure** | Describe the link between loudness and amplitude (Level 6). | 2 | Starter 2, Main 1 |
| | Describe the link between pitch and frequency (Level 6). | 2 | Starter 2, Main 1 |
| | State the range of human hearing and describe how it differs from the range of hearing in animals (Level 5). | 3 | Maths, Main 1 |
| | Explain how sounds will differ in different situations (Level 6). | | Main 1, Plenary 1 |
| **Extending** | Compare and contrast waves of different loudness using a diagram (Level 7). | | Main 1, Plenary 1 |
| | Compare and contrast waves of different frequency using a diagram (Level 7). | | Main 1, Plenary 1 |
| | Explain how animals hear the same sounds differently (Level 7). | 3 | Main 1 |
| | Present a reasoned prediction using data of how sounds will be differently heard by different animals (Level 7). | | Main 1 |

**Maths**
In the student-book activity students carry out simple conversions between Hz and kHz, demonstrating their understanding of number size and scale and the quantitative relationship between units.

**Literacy**
Students explain in writing how mosquito alarms are used for their homework.

**APP**
Students use secondary data to make further predictions (AF5).

**Key Words**
pitch, loudness, microphone, oscilloscope, hertz, kilohertz, audible range, infrasound, ultrasound

## Answers from the student book

| In-text questions | **A** amplitude |
| | **B** frequency |
| Activity | **Conversions** |
| | **a** 0.02 kHz–20 kHz |
| | **b** 1 kHz–123 kHz |

# P1 Chapter 2: Sound

| Summary questions | 1 amplitude, frequency, hertz, audible (4 marks) |
|---|---|
| | 2 Human hearing range is 20–20 000 Hz. Dolphins hear frequencies much higher than humans but cannot hear as low frequencies as humans. (2 marks) |
| | 3 QWC question. Example answers (6 marks): |
| | Vocal chords vibrate to produce sound. |
| | Sound waves are made when air is squashed and stretched. |
| | Pitch depends on frequency. |
| | To make a higher note her vocal chords vibrate more times per second. |
| | That makes the frequency of a sound wave higher. |
| | Loudness depends on amplitude. |
| | To make a louder note her vocal chords vibrate with a bigger amplitude. |
| | That makes the amplitude of a sound wave bigger. |

| Starter | Support/Extension | Resources |
|---|---|---|
| **Loudness and pitch** (5 min) The interactive resource asks students to categorise ways to change the pitch or loudness of sounds based on everyday observations and musical instruments. | **Extension**: Students supply their own suggestions to add to the lists. | **Interactive**: Loudness and pitch |
| **Sound rulers** (5–10 min) This can be done either as a demonstration or as a quick practical activity (depending on the number of rulers available). Securely hold the ruler overhanging the end of a bench and twang the free end to produce a sound. Show how to change the pitch by changing the length of the ruler that is overhanging, and the loudness by changing the size of vibration or by increasing the force. | **Extension**: Students investigate sound from rulers independently and state a clear relationship between the variables. | |

| Main | Support/Extension | Resources |
|---|---|---|
| **Wave diagrams** (30 min) Students find drawing wave diagrams difficult so a lot of practice of this skill is essential. Use simple examples, changing one factor at a time to begin with. Keep checking diagrams drawn to make sure students keep wavelengths and amplitudes consistent. Connect the signal generator and loudspeaker to the output of an oscilloscope. Show the shape of the wave for a frequency of about 400–600 Hz. Change the pitch to demonstrate how the wavelength changes and change the volume to demonstrate how the amplitude changes. Students then complete the activity sheet. | **Support**: A support sheet is available as a reference for key terms used during this activity.<br>**Extension**: Students should be able to draw wave diagrams where both pitch and loudness are changed. | **Activity**: Wave diagrams<br>**Skill sheet**: Converting units |
| **Human hearing** (10 min) Explain that there is a limit to the pitch of notes we can hear. Use the signal generator to generate a sound that is audible – the lowest frequency is about 20 Hz. Increase the pitch until students cannot hear the sound (about 20 000 Hz). Be aware some pitches are unpleasant – ask students to indicate noises that cause discomfort – and move quickly through these. Near the upper range students indicate when they stop hearing the sounds. This can be between 15 kHz and 20 kHz. Explain that 1 kHz is 1000 Hz. Older adults may not be able to hear the upper ranges in pitch. | | |

| Plenary | Support/Extension | Resources |
|---|---|---|
| **Changing waves** (10 min) Students sketch a wave on a mini-whiteboard and then draw a louder wave. Check answers, then repeat but ask students to draw a higher pitched wave, and so on. | **Support**: Present a choice of waves for students to choose the loudest, the highest pitched, and so on. | |
| **What do you know?** (10 min) Students write down three things they have learned this lesson. This is a useful chance to check misconceptions, for example, confusing amplitude with wavelength. | | |

| Homework | | |
|---|---|---|
| Students write a short paragraph explaining how high-pitched 'mosquito' alarms can be used to deter anti-social teens from loitering outside shops. | | |

# 2.4 Detecting sound

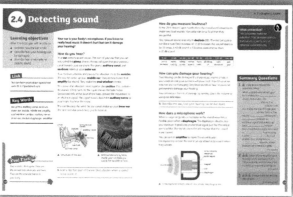

## Physics NC link:
- pressure waves transferring energy; waves transferring information for conversion to electrical signals by microphone
- sound produced by vibrations of objects, in loudspeakers, detected by their effects on microphone diaphragm and the ear drum.

## Working Scientifically NC link:
- evaluate risks.

| Band | Outcome | Checkpoint | |
|---|---|---|---|
| | | Question | Activity |
| **Developing** | Name some parts of the ear (Level 4). | A, 1 | Main 2 |
| | State some ways that hearing can be damaged (Level 4). | B, 2 | Main 2 |
| | State that a microphone detects sound waves (Level 4). | 1 | Main 1 |
| ↓ | Describe some risks of loud music (Level 4). | | Main 2 |
| **Secure** | Describe how the ear works (Level 5). | 1 | Main 2, Plenary 1 |
| | Describe how your hearing can be damaged (Level 5). | B, 2 | Main 2 |
| | Describe how a microphone detects sound (Level 5). | 1, 3 | Main 1 |
| ↓ | Explain some risks of loud music (Level 6). | | Main 2, Plenary 2 |
| **Extending** | Explain how parts of the ear transfer vibrations (Level 7). | 1 | Main 1, Main 2, Plenary 1 |
| | Explain how your hearing can be damaged (Level 7). | 2 | Main 2, Plenary 2 |
| | Compare and contrast the ear and the microphone (Level 7). | 3 | Main 1 |
| ↓ | Explain, in detail, risks of hearing damage linked to sound level and time of exposure (Level 8). | | Main 2, Plenary 2 |

### Literacy
For homework students summarise information from this lesson in a leaflet on the dangers of loud music.

Students extract information from text, and use this information when answering comprehension questions in the activity.

### APP
In the student-book activity students plan an experiment and suggest variables when testing ear defenders (AF4).

Students make suggestions to reduce risks to hearing on the activity sheet (AF4).

Students use appropriate terminology in communicating ideas to primary school children in their leaflet for homework (AF3).

### Key Words
ear, pinna, auditory canal, eardrum, outer ear, ossicles, middle ear, amplify, oval window, cochlea, auditory nerve, inner ear, decibel, diaphragm, amplifier

## Answers from the student book

| In-text questions | **A** ear drum **B** One of: inserting a sharp object, exposure to a very loud sound, wax build-up |
|---|---|
| Activity | **What protection?**<br>Example: somebody wears the ear defenders, another person reduces a loud sound until the person with the ear defenders cannot hear it. Change ear defenders and repeat. The independent variable is the ear defenders. The control variables are person, distance to loudspeaker, frequency of sound. Repeat with different people and compare the results. |

# P1 Chapter 2: Sound

| Summary questions | 1 ear drum, ossicles, oval window, cochlea, hairs, cochlea, auditory nerve, decibels, damaged, diaphragm (10 marks) <br> 2 Not permanent: ear wax, perforated ear drum, ear infection. <br> Permanent: listening to loud music, head injury. (2 marks) <br> 3 QWC question. Example answers (6 marks): <br> Both detect vibration. <br> Both produce an electrical signal. <br> The ear contains bones/membranes/liquid and the microphone does not. <br> The ear amplifies the sound and the microphone does not. <br> The ear contains cells that produce a signal and the microphone does not. <br> A microphone contains magnets and wire and the ear does not. <br> A microphone can be attached to an amplifier and the ear already amplifies sound. <br> The ear drum in the ear is like the diaphragm in the microphone. |
|---|---|

| Starter | Support/Extension | Resources |
|---|---|---|
| **Measuring loudness** (10 min) Display a decibel scale, which indicates safe sound levels and everyday examples. Discuss the display, explaining how loudness is measured in decibels and suggest ways to reduce harm. <br><br> **Parts of the ear** (10 min) As a class, play hangman using the names of the different parts of the ear (e.g., pinna, eardrum, cochlea). As students guess each part, identify where it is within the ear, and how vibrations pass through the different parts of the ear. | **Extension**: Discuss whether the link between decibels and exposure-time is as clear-cut as diagrams suggest. <br><br> **Support**: Students describe parts of the ear rather than naming them. <br> **Extension**: Discuss additional structures in the ear and balance. | |
| **Main** | **Support/Extension** | **Resources** |
| **Detecting sounds** (10 min) Connect the microphone to the input of the oscilloscope. Demonstrate sound waves produced when a noise is made. Explain links between the microphone and ear (if possible, unscrew the microphone's cover to show the diaphragm corresponding to the human ear drum). Recap the parts of the ear and how sounds are measured in decibels. <br><br> **Hearing and how it is damaged** (30 min) If a sound level meter is available, measure sound levels during the lesson. Students complete the activity sheet identifying parts of the ear and then extract information from text to identify ways the ear can be damaged, suggesting methods to reduce harm. | **Support**: Keep to the obvious comparisons between the microphone and ear to avoid confusion. <br><br> **Extension**: Students may choose to add descriptions to their diagram explaining the function of each part of the ear. | **Activity**: Hearing and how it is damaged |
| **Plenary** | **Support/Extension** | **Resources** |
| **Hearing** (5 min) Students rearrange sentences to explain how sounds travel from the pinna to the brain in the interactive resource. <br><br> **How loud was the lesson?** (10 min) Display sound levels during the lesson against a decibel scale. Discuss implications, for example, duration and levels, impact on concentration, the need to reduce levels so instructions can be heard, and so on. | **Extension**: Ask students to give additional details <br><br> **Extension**: Discuss implications in more detail (e.g., varied impact on people, factors beyond control). | **Interactive**: Hearing |
| **Homework** | | |
| Students write a leaflet for primary students on the dangers of loud music and list ways to reduce the harm. <br><br> An alternative WebQuest homework activity is also available on Kerboodle where students research the science of music. | | **WebQuest**: The science of music |

# 2.5 Echoes and ultrasound

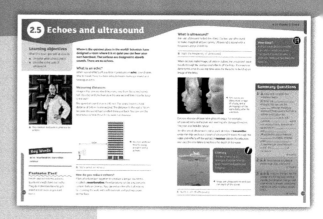

**Physics NC link:**
- pressure waves transferring energy; use for cleaning and physiotherapy by ultra-sound
- frequencies of sound waves measured in hertz (Hz); echoes, reflection, and absorption of sound.

**Working Scientifically NC link:**
- present reasoned explanations, including explaining data in relation to predictions and hypotheses.

| Band | Outcome | Checkpoint | |
|---|---|---|---|
| | | Question | Activity |
| **Developing** | State simply what ultrasound is (Level 4). | | Plenary 1 |
| | State some uses of ultrasound (Level 4). | C, 1 | Starter 1, Main, Plenary 1, Plenary 2 |
| | Suggest reasons why animals use ultrasound (Level 4). | | Main |
| **Secure** | Describe what ultrasound is (Level 5). | B | Main, Plenary 1 |
| | Describe some uses of ultrasound (Level 5). | 1, 3 | Starter 1, Main, Plenary 1, Plenary 2 |
| | Explain, with reasons, why animals use echolocation (Level 6). | | Main |
| **Extending** | Explain how ultrasound can be analysed (Level 7). | 3 | Maths, Main |
| | Explain some uses of ultrasound (Level 7). | 3 | Starter 1, Main, Plenary 2 |
| | Explain, with reasons, different ways animals use echolocation (Level 7). | | Main |

**Maths**
In the student-book activity students carry out simple calculations, substituting numerical values in the speed–time equation to deduce the depth of the sea, given values for speed and time.

**Literacy**
Students extract information from text and apply this information to answer questions on examples of echolocation.

For homework students summarise what they know about echoes, using a range of scientific terminology and diagrams.

**APP**
Draw valid conclusions that utilise more than one piece of supporting evidence, including numerical data and line graphs (AF4).

**Key Words**
echo, reverberation, transmitter, receiver

## Answers from the student book

| In-text questions | A A reflection of sound.  B sounds above 20 000 Hz |
| | C One of: to make an image of a fetus/find the depth of the ocean/find fish/find cancer/destroy kidney stones. |
| Activity | **How deep?** |
| | Total distance travelled = 1.6 s × 1500 m/s = 2400 m |
| | So the distance to the bottom = 2400 m ÷ 2 = 1200 m |

# P1 Chapter 2: Sound

| Summary questions | |
|---|---|
| | 1 reflection, time, distance, absorb, communicate, hunt, image, kidney stones, depth (9 marks) |
| | 2 To image a newborn baby by ultrasound waves reflecting off the fetus, with the differing time taken to detect the echo is used to build an image of the fetus. (2 marks) |
| | 3 Example answers (6 marks): <br> Fix a transmitter and receiver to a boat. <br> Use ultrasound not sound. Ultrasound is more focused than sound. <br> Use a transmitter to send out a pulse of ultrasound. <br> Time how long it takes to hear the echo. <br> Work out the distance. <br> Divide by two. <br> Ignore later echoes as they could be from the sea floor. <br> Characteristics of a reflected wave change dependent on the material it is reflected from. |

| Starter | Support/Extension | Resources |
|---|---|---|
| **Ultrasound scans** (10 min) Show an image or video clip of an ultrasound scan. Explain ultrasound are sound waves too high pitched to hear. The image is created because ultrasound waves partly reflect from different surfaces. | **Extension**: Discuss other uses of ultrasound, for example, in engineering. | |
| **Echoes** (10 min) Students write down three things they know about echoes. Compare their answers to bring out these points: echoes are sound reflections, the echo is the same as the original sound but quieter and heard later, echoes are heard where there are lots of hard surfaces. Make sure students realise there must be a sound wave and a reflecting surface. | **Extension**: Students give examples of echolocation. They may realise that echoes from more distant reflecting surfaces arrive later or that soft surfaces will absorb sound. | |

| Main | Support/Extension | Resources |
|---|---|---|
| **Using echoes** (35 min) Demonstrate that a dropped ball takes longer to fall, bounce, and return to its original height when it falls a greater distance. Explain distances can be measured using echoes, where the ball is replaced by a sound wave. Remind students the signal travels to the surface and returns, so times measured are twice the time taken to reach the surface. Discuss uses of echolocation (bats, whales, sonar, finding flaws inside materials, scanning a patient) and how hard surfaces reflect waves, whilst soft surfaces absorb waves. Remind students that ultrasound is very high frequency (above 20 000 Hz). Students then complete tasks and questions on the activity sheet. | **Support**: An access sheet is available with simpler text and supporting comprehension questions. <br> **Extension**: Students can evaluate the safety of medical scans that use ultrasound. | **Activity**: Using echoes |

| Plenary | Support/Extension | Resources |
|---|---|---|
| **Ultrasound and echoes** (5 min) Interactive resource in which student link together sentences on ultrasound, echoes, and their uses. | **Extension**: Students can suggest further halves of sentences for others in the class to match. | **Interactive**: Ultrasound and echoes |
| **Ultrasound or echoes** (10 min) Present some applications and ask students to identify the ones which use echoes (sonar, echolocation) and the ones which use ultrasound (medical scans). | **Support**: Stress whether the sound can be heard in each application. <br> **Extension**: Students prepare lists of uses of echoes/ultrasound. | |

| Homework | | |
|---|---|---|
| Students prepare a sheet summarising what they have learned about ultrasound and echoes using diagrams and text to explain their ideas. | | |

# P1 Chapter 2 Checkpoint

## Checkpoint lesson routes

The route through this lesson can be determined using the Checkpoint assessment. Percentage pass marks are supplied in the Checkpoint teacher notes.

**Route A (support)**
Resources: P1 Chapter 2 Checkpoint Revision
Students will work through a revision activity that allows them to gradually revisit and consolidate their understanding of sound and waves.

**Route B (extension)**
Resources: P1 Chapter 2 Checkpoint Extension
Students will be asked to prepare a poster explaining how people hear music at a concert in detail. They will use scientific language to include full explanations accompanied by diagrams.

## Progression to *secure*

| No. | Developing outcome | Secure outcome | Making progress |
|---|---|---|---|
| 1 | State some features of waves. | Describe the different types of waves and their features. | Demonstrating longitudinal and transverse waves using a slinky spring will help students to visualise the two types of waves. Students can then begin to complete Task 1. |
| 2 | State what happens when a wave hits a barrier. | Describe what happens when water waves hit a barrier. | Using a tray of water, remind students what happens when waves hit a barrier. Students are then able to start the cloze activity in Task 2. |
| 3 | State that waves in the same place affect each other. | Describe what happens when waves superpose. | The tray of water can again be used for demonstration. Students can complete the sentence about superposition in the cloze activity in Task 2. |
| 4 | Name some sources of sound. | Describe how sound is produced and travels. | Students complete a description using key words of how sound is produced in the cloze activity in Task 2. |
| 5 | Name materials that sound can travel through. | Explain why the speed of sound is different in different media. | Before completing the cloze activity in Task 3, students should draw diagrams of particle arrangements in the boxes provided. |
| 6 | State that sound travels slower than light. | Contrast the speed of sound and the speed of light. | Show students video clips of lightning and thunder reaching the observer at different times. |
| 7 | State the link between loudness and amplitude. | Describe the link between loudness and amplitude. | Demonstrate the link between loudness and amplitude using an oscilloscope, signal generator, and loudspeaker if available. Students often confuse amplitude with wavelength. Students should write a full description of the link in Task 4. |
| 8 | State that frequency is measured in hertz. | Describe the link between pitch and frequency. | Demonstrate the link between pitch and frequency using an oscilloscope, signal generator, and loudspeaker. Students can complete descriptions in Task 4. |
| 9 | State the range of human hearing. | State the range of human hearing and describe how it differs from the range of hearing in animals. | A basic graphical representation of hearing ranges is given in the support sheet. Students can then complete Task 5. |
| 10 | Name some parts of the ear. | Describe how the ear works. | In Task 6, students can annotate a diagram of the ear and describe the role of each part. |
| 11 | State some ways that hearing can be damaged. | Describe how your hearing can be damaged. | In Task 6, students first complete a table of parts of the ear and how they can be damaged. They can then use this information to write a full paragraph. |
| 12 | State that a microphone detects sound. | Describe how a microphone detects sound. | Students need to consider the sequence to write a full description. Guidance is provided in Task 7. |
| 13 | State simply what ultrasound is. | Describe what ultrasound is. | Give students the frequency range of ultrasound, and ask students to look back to the hearing range information in Task 5. Students can then work through Task 7. |
| 14 | State some uses of ultrasound. | Describe some uses of ultrasound. | Students can complete a guided paragraph to describe uses of ultrasound in Task 7. |

● P1 Chapter 2: Sound

## Answers to end-of-chapter questions

1 Diagram with correct label of amplitude and correct label of wavelength. (2 marks)
2a Diagram with the same wavelength but larger amplitude. (1 mark)
 b Diagram with the same amplitude but smaller wavelength. (1 mark)
3 400 (1 mark)
4a it reflects (1 mark)
 b They add up or cancel out. (2 marks)
5a The oscillation is at 90° to the direction of travel. (1 mark)
 b The oscillation is parallel to the direction of travel. (1 mark)
6 Credit a sensible situation, such as a concert. (1 mark)
7a C (1 mark)   b B (1 mark)
 c The particles in C are closer together than the particles in A. The particles in A are closer together than the particles in B. Sound travels better through materials where the particles are closer together. (3 marks)
8a How does the intensity of a sound vary with distance from the source? (1 mark)
 b Independent – distance from sound source; dependent – loudness of sound; controls – frequency and loudness of sound from source (1 mark)
 c line graph (1 mark)
9 This is a QWC question. Students should be marked on the use of good English, organisation of information, spelling and grammar, and correct use of specialist scientific terms. The best answers will have scientific ideas clearly and correctly organised to give a detailed description of sound travel (maximum of 6 marks).
 Examples of correct scientific points:
 The loudspeaker vibrates/moves in and out.
 This squashes and stretches the air.
 This is a longitudinal wave, with compressions (where air molecules are close together) and rarefactions (where they are far apart).
 The wave travels through the air as the molecules pass on the vibration.
 The wave is guided into your auditory canal by the pinna.
 This makes your ear drum vibrate.
 This makes the ossicles vibrate.
 This makes the oval window vibrate.
 This makes the liquid in the cochlea vibrate.
 Produces an electrical signal.
 The signal travels up your auditory nerve to your brain.

## Answer guide for Sound campaign

| Developing | Secure | Extending |
|---|---|---|
| 1–2 marks | 3–4 marks | 5–6 marks |
| • Includes basic ideas related to each situation e.g., vibrating source, older people don't hear higher frequencies, barriers reflect sound, loud sounds can damage hearing.<br>• Lacks organisation and detail. | • Includes more complex ideas e.g., defines wave properties, links frequency to pitch and amplitude to loudness, defines ultrasound and how images are produced.<br>• Lacks some detail and organisation. | • Includes complex ideas related to each situation e.g., changes in cochlea to hearing in old age, explanation of scanning in terms of echoes and linking to distance, reduction of risk of damage by using material to shield houses from the road.<br>• The written passage is organised and detailed. |

### kerboodle

P1 Chapter 2 Checkpoint assessment (automarked)
P1 Chapter 2 Checkpoint: Revision
P1 Chapter 2 Checkpoint: Extension
P1 Chapter 2 Progress task (Maths)

# 3.1 Light

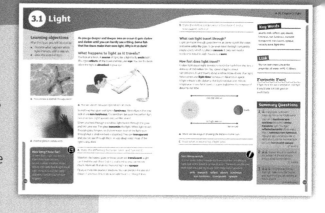

**Physics NC link:**
- the similarities and differences between light waves and waves in matter
- light waves travelling through a vacuum; speed of light
- the transmission of light through materials: absorption, diffuse scattering, and specular reflection at a surface.

**Working Scientifically NC link:**
- evaluate data, showing awareness of potential sources of random and systematic error.

| Band | Outcome | Checkpoint | |
|---|---|---|---|
| | | Question | Activity |
| **Developing** | Describe some ways that light interacts with materials (Level 4). | A, B, 1 | Starter 2, Main |
| | State that light travels very fast (Level 4). | | Starter 1 |
| | Compare results with other groups, stating if there is a spread in results (Level 4). | | Plenary 2 |
| **Secure** | Describe what happens when light interacts with materials (Level 5). | A, B, 1–3 | Starter 1, Starter 2, Main |
| | State the speed of light (Level 5). | 2 | |
| | Compare results with other groups, suggesting reasons for differences (Level 5). | | Plenary 1 |
| **Extending** | Predict how light will interact with different materials (Level 7). | | Starter 2, Main, Plenary 2 |
| | Calculate the distance travelled by light in a light-year (Level 7). | C | |
| | Evaluate results suggesting reasons for errors (Level 7). | | Plenary 1 |

**Maths**
The student-book activity asks students to compare light-time to sound-time, carrying out simple calculations and change of units.
Students also extract and interpret information and from tables.

**Literacy**
The literacy activity in the student book requires students to use scientific terms accurately in a given context.

**APP**
Carry out an experiment to investigate properties of different materials, displaying data in a table (AF4).
Interpret light intensity/resistance data to group results obtained, form a conclusion, and evaluate the experiment (AF5).

**Key Words**
source, emit, reflect, eye, absorb, luminous, non-luminous, transmit, transparent, translucent, opaque, vacuum, wave, light-time

## Answers from the student book

| In-text questions | A Emit means to give out light, transmit means to allow light to pass through it. |
|---|---|
| | B You can see clearly through a transparent material but not through a translucent material, even though light travels through both. |
| | C The distance light travels in a year. |

38

| | |
|---|---|
| Activity | **How long? How far?**<br>Sound takes a million times longer: 8 million minutes<br>8 000 000/(60 × 24 × 365) = 15.2 years<br>**Sort those words**<br>For example, the light bulb emits light because it is luminous.<br>The flower reflects light because it is non-luminous and opaque. This light is then absorbed by your eye.<br>The water transmits light and is transparent. |
| Summary questions | **1** luminous, emits, reflects, non-luminous, opaque (5 marks)<br>**2** Light is absorbed by water even though you can see through it.<br>Only a small amount is absorbed, so you need a lot of water for it to become dark. (2 marks)<br>**3** QWC question (6 marks). Example answers:<br>The Sun emits light.<br>The light travels through space to the Earth.<br>The light travels through the air.<br>The light (is refracted as it) goes into the water.<br>The fish reflects light.<br>The light (is refracted as it) comes out of the water.<br>The light enters your eye and is absorbed. |

| Starter | Support/Extension | Resources |
|---|---|---|
| **Sun's light** (5 min) Discuss how the Sun's light travels into the classroom and how we see it. Key points: It travels through a vacuum, air, and glass; it takes about 8 minutes to reach us; it reflects off surfaces into our eyes. (Students may not realise there is a vacuum between Earth and the Sun.) | **Support**: Make sure key terms are understood (e.g., vacuum).<br>**Extension**: Discuss how we can see the Moon, planets, and stars other than the Sun. | |
| **Types of material** (5 min) Students use the interactive resource to classify different objects using the terms translucent, opaque, and transparent. Discuss answers to check understanding. | **Extension**: Students can offer further examples of materials in each category. | **Interactive**: Types of material |

| Main | Support/Extension | Resources |
|---|---|---|
| **How bright is the light?** (40 min) Measure the light transmitted through different materials using a light dependent resistor (LDR) and multimeter to measure resistance, or a light meter. Many light meters give readings in lux. An LDR is a resistor with lower resistance for higher light levels. Set the multimeter to read resistance and aim the LDR towards the light source. Resistance is not directly proportional to light levels, so this is best for ranking materials rather than quantitative comparisons.<br>Students check equipment by seeing how light levels vary in the room first. Use clamp stands to fix the LDR/light meter and light source about 5–10 cm apart. Place samples of different materials between the light and LDR/light meter and record measurements. Students rank materials on a scale from transparent to opaque. | **Support**: A suggested results table is provided, using a simplified practical procedure.<br>**Extension**: Students can investigate the effect of thickness on opacity using layers of tissue paper. | **Practical**: How bright is the light?<br>**Skill sheet**: Recording results<br>**Skill sheet**: Accuracy and precision<br>**Skill sheet**: Calculating means |

| Plenary | Support/Extension | Resources |
|---|---|---|
| **Comparing results** (10 min) Students compare results from their experiment. Discuss why results vary, suggesting improvements. | | |
| **Comparing materials** (5–10 min) Students compare materials that light or sound travels easily through. These may not be the same (e.g., double glazing does not transmit sound well but does transmit light well). | **Support**: Students have a list of materials and they have to decide whether the material will let light or sound through. | |

| Homework | | |
|---|---|---|
| Students list 10 materials used at home, classifying them as opaque, transparent, and translucent. They write a sentence for each material, explaining why being opaque, transparent, or translucent makes it suitable for its purpose. | | |

# 3.2 Reflection

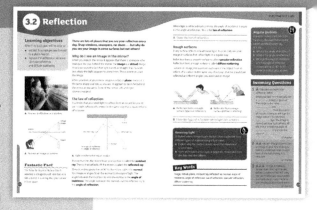

**Physics NC link:**
- the transmission of light through materials: absorption, diffuse scattering, and specula reflection at a surface
- use of ray model to explain imaging in mirrors
- differential colour effects in absorption and diffuse reflection.

**Working Scientifically NC link:**
- use appropriate techniques and apparatus during fieldwork and laboratory work, paying attention to health and safety.

| Band | Outcome | Checkpoint | |
|---|---|---|---|
| | | Question | Activity |
| **Developing** | Describe the features of a mirror image (Level 4). | 1 | Starter 1 |
| | Identify examples of specular reflection and diffuse scattering (Level 4). | B, 2 | Starter 2 |
| | Use appropriate equipment safely with guidance (Level 4). | | Main |
| **Secure** | Explain how images are formed in a plane mirror (Level 5). | 1 | Plenary 2 |
| | Explain the difference between specular reflection and diffuse scattering (Level 6). | | Main |
| | Use appropriate equipment and take readings safely without help (Level 6). | | Main |
| **Extending** | Draw a ray diagram showing how an image is formed in a plane mirror (Level 7). | | Plenary 2 |
| | Extend the concept of specular reflection and diffuse scattering by applying this to models and other examples (Level 8). | 3 | Main |
| | Take accurate readings using appropriate equipment and working safely (Level 7). | | Main |

**Maths**
Students carry out simple calculations with angles in the student-book activity, applying existing knowledge of geometry.

**Literacy**
Students use scientific terminology in explaining their reflection experiment and when answering corresponding questions.

**APP**
In the student-book activity students must choose the correct graph to use when investigating reflection (AF3).

Students carry out experiments to investigate concepts in reflection (AF4).

Students interpret data to explain and evaluate the reflection experiment and form a conclusion (AF5).

**Key Words**
image, virtual, plane, incident ray, reflected ray, normal, angle of incidence, angle of reflection, law of reflection, specular reflection, diffuse scattering

## Answers from the student book

| In-text questions | A When light is reflected from a mirror, the angle of incidence is equal to the angle of reflection.<br>B specular reflection |
|---|---|
| Activity | **Angular problem**<br>a 50° b 50° c No, the angle of incidence is equal to the angle of reflection and the angle between them can be anything from nearly 180° to 0°. |

# P1 Chapter 3: Light

| | |
|---|---|
| | **Bouncing light**<br>**a** Repeating readings helps to eliminate the effect of random errors and makes results more precise.<br>**b** A bar chart, because the data are categorical (name of material) and are not both continuous. |
| Summary questions | **1** virtual, size, shape, distance, right, incidence, reflection (7 marks)<br>**2** The light hits the wall and is reflected at lots of different angles. The light needs to reflect in a regular way to form an image. (2 marks)<br>**3** Example answers (6 marks):<br>A design showing an uneven surface, made by footballs lined up in a row.<br>A marble can be reflected from the surface of the footballs.<br>At each part of the surface the marble is reflected according to the law of reflection.<br>The surfaces of the footballs are at different angles to each other so the marble ends up scattered in lots of directions. |

| Starter | Support/Extension | Resources |
|---|---|---|
| **Mirror images** (5 min) Hand students mirrors and ask them to describe the image of an object, for example, which way up, which way round, its size. | **Support**: Ask structured questions, for example, which way up is it?<br>**Extension**: Students explain why the image is the same size, right way up, and laterally inverted. | |
| **Different reflections** (10 min) Explain the difference between specular reflection (as in mirrors) and diffuse scattering (as from rougher surfaces). Students classify examples, for example, specular reflection from surface of still water, from mirrors, or from glass surfaces. Diffuse scattering from painted walls, from clothes, from whiteboards, or pages in a book. | **Support**: Show images that students can classify as specular reflection or diffuse scattering. | |

| Main | Support/Extension | Resources |
|---|---|---|
| **Investigating reflection** (40 min) This works best if black out blinds are used. Start by demonstrating the law of reflection using a mirror. Students predict and explain results. Students follow this by investigating specular reflection and diffuse scattering. They shine a torch onto a selection of different flat surfaces and observe the reflected light on a nearby white surface. The experiment shows that a clear image will form from a mirror (specular reflection) and that coloured surfaces reflect their own colour of light, while dull, dark surfaces absorb light. | **Support**: Students are given a choice of reflected rays on the practical sheet when considering specular reflection. Demonstrate the practical procedure for diffuse scattering beforehand to ensure students understand the task fully. | **Practical**: Investigating reflection |

| Plenary | Support/Extension | Resources |
|---|---|---|
| **Reflection experiment** (5 min) Interactive resource where student choose words to complete a paragraph on the reflection experiment. | | **Interactive**: Reflection experiment |
| **Forming images in mirrors** (10 min) Demonstrate how mirror images are formed. Draw a triangle on one half of an OHP sheet. Fold the plastic down the centre (the fold represents the mirror). Trace the triangle on the other half of the sheet. Unfold the sheet to compare the image's position, size, and so on with the object. Add lines to represent the path of the rays of light. Students copy down the ray diagram. | **Extension**: Students apply this concept to explain how a kaleidoscope works. | |

| Homework | Support/Extension | |
|---|---|---|
| Set questions showing the position of an object and the position of a mirror. Students draw the position they expect to see the images formed in the mirror, and check their answers using a mirror if possible. | **Extension**: Students should add light rays to their diagrams. | |

# 3.3 Refraction

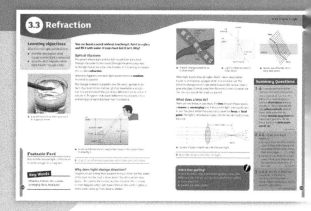

**Physics NC link:**
- the refraction of light and action of convex lens in focusing (qualitative); the human eye.

**Working Scientifically NC link:**
- present observations using appropriate methods, including tables and graphs.

| Band | Outcome | Checkpoint | |
|---|---|---|---|
| | | Question | Activity |
| **Developing** | Describe what happens when light is refracted (Level 4). | 1 | Starter 1, Main, Plenary 1 |
| | Describe features of the image formed by a lens (Level 4). | | Plenary 2 |
| | Record some observations as a diagram with help (Level 4). | | Main |
| **Secure** | Describe and explain what happens when light is refracted (Level 6). | 1 | Starter 1, Main, Plenary 2 |
| | Describe what happens when light travels through a lens (Level 6). | B | Plenary 2 |
| | Record observations using a labelled diagram (Level 5). | | Main |
| **Extending** | Predict the path of light using a model of light refraction (Level 7). | 2, 3 | Plenary 1 |
| | Explain what happens when light travels through a lens (Level 7). | B | Plenary 2 |
| | Record observations using labelled diagrams, and apply this to other situations (Level 7). | | Main |

**Literacy**
Students identify the correct spellings of key words in the student-book activity.

**APP**
Students carry out an experiment to investigate refraction, displaying observations using ray diagrams (AF4).

Students interpret results obtained from the refraction experiment to draw a conclusion (AF5).

**Key Words**
refraction, medium, lens, convex, converging, focus, focal point, critical angle, total internal reflection, optical fibres, endoscope

## Answers from the student book

| In-text questions | **A** In reflection light bounces off something, in refraction it changes direction. |
| | **B** A lens focuses or bends the rays of light to a focal point. |
| Activity | **Watch that spelling!**<br>**a** lens<br>**b** parallel |

| Summary questions | 1 above, refracts, away from, speeds up (4 marks) |
| --- | --- |
| | 2 a Speed would decrease; direction would stay the same. (2 marks) |
| | b Speed would decrease; direction would stay the same. (2 marks) |
| | 3 QWC question (6 marks). Example answers: |
| | Draw a line on the ground to show the boundary between air and glass. |
| | Draw another one further on to show the boundary between glass and air. |
| | Make lines of people about a metre apart. |
| | They march at an angle towards the line on the ground. |
| | As they get to the line on the ground they slow down. |
| | The people who reach it first slow down first. |
| | This changes the direction that they are marching in. |
| | As they cross the second line they speed up. |
| | This changes the direction again. |
| | They should be marching in the same direction as they were originally. |

**kerboodle**

| Starter | Support/Extension | Resources |
| --- | --- | --- |
| **Becoming invisible** (5 min) We can only see transparent objects if light changes direction (refracts) when it passes through them. Place a test tube in a beaker. Pour glycerol in the beaker. Then pour glycerol inside the test tube – the test tube becomes invisible. Explain light doesn't refract (change direction) when it travels between the test tube and the glycerol, so we cannot detect the test tube. | **Extension**: Show that the test tube is not invisible if water is used, even though both the test tube and the water are transparent. Ask for suggestions why (light refracts when travelling from one medium to another). | |
| **Key words in light** (5 min) The interactive resource provides a crossword on key words from this topic so far for students to complete. | | **Interactive**: Key words in light |
| **Main** | **Support/Extension** | **Resources** |
| **Investigating refraction** (40 min) Students investigate the path of light through a glass or perspex block, changing the angle of incidence. For accuracy, students mark the path of each emerging ray using dots, then remove the block and draw the rays using a ruler. Students then complete practical sheet questions. The ray of light arriving along the normal (at right angles to the block) goes straight through; light arriving at an angle changes direction at the boundary. It moves towards the normal. It emerges parallel to the original ray. | **Support**: An access sheet is available where students are required to carry out the experiment along pre-drawn incident rays, then answer a series of multiple-choice statements. | **Practical**: Investigating refraction |
| **Plenary** | **Support/Extension** | **Resources** |
| **What is happening?** (10 min) Students can model refraction by marching in groups of three towards a boundary. As each row passes a boundary marked on the floor, it slows down to simulate light travelling in a medium. If all students in the row arrive simultaneously, their row does not change direction. If one side of the row reaches the boundary first, this end slows down and the row changes direction. To keep rows in line, students can hold a metre ruler horizontally. | **Support**: Help students spot which part of the row slows down and predict the change in direction. **Extension**: Students explain how this activity relates to a ray of light travelling through a glass block. Students predict how the angle changes if they approach at different angles. | |
| **Water lenses** (5 min) Place a drop of water on an image drawn on a shiny surface (e.g., mini-whiteboard with a small picture on it). The water magnifies the image. Explain that this is due to refraction through the lens. | **Extension**: Students explain why the lens magnifies the image. | |
| **Homework** | | |
| Students identify equipment that uses lenses (or refraction) at home. They write a sentence explaining what the job of the lens is in each example. | | |

# 3.4 The eye and the camera

**Physics NC link:**
- light transferring energy from source to absorber leading to chemical and electrical effects; photo-sensitive material in the retina and in cameras
- use of ray model to explain the pinhole camera
- the refraction of light and action of convex lens in focusing (qualitative); the human eye.

**Working Scientifically NC link:**
- use appropriate techniques, apparatus, and materials during fieldwork and laboratory work, paying attention to health and safety.

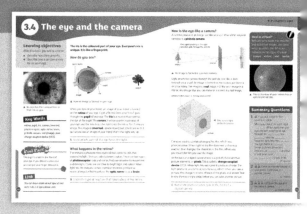

| Band | Outcome | Checkpoint | |
|---|---|---|---|
| | | Question | Activity |
| **Developing** | Name parts of the eye (Level 4). | A, 1 | Starter 2, Main |
| | Name parts of the camera (Level 4). | C | Starter 2, Main |
| | Use suitable materials to make models of the eye and the camera (Level 4). | | Main |
| **Secure** | Describe how the eye works (Level 5). | B, 1 | Main, Plenary 1 |
| | Describe how a simple camera forms an image (Level 5). | | Main |
| | Choose suitable materials to make models of the eye and the camera (Level 5). | | Main |
| **Extending** | Explain how the eye forms an image (Level 7). | 1 | Plenary 1 |
| | Compare a simple camera with the eye (Level 7). | 4 | |
| | Justify the choice of materials used to make models of the eye and the camera (Level 7). | | Main |

**Literacy**
In the student-book activity students use scientific terminology to explain the difference between real and virtual images. Students describe how parts of the eye and camera are similar and different. Students research about the eyes of other animals and write a short summary with a labelled diagram.

**APP**
Students use models to explain how the eye and camera work (AF1).

**Key Words**
iris, retina, pupil, cornea, inverted, photoreceptors, optic nerve, brain, pinhole camera, real (image), pixel, charge-coupled device (CCD)

## Answers from the student book

| In-text questions | A the cornea and the lens |
| | B chemical reaction |
| | C charge-coupled device (CCD) |
| Activity | **Real or virtual** |
| | A real image is an image that you can put on a screen whereas a virtual image is one that you see in a mirror. |

| Summary questions | 1 reflects, pupil, cornea, lens, retina, real, electrical, optic nerve (9 marks) |
|---|---|
| | 2 The camera in your phone contains a CCD not a screen. The camera stores an image but the pinhole camera does not. (2 marks) |
| | 3 QWC question (6 marks). Example answers: |
| | Similarities: |
| | They both have a hole at the front to let the light in. |
| | There is a pinhole in the camera and a pupil in the eye. |
| | Both have a screen or place where the image is formed. |
| | Differences: |
| | There is no focusing of the image in the pinhole camera. |
| | The retina has light-sensitive cells where there is a chemical reaction. |
| | The eye produces an electrical signal. |
| | Lots of people can see the same image on the screen of the camera but only you can see the image on your retina. |

| Starter | Support/Extension | Resources |
|---|---|---|
| An alternative question-led lesson is also available.<br>**What do lenses do?** (10 min) Students look through convex lenses and describe the images seen when objects are varying distances away. Nearby objects are magnified, distant objects are smaller. If they are focused on a screen, images are upside down.<br>**The camera and the eye** (5 min) The interactive resource allows students to sort parts of the eye, parts of the camera, and parts that appear in both. | **Support**: Target students with easier questions.<br>**Extension**: Link shape of lens (thickness) with focal length.<br>**Support**: Allow students to use the image in the student book.<br>**Extension**: Students match parts of the eye to their function. | **Question-led lesson:** The camera and the eye<br><br>**Interactive**: The camera and the eye |

| Main | Support/Extension | Resources |
|---|---|---|
| **Modelling the eye and the camera** (40 min) Explain that the eye and the camera perform similar jobs. Explain what each part of the eye and the camera do, and identify these on a diagram.<br>Students then make a model of an eye and a model of a camera, describing similarities and differences. Each model has an aperture, a lens, a light-detecting surface, and a space between the lens and light-detecting surface.<br>It is important to explain that the cornea and the fluid inside the eyeball help focus light, as well as the lens. Compare changing the distance between the lens and the film in a camera with changing the shape of the lens in the eye to focus on different objects.<br>At the end of the activity students should draw ray diagrams of the camera and the eye in their books. | **Support**: The support sheet includes a list of parts of the camera and the eye to help students label diagrams, and to help them decide on parts to show on their models. | **Activity**: Modelling the eye and the camera |

| Plenary | Support/Extension | Resources |
|---|---|---|
| **The journey through the eye** (5 min) Students describe how light travels from an object to the retina using scientific terminology.<br><br>**Why we have two eyes** (10 min) Students view an object across the room using each eye in turn, then both eyes. Ask how the image seemed to change, for example, if it seemed to change position, appear 2D rather than 3D, and so on. Discuss why we need two eyes, for example, to judge the speed of approaching objects. | **Support**: Use the list on the support sheet provided for the main activity.<br><br>**Extension**: Students discuss why predators have eyes at the front of their heads and prey have eyes at the side of their heads. | |

| Homework | | |
|---|---|---|
| Students research eyes of another animal to write a short article with a labelled diagram. The article should include comparisons between the ray diagram for the eye and that of the pinhole camera. | | |

# 3.5 Colour

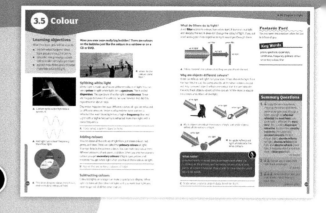

**Physics NC link:**
- colours and the different frequencies of light, white light, and prisms (qualitative only); differential colour effects in absorption and diffuse reflection.

**Working Scientifically NC link:**
- make predictions using scientific knowledge and understanding.

| Band | Outcome | Checkpoint | |
|---|---|---|---|
| | | Question | Activity |
| **Developing** | State what happens to light when it passes through a prism (Level 4). | 1 | Starter 1, Starter 2 |
| | State the primary and secondary colours of light (Level 4). | A | Main, Plenary 2 |
| | State the effect of coloured filters on light (Level 4). | 1 | Main |
| | Predict how red light will appear on a white surface (Level 4). | | Main |
| **Secure** | Explain what happens when light passes through a prism (Level 6). | 1 | Starter 1, Starter 2 |
| | Describe how primary colours add to make secondary colours (Level 6). | | Main, Plenary 2 |
| | Explain how filters and coloured materials subtract light (Level 6). | 1, 2 | Main, Plenary 1 |
| | Predict the colour of objects in red light and the colour of light through different filters (Level 6). | | Main, Plenary 1 |
| **Extending** | Explain why a prism forms a spectrum (Level 7). | 1, 3 | Starter 1, Starter 2 |
| | Explain the formation of secondary colours (Level 8). | | Main, Plenary 1 |
| | Predict how coloured objects will appear given different coloured lights and filters (Level 7). | 1 | Main, Plenary 1 |
| | Predict the colour of objects in lights of secondary colours, giving a reason for the prediction (Level 7). | | Main, Plenary 1 |

**Literacy**
Students use scientific terminology to explain how filters work in summary questions, on their practical sheet, and in their homework.

**APP**
Students suggest a suitable table of results given an experiment on primary and secondary colours in the student-book activity (AF3).

Students make predictions and carry out an experiment to investigate colour mixing (AF4).

Students interpret observations and data from their experiments to draw a conclusion, and apply this to other scenarios (AF5).

**Key Words**
prism, spectrum, dispersion, continuous, frequency, primary colour, secondary colour, tertiary colour, filter

## Answers from the student book

| In-text questions | A Splits white light into a spectrum  B cyan, yellow, magenta  C A black object absorbs all colours of light. |
|---|---|
| Activity | **What table?** |

| Colour of material | Appearance in red light | Appearance in green light | Appearance in blue light | Appearance in cyan light | Appearance in magenta light |
|---|---|---|---|---|---|
| | | | | | |

| Summary questions | 1 refracted, least, most, dispersion, transmits, absorbs, absorbs, reflects, reflects, green (10 marks) |
|---|---|
| | 2 The green shirt only reflects green light. |
| | It absorbs the red light and reflects no light, which we see as black. (2 marks) |
| | 3 QWC question (6 marks). Example answers: |
| | Filters subtract colours from white light. You cannot subtract a colour and still have white. White consists of all the colours mixed together. A white filter would be like a piece of transparent material, like glass. To see black there must be no light reaching your eye. A black filter would absorb all the colours. A black filter would be like an opaque material like brick. |

| Starter | Support/Extension | Resources |
|---|---|---|
| **Big prism** (10 min) Use a very bright light source (e.g., the Sun, an OHP) to project a spectrum using a prism. This is dispersion. Ask why the colours appeared (white light travelling through the prism is a mixture of coloured light). The prism does not create coloured light – it splits white light into a spectrum. | **Support**: Prompt students towards the colours seen (and link to a rainbow). **Extension**: Students give examples of other spectra, for example, rainbows in waterfalls. | |
| **Rainbows** (10 min) Class discussion: Where do we see rainbows? Why do they occur? This can be used as a consolidation of refraction as well as a short introduction to dispersion. | **Support**: Prompt students with 'Under what circumstances do you see rainbows?' to help students make the link between water, light, and refraction. | |

| Main | Support/Extension | Resources |
|---|---|---|
| **Colour mixing** (40 min) Introduce the concept by asking students to look around the room using coloured filters. They should see that objects appear different colours. Students then carry out the experiment on the practical sheet. This works best if black out blinds are used. If these are not available, place the experiments in boxes. Remind students we see light reflecting off objects. Explain black is not a colour – black objects absorb all light. Students predict the colour of a red object in different coloured light and predict the colour of light through two coloured filters. They then test their predictions. Students then move on to testing colours of objects by shining different coloured lights onto them, against a black background. | **Support**: The support sheet includes a suggested table of results, guiding students through a simpler experimental procedure. **Extension**: Some students may be able to predict a pattern based on the preliminary experiment. | **Practical**: Colour mixing |

| Plenary | Support/Extension | Resources |
|---|---|---|
| **How can you see colours?** (5 min) Students suggest ways to make an object appear red (e.g., it is red so it reflects red light, a red light source shines on a red or white object, or white light passes through a red filter onto a red or white object). | | **Interactive**: Types of colours |
| **Types of colours** (5 min) Interactive resource where students sort colours into primary, secondary, or neither. | **Extension**: Students suggest additional ways to make something appear yellow (combining two primary colours). | |

| Homework | | |
|---|---|---|
| Students write a guide telling police how to collect accurate witness statements for crimes committed in yellow street light, suggesting mistakes witnesses may make describing colours. | | |
| An alternative WebQuest homework activity is also available on Kerboodle where students research how lights can be used during concerts on stage. | | **WebQuest**: Stage lighting |

# P1 Chapter 3 Checkpoint

## Checkpoint lesson routes

The route through this lesson can be determined using the Checkpoint assessment. Percentage pass marks are supplied in the Checkpoint teacher notes.

**Route A (support)**
Resources: P1 Chapter 3 Checkpoint Revision.

Students will work through a revision activity that allows them to gradually revisit and consolidate their understanding of reflection and refraction, coloured light, and the eye and camera. Include simple demonstrations throughout the lesson to reinforce different points.

**Route B (extension)**
Resources: P1 Chapter 3 Checkpoint Extension.

Students will be asked to prepare a poster describing the journey of light when a person looks at a view through a window. This allows students to describe in detail how sunlight is reflected, travels through the glass, and into the person's eyes or a camera. Students should use scientific language in their poster to explain how the image is formed and describe what happens at the different stages.

## Progression to *secure*

| No. | Developing outcome | Secure outcome | Making progress |
|---|---|---|---|
| 1 | Describe some ways that light interacts with materials. | Describe what happens when light interacts with materials. | In Task 1 students can complete a cloze activity using the key words they need for a full description. |
| 2 | State that light travels very fast. | State the speed of light. | Task 2 is a cloze activity using numbers. Students will need to consider the magnitude of each number. The speed is given in metres per second. Students may have previously met it in kilometres per second or miles per hour. |
| 3 | Describe what happens when light is reflected. | State the law of reflection. | Students should complete a labelled ray diagram in Task 2 and state the law of reflection. They will use the law of reflection to complete the cloze activity. Students may benefit from repeating simple reflection light experiments. |
| 4 | Identify examples of specula and diffuse reflection. | Compare specula and diffuse reflection. | Students may struggle with the correct use of terminology for diffuse and specula reflection. Students should complete the cloze activity in Task 3, and then note down ways of remembering the two terms in the space provided. |
| 5 | Describe what happens when light is refracted. | Describe and explain what happens when light is refracted. | For students to understand this enough to produce an explanation, they need to think about light travelling as a wave. Draw a diagram for students, or demonstrate with a water tray or ripple tank if available. Students can write a full explanation in Task 5. |
| 6 | Describe features of the image formed by a lens. | Describe what happens when light travels through a lens. | Students should draw and annotate a diagram in Task 5. They should then write a description. |
| 7 | Name parts of the eye. | Describe how the eye works. | In the table in Task 6, students will need to describe what each part of the eye does. They can use this information to form a full description, supported by prompts in Task 6. |
| 8 | Name parts of the camera. | Describe how a simple camera forms an image. | Students complete a similar task to the previous outcome in Task 6. Students may benefit from having a video clip available to watch during this part of the activity. |
| 9 | Name some parts in the eye and in the camera. | Compare the eye and the camera. | The table in Task 6 will help students to draw comparisons between the eye and the camera. |
| 10 | State what happens to light when it passes through a prism. | Explain what happens when light passes through a prism. | Students should be able to remember what happens with a prism visually, and then need to ensure they have the correct vocabulary for a description. Support is given in Task 7. |
| 11 | State the primary and secondary colours of light. | Describe how primary colours add to make secondary colours. | Students will benefit from visual demonstrations and representations of colour. If available, provide students with coloured lenses and reinforce key points with coloured board pens. Students can then complete Task 7. |
| 12 | State the effect of coloured filters on light. | Explain how filters and coloured materials subtract light. | Students can complete the table in Task 7. They can use the information given in the table to help them write a full explanation. |

## Answers to end-of-chapter questions

1. A, H, I, M, O, T, U, V, W, X, Y (1 mark)
2. **a** Blue jacket and red trousers. All colours are in white light, the blue jacket reflects blue and the red trousers reflect red. (2 marks)
   **b** Black jacket and black trousers. The blue jacket and red trousers would absorb green light so no light is reflected. (2 marks)
3. **a** The light is refracted so the image of the fish is below where it really is. (2 marks)
   **b** The light does not change direction so the fish is below the bird. (2 marks)
4. **a** angle of incidence (1 mark)
   **b** mass of plastic (1 mark)
   **c** angle of refraction (1 mark)
   **d** The bigger the mass, the smaller the angle of refraction. (1 mark)
   **e** Put the results in order of increasing mass. (1 mark)
5. Rays brought to focus, as shown on page 143 of the Student Book. (4 marks)
6. Angle would be bigger in water. Water slows light down less. (2 marks)
7. This is a QWC question. Students should be marked on the use of good English, organisation of information, spelling and grammar, and correct use of specialist scientific terms. The best answers would present clear, detailed, and well organised descriptions and explanations of light through the lenses (maximum of 6 marks).
   Examples of correct scientific points:
   Light is refracted as it goes from air into each of the materials.
   The materials would refract light by different amounts.
   A lens is a piece of glass that focusses light.
   The rays cross at the focal point.
   If the material slows light down more, it would refract light more.
   Diamond slows down light the most, so would refract light the most.
   The focus would be closest for a diamond lens.
   Glass would refract light the least because it slows light down the least.
   The focus would be furthest for glass.

## Answer guide for the Big write

| Developing | Secure | Extending |
|---|---|---|
| 1–2 marks | 3–4 marks | 5–6 marks |
| • Uses coloured lights to 'change' the colours of clothing, writing on posters, and writing on programmes.<br>• Shows an understanding of how mirrors reflect light.<br>• Plan lacks detail and organisation. | • Uses simple ideas about reflection to suggest ways to use mirrors to produce images that the audience could see.<br>• Produce examples of materials that could be used on a programme/poster that would change colour.<br>• Plan lacks organisation of ideas. | • Uses ideas of partial reflection in glass to explain how to produce a ghostly image e.g., pepper's ghost where you could have an image and a person in the same place.<br>• Describes in detail how it could be done practically.<br>• Plan is clearly organised and has sufficient detail. |

### kerboodle

P1 Chapter 3 Checkpoint assessment (automarked)
P1 Chapter 3 Checkpoint: Revision
P1 Chapter 3 Checkpoint: Extension
P1 Chapter 3 Progress task (Literacy)

# 4.1 The night sky

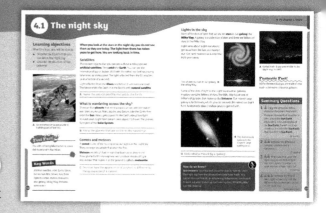

**Physics NC link:**
- our Sun as a star, other stars in our galaxy, other galaxies
- the light year as a unit of astronomical distance.

**Working Scientifically NC link:**
- understand that scientific methods and theories develop as earlier explanations are modified to take account of new evidence and ideas, together with the importance of publishing results and peer review.

| Band | Outcome | Checkpoint | |
|---|---|---|---|
| | | Question | Activity |
| **Developing** | Name some objects seen in the night sky (Level 3). | A, 3 | Starter 1, Starter 2 |
| | Place some objects seen in the night sky in size order (Level 4). | | Plenary 2 |
| | Identify scientific evidence from secondary evidence (Level 4). | | Starter 1 |
| **Secure** | Describe the objects you can see in the night sky (Level 5). | D, 1 | Starter 1, Starter 2, Main 1 |
| | Describe the structure of the Universe (Level 5). | B | Main 1 |
| | Draw valid conclusions that utilise more than one piece of supporting evidence (Level 5). | | Main 2 |
| **Extending** | Use the speed of light to describe distances between astronomical objects (Level 7). | 4 | Plenary 1 |
| | Describe the structure of the Universe in detail, in order of size and of distance away from the Earth (Level 7). | | Main 1, Plenary 2 |
| | Assess the strength of evidence, deciding whether it is sufficient to support a conclusion (Level 7). | | Main 2 |

**Maths**
Understand number size and scale with reference to a billion.

**Literacy**
Read information from a range of sources about the objects in the night sky and prepare a podcast for the public.

**APP**
Draw valid conclusions that utilise more than one piece of supporting evidence such as photographs of objects in space (AF4).

**Key Words**
star, artificial satellite, orbit, Earth, Moon, natural satellite, planet, Sun, Solar System, comet, meteor, meteorite, star, galaxy, Milky Way, Universe, astronomer

## Answers from the student book

| In-text questions | A the Moon |
|---|---|
| | B Mercury, Venus, Mars, Jupiter, Saturn |
| | C A comet is an object with a tail that stays in the night sky and returns. A meteor produces a streak of light that lasts a very short time. |
| | D A galaxy contains millions of stars. |

# P1 Chapter 4: Space

| Summary questions | |
|---|---|
| | 1  Earth, Earth, Sun, Sun (4 marks) |
| | 2  A meteor is a piece of rock or dust that burns up in the atmosphere. A meteorite is a piece of rock that reaches the ground. (2 marks) |
| | 3  Any two from: stars, galaxies, planets |
| | 4  QWC question (6 marks). Example answers: <br> It takes fractions of a second for light to reach us from objects in orbit around the Earth, such as satellites or the International Space Station. Light takes minutes to reach us from planets close to us in the Solar System, such as Mercury, Venus, Mars, Jupiter. Light takes hours to reach us from distant planets in the Solar System. Light takes years to reach us from stars in the Milky Way galaxy. Our nearest star is about 4 light-years away. Light takes millions of years to reach us from other galaxies. |

| Starter | Support/Extension | Resources |
|---|---|---|
| **What is in the night sky?** (10 min) Students list what they can see in the night sky. Then use the interactive resource where students match items in the night sky with their definition. Discuss why there objects are visible. | **Support**: Suggest ideas and ask students what they have seen. <br> **Extension**: Students identify reasons why they cannot see things well at night, for example, light pollution, clouds, or buildings. | **Interactive**: What is in the night sky? |
| **What is in the sky tonight?** (5–10 min) Use a star map to show what is visible in tonight's sky (e.g., from the National Schools Observatory website) or show a current video of Tonight's Sky from Hubble's website. Free downloadable programs such as Celestia and Stellarium make good alternatives. | **Extension**: Discuss if it is possible to tell between planets or stars using a telescope. | |

| Main | Support/Extension | Resources |
|---|---|---|
| **What is in the Universe?** (20 min) Use the Hubble website image gallery to show objects in the night sky (planets, nebulae – gas clouds where stars form, stars, black holes – remnant of collapsed giant stars, galaxies). Explain how objects fit together to form the Universe. This can be prepared in advance as a slide show with images and titles. Use the activity sheet to reinforce student perception of our place in the Universe. | **Support**: Show animations of satellites. An access sheet is available with easier text and comprehension questions. Graph paper is useful to give students an idea of one billion. <br> **Extension**: Discuss different orbits for satellites (vary in height, orientation, uses), for example, geostationary orbits, low polar orbits. Ask students to suggest benefits for scientists of sharing their ideas. | **Activity**: What is in the Universe? <br> **Skill sheet**: Converting units |
| **Satellites** (20 min) Define a satellite as a smaller object orbiting a larger one. Give examples of natural satellites such as the Moon orbiting the Earth or planets orbiting stars. Remind students satellites always move and that they orbit the widest point of Earth but not necessarily over the equator. Discuss uses of man-made satellites and describe how scientists share data from these. | | |

| Plenary | Support/Extension | Resources |
|---|---|---|
| **How far are they?** (10 min) Students rank objects in order of distance from Earth and matching distances in light-time, for example, Sun (8 light-minutes), Moon (1 light-second), Proxima Centuri (our nearest star, 4 light-years). Planet light-times vary as position in orbit varies, for example, Neptune (4 light-hours ±8 light-minutes) or Mars about 4–20 light-minutes. | **Support**: Provide a diagram for reference. <br> **Extension**: Students estimate distances in light-time before you provide a list. | |
| **What is in the Universe?** (5 min) Students list objects found in the Universe. Rank them in size order, (e.g., Moon, planet, star, black hole, galaxy, Universe). | **Support**: Provide the list for students to rank. | |

| Homework | Support/Extension | |
|---|---|---|
| Make a model of a satellite identifying solar panels for power, rockets to control direction, communication antenna, and battery for power supply. | **Support**: Use Met Office template for satellite model, available from their website. <br> **Extension**: Model a named satellite. | |

# 4.2 The Solar System

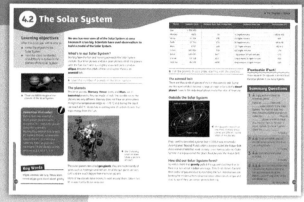

**Physics NC link:**
- gravity force, gravity forces between Earth and Moon, and between Earth and Sun (qualitative only).

**Working Scientifically NC link:**
- interpret observations and data, including identifying patterns and using observations, measurements and data to draw conclusions.

| Band | Outcome | Checkpoint | |
|---|---|---|---|
| | | Question | Activity |
| **Developing** | Name some objects in the Solar System (Level 3). | | Starter 1, Plenary 1 |
| | Name the planets in the Solar System (Level 4). | A, B | |
| | Identify some patterns in the Solar System (Level 3). | | Main 2 |
| **Secure** | Describe how objects in the Solar System are arranged (Level 5). | 1 | Main 1, Main 2 |
| | Describe some similarities and differences between the planets of the Solar System (Level 5). | 2 | Main 2 |
| | Identify patterns in the spacing and diameters of planets (Level 6). | | Main 2 |
| **Extending** | Explain how the properties and features of planets are linked to their place in the Solar System (Level 7). | | Main 2, Plenary 2 |
| | Compare features of different objects in the Solar System (Level 7). | 2, 3 | |
| | Use data to make predictions about features of planets (Level 7). | | Main 2 |

**Literacy**
Students retrieve and collate information from a range of sources on space exploration, exploring the advantages and disadvantages of space travel, to summarise the information in a table.

**APP**
Students use the model of the orrery to explain the movement of the Earth and the Moon relative to the Sun (AF1).

Students choose different methods of representing scientific data in the activity, transferring data from a table to a graph (AF3).

**Key Words**
ellipse, asteroid, Mercury, Venus, Mars, terrestrial, gas giant, dwarf planet, gravity

## Answers from the student book

| In-text questions | A There are eight planets in the Solar System. <br> B Mercury, Mars, Venus, Earth, Neptune, Uranus, Saturn, Jupiter |
|---|---|
| Activity | **Remember that order!** <br> Students should choose a suitable mnemonic with the correct initial letters. |
| Summary questions | 1 four, four, asteroid belt, dwarf, Oort Cloud (5 marks) <br> 2 Similarities: They all orbit the Sun. They are round. Differences: The inner planets are made of rock, the outer planets, of gas. Outer planets are colder. You cannot see some of the outer planets with the naked eye. (2 marks) <br> 3 Planets and asteroids both orbit the Sun. Some of the planets are made of rock like some asteroids. Asteroids are not spherical. <br> 4 QWC question (6 marks). Example answers: <br> As you move away from the Sun the temperature decreases. Less light reaches objects that are further away. Less energy is transferred from the Sun to objects that are further away. More distant planets should be colder than nearer planets. Venus should be colder than Mercury because it is further from the Sun. It is hotter than Mercury because it has an atmosphere that traps energy transferred the Sun. |

● P1 Chapter 4: Space

| Starter | Support/Extension | Resources |
|---|---|---|
| **What do you know?** (5 min) Students sketch a diagram showing the objects they think are in the Solar System and their orbits. Use this to assess prior knowledge and draw out misconceptions.<br><br>**Models of the Solar System** (10 min) Show the video clip 'Models of the Solar System – Earth, Sun and Moon' from the Institute of Physics website. Students list 3–5 points from the video. | **Support**: Provide a diagram for students to add labels to.<br><br>**Support**: Point out models of Sun, Moon, and Earth in video.<br>**Extension**: Students explain why we see 'wandering stars' (planets). | |

| Main | Support/Extension | Resources |
|---|---|---|
| **The moving Solar System** (15 min) Students make an orrery (moving model of Sun, Earth, and Moon) in their books. This can also be done as a large demonstration model. One paper fastener fixes the Sun and the longer paper strip to the page so the strip can turn. The other paper fastener fixes Earth and the short strip to the other end of the longer strip, so Earth orbits the Sun. Glue the Moon to the other end of the shorter paper strip so it orbits Earth.<br><br>Students use the orrery to explain phenomena in the Solar System. They suggest improvements to their models, for example, scale.<br><br>**The Solar System to scale** (25 min) At this point, it is important to introduce the difference between inner planets and outer planets, in particular about the materials they are made from. This can be done from the student book.<br><br>Using a long, narrow strip of paper, students can display relative distances of planets from the Sun by folding the paper, or by using a scale diagram. Discuss patterns in the separations and the scale of the Solar System.<br><br>Students then work through the activity sheet individually. | **Extension**: Students add another planet, and use the orrery to explain why it seems to move forwards and backwards relative to Earth.<br><br><br>**Support**: Introduce the idea of scale and give students 30-cm rulers. The support sheet includes a table of data to help students answer the questions.<br>**Extension**: Calculate space-time to planet, discussing problems with space travel. | **Activity**: The Solar System to scale<br>**Skill sheet**: Choosing scales |

| Plenary | Support/Extension | Resources |
|---|---|---|
| **Objects in the Solar System** (5 min) Interactive resource where students order objects in the Solar System according to size.<br><br>**What planet am I?** (5 min) Each student writes down clues so their partner can guess which planet they are thinking of. | **Support**: Ask students to focus on the relative sizes of the Sun, Earth, and Moon. | **Interactive**: Objects in the Solar System |

| Homework | Support/Extension | |
|---|---|---|
| Students research benefits and costs of space travel (e.g., spin-off technology, cost of manned versus unmanned expeditions).<br><br><br><br><br>An alternative WebQuest homework activity is also available on Kerboodle where students research the planets of the Solar System. | **Support**: Students fill out a table with two columns: advantages and disadvantages.<br>**Extension**: Students can add extra columns based on evidence and evaluation. | **WebQuest**: Solar System tourist |

53

# 4.3 The Earth

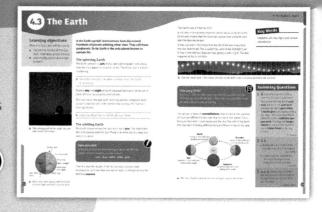

**Physics NC link:**
- the seasons and the Earth's tilt, day length at different times of the year, in different hemispheres.

**Working Scientifically NC link:**
- interpret observations and data, including identifying patterns and using observations, measurements, and data to draw conclusions.

| Band | Outcome | Checkpoint | |
|---|---|---|---|
| | | Question | Activity |
| **Developing** | Describe differences between seasons (Level 3). | 2 | Starter 1 |
| | Describe the motion of the Sun, stars, and Moon across the sky (Level 4). | B, 1 | Starter 2 |
| | Describe patterns in data linking day-length and month (Level 4). | | Main 3 |
| **Secure** | Explain the motion of the Sun, stars, and Moon across the sky (Level 5). | A, B, 1 | |
| | Explain why seasonal changes happen (Level 6). | | Main 1, Main 2 |
| | Use data to show the effect of the Earth's tilt on temperature and day-length (Level 5). | | Main 3 |
| **Extending** | Predict the effect of the Earth's tilt on temperature and day-length (Level 7). | | Main 3 |
| | Predict how seasons would be different if there were no tilt (Level 7). | 3 | Plenary 2 |
| | Interpret data to predict how the Earth's tilt affects temperature and day-length (Level 7). | | Main 3 |

### Maths
The student-book activity allows students to carry out simple calculations to work out the occurrence of a leap year.

During the activity students extract and interpret information from charts, graphs, and tables. They also represent changes in temperature and day-length with changes in season graphically.

In order to answer questions, students must interpret graphs comparing day-length, temperature, and season.

### Literacy
The student-book activity asks students to summarise information using key words.

Students explain to each other phenomena caused by the moving Earth.

For homework students write an account of changes experienced travelling from the equator to the North Pole.

### APP
Use of globes, paper Pole Stars, and thermofilm to explain phenomena when explaining the seasons (AF1).

Students display tabulated data as graphs to show trends and patterns (AF3).

### Key Words
exoplanet, axis, day, night, year, season, constellation

## Answers from the student book

| In-text questions | **A** Take a picture of the night sky over many hours. The stars make circular tracks. **B** east |
|---|---|
| Activity | **Spin and orbit** <br> For example, one day is the time it takes for the Earth to spin once. The half of the Earth where sunlight does not reach is night. One year is the time it takes the Earth to orbit the Sun once. <br> **February 29th?** <br> $21\,600 \times 4 = 86\,400$ so $86\,400 \div (24 \times 60 \times 60)$ days = 1 day |

● P1 Chapter 4: Space

| Summary questions | 1 east, west, spins, year, orbit the Sun, longer, higher (7 marks)<br>2 a It is hotter because the days are longer so the Sun warms the Earth for longer. The rays from the Sun are more concentrated than they are in winter. (2 marks)<br>   b The Sun is lower in the sky in the winter so shadows are longer. (1 mark)<br>3 QWC question (6 marks). Example answers:<br>You would not have seasons. Days and nights would be equal length throughout the year. Shadow-length at noon would be the same throughout the year. The height of the Sun in the sky at noon would be the same throughout the year. There would be no difference between the angle at which the Sun's rays hit the Earth at different times of the year. Temperature changes depend on the Sun's rays spreading out over a bigger area in the winter than the summer. |
|---|---|

*kerboodle*

| Starter | Support/Extension | Resources |
|---|---|---|
| An alternative question-led lesson is also available.<br>**Different seasons** (5 min) Students list differences in seasons, for example, day-length, position of Sun, and weather. Students suggest why changes happen.<br><br>**The Pole Star** (5 min) Discuss navigation without a compass. The North Pole always points towards the Pole Star because Earth tilts that way. Use a video clip from the Internet to show how to find the Pole Star and navigate using it. | **Support**: Students identify differences in day-length and temperature.<br>**Extension**: Students suggest differences on the same date in different parts of the Earth. | **Question-led lesson**: The Earth |
| **Main** | **Support/Extension** | **Resources** |
| **Why we have seasons** (15 min) Ensure students know the Earth always tilts towards the Pole Star, not towards the Sun. Use a paper star on a wall as the Pole Star. Move a globe (Earth) to tilt towards this star as it orbits around a central lamp (Sun). The North Pole tilts towards the Sun for part of the year only. Add a sticker on the globe to show the UK. Students should identify when the UK has winter and summer, and predict changes in day-length.<br><br>**Seasons and temperature** (10 min) Students may think winter is cooler because the Earth is further away from the Sun but it is because the Sun's rays spread over a larger area when Earth tilts away from the Sun.<br><br>Stick a 1-cm wide strip of thermofilm from pole to pole, including the UK. Tilt the globe towards the lamp. The thermofilm by the UK warms up changing colour (summer). Tilt the globe away from the lamp, light spreads over a larger area and the thermofilm is cooler (winter). It is important to keep the separation of the lamp and section of the globe the same.<br><br>**The seasons** (20 min) Students complete questions on the activity sheet. | **Extension**: Students design their own model on paper to show this idea.<br><br><br><br><br><br><br><br><br><br>**Support**: A support sheet is provided with labelled graph grids and fewer sets of data. | **Activity**: The seasons |
| **Plenary** | **Support/Extension** | **Resources** |
| **The Sun and the seasons** (5 min) Students complete the gap fill on the interactive resource to explain how seasons occur.<br><br><br>**A changing tilt** (5 min) Students predict what would be different if Earth was not tilted (we would still be cooler than the equator but day-length/temperature would be the same all year). | **Support**: Set as cloze exercise.<br>**Extension**: Students draw diagrams explaining why some countries are cooler.<br>**Support**: Structure using questions with yes/no answers.<br>**Extension**: Predict changes if Earth's tilt were greater. | **Interactive**: The Sun and the seasons |
| **Homework** | | |
| Give students the temperature and day-length in a particular month for four countries between the equator and the North Pole. They write an account or postcards describing changes from the point of view of a tourist. | | |

# 4.4 The Moon

**Physics NC link:**
- use of ray model.

**Working Scientifically NC link:**
- make predictions using scientific knowledge and understanding.

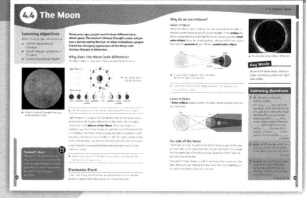

| Band | Outcome | Checkpoint | |
|---|---|---|---|
| | | Question | Activity |
| **Developing** ↓ | Name some phases of the Moon (Level 4). | A, 1 | |
| | Explain simply why we see the Moon from Earth (Level 4). | | Main |
| | Describe what a total eclipse is (Level 4). | 1 | |
| | Show the different phases of the Moon using models provided (Level 4). | | Main |
| **Secure** ↓ | Describe the phases of the Moon (Level 5). | 1 | Main, Starter 2, Plenary 2 |
| | Explain why we see the phases of the Moon (Level 6). | | Main |
| | Explain why total eclipses happen (Level 6). | 1, 3 | Main |
| | Explain phases of the Moon using the models provided (Level 6). | | Main |
| **Extending** ↓ | Predict phases of the Moon at a given time (Level 7). | | Plenary 1 |
| | Explain how total eclipses are linked to phases of the Moon (Level 8). | | Main |
| | Explain why it is possible to see an eclipse on some of the planets in the Solar System but not others (Level 7). | 2 | |
| | Predict the phases of the Moon using models provided (Level 8). | | Main |

**Maths**
The student-book activity asks students to carry out a simple calculation to work out the distance between the Moon and the Earth at a given time.

**Literacy**
Students use scientific vocabulary when writing about the phases of the Moon in the starter and plenary tasks.

Students summarise scientific text for key ideas in their homework.

**APP**
Use of models to demonstrate the phases of the Moon (AF1).

Students choose appropriate methods to present observations (AF3).

**Key Words**
solar eclipse, phases of the Moon, total eclipse, partial eclipse, lunar eclipse

## Answers from the student book

| In-text questions | **A** full moon, waning gibbous, last quarter, waning crescent, new moon, waxing crescent, first quarter, waxing gibbous<br>**B** Half the Moon is lit up at all times.<br>**C** umbra |
|---|---|
| Activity | **Farewell, Moon**<br>Distance = your age × 3.8 cm/year<br>  = 11 years × 3.8 cm/year<br>  = 41.8 cm |

| Summary questions | 1 full, new, Moon, Earth, Earth, Moon (6 marks) |
| --- | --- |
| | 2 There will be eclipses on any other planet that has one or more moons. |
| | 3 QWC question (6 marks). Example answers: |
| | Put the torch on the desk and switch it on. |
| | Label the tennis ball 'Moon'. |
| | Label the beach ball 'Earth'. |
| | For a solar eclipse, hold the tennis ball between the beach ball and the torch. |
| | There is a shadow cast by the tennis ball on the beach ball. |
| | For a lunar eclipse, hold the beach ball between the tennis ball and the torch. |

| Starter | Support/Extension | Resources |
| --- | --- | --- |
| **Check the facts** (5 min) Check misconceptions/prior knowledge with five short questions. Students may think that the Moon changes shape or clouds change its appearance, that it always appears in the same part of the sky, and that it gives out its own light. Possible questions: Does the Moon change shape? Is the Moon bigger/closer than the Sun? What is a full/new moon? Is the Moon seen in the same place each night/during the night? <br><br> **How does the Moon change?** (5 min) Students write down how the Moon changes in as much detail as possible, for example, timescale, what they see, where it is, and when it is seen. | **Support**: Provide multiple choice answers. <br><br> **Extension**: Students explain answers and offer more detail. | |

| Main | Support/Extension | Resources |
| --- | --- | --- |
| **The Moon and eclipses** (40 min) Students model the phases of the Moon and eclipses using the instructions on the practical sheet. <br><br> Students then answer the questions on the practical sheet. | **Support**: Clarify these concepts using animations and diagrams. A support sheet is available with partially drawn diagrams for students to complete. <br><br> **Extension**: Students suggest why we don't see eclipses every day/month. | **Practical**: The Moon and eclipses |

| Plenary | Support/Extension | Resources |
| --- | --- | --- |
| **What does it look like?** (10 min) Draw a phase of the Moon (e.g., full moon). Students describe its appearance in future or the past, for example, in a week's time/two weeks' time/a week ago. This can be done in conjunction with the interactive gap fill as a summary. <br><br> **How does the Moon change? (Part 2)** (5 min) Students revisit their answers at the start of the lesson to see how much more detail they can add. | **Support**: Provide cards with images to sort. <br><br> **Extension**: Predict appearance (phases) of Earth for an astronaut on the Moon. | **Interactive**: What does it look like? |

| Homework | Support/Extension | |
| --- | --- | --- |
| Provide students with accounts to read from people/news articles of solar or lunar eclipses. Students must then write a summary paragraph explaining what was seen. | **Extension**: Students should relate their summary to the relative positions of the Sun, Earth, and Moon. | |

# P1 Chapter 4 Checkpoint

## Checkpoint lesson routes

The route through this lesson can be determined using the Checkpoint assessment.
Percentage pass marks are supplied in the Checkpoint teacher notes.

**Route A (support)**
Resource: P1 Chapter 4 Checkpoint Revision

Students will create a poster about space, using the prompts and questions provided in the revision activity, to help them revisit and consolidate their understanding of this chapter.

**Route B (extension)**
Resource: P1 Chapter 4 Checkpoint Extension

Students will be asked to write an account of a journey through the Solar System playing attention to the forces involved, and comparing the planets they visit. Prompts and guidance are given in the extension sheet.

## Progression to *secure*

| No. | Developing outcome | Secure outcome | Making progress |
| --- | --- | --- | --- |
| 1 | Name some objects seen in the night sky. | Describe the objects you can see in the night sky. | Before completing this section of their poster students can complete the cloze activity in Task 1. |
| 2 | Place some objects seen in the night sky in size order. | Describe the structure of the Universe. | Key words are given as prompts in Task 1 for students to add to their poster. Task 3 looks at the numbers involved in describing the Universe. |
| 3 | Name some objects in the Solar System. | Describe how objects in the Solar System are arranged. | In Task 2 prompts are given for the students to draw and annotate objects in the Solar System. |
| 4 | Name the planets in the Solar System. | Describe some similarities and differences between the planets of the Solar System. | Students are encouraged to include facts and comparisons in their poster using the prompts given in Task 2. |
| 5 | Describe differences between seasons. | Explain why seasonal changes happen. | Students may benefit from a model demonstration using a globe and a light source. They should write clear explanations on the poster. Further support is given in Task 4. |
| 6 | Describe the motion of the Sun, stars, and Moon across the sky. | Explain the motion of the Sun, stars, and Moon across the sky. | You may wish to demonstrate relative movement by getting students to stand and turn round in their places to see objects in the room appear to move. Support is given in Task 5. |
| 7 | Name some phases of the Moon. | Describe the phases of the Moon. | Students could include a Moon calendar, with named phases, in their poster. Support is given in Task 5. |
| 8 | Explain simply why we see the Moon from Earth. | Explain why we see the phases of the Moon. | You may wish to demonstrate different phases of the Moon using a light source, globe, and ball. |
| 9 | Describe what a total eclipse is. | Explain why total eclipses happen. | You may wish to demonstrate how eclipses occur using a light source, globe, and ball. Support is given in Task 5. |

## Answers to end-of-chapter questions

1. Orbit the Earth: Moon, satellite, International space station.
   Orbit the Sun: planet, asteroid, comet. (2 marks)
2. **a** One mark for each correct label. (3 marks)
   **b** winter (1 mark)
   **c** 9 (1 mark)
3. **a** Left of diagram labelled east and sunrise. Centre of diagram labelled noon. Right of diagram labelled west and sunset. (2 marks)
   **b** Winter path has the same shape as the summer path but will be lower in the sky (2 marks)
   **c** Earth orbits around the Sun in one year, and rotates around a tilted axis. (2 marks)
4. **a** light-second away: Moon (1 mark)
   light-years away: galaxy (1 mark)
   **b** It would take minutes or hours for the signal to reach the spacecraft. There would be a long delay between asking a question and receiving an answer. (2 marks)
5. This is a QWC question. Students should be marked on the use of good English, organisation of information, spelling and grammar, and correct use of specialist scientific terms. The best answers will be well presented and clearly organised, making references to the information provided in the table as well as to their scientific knowledge (maximum of 6 marks).
   Examples of correct scientific points:
   The seasons would be would be longer or shorter depending on the angle.
   The angle of tilt of Mars, Saturn, and Neptune is about the same as Earth.
   The seasons on Mars, Saturn, and Neptune would be similar to Earth.
   The axis of Mercury is not tilted.
   Mercury would not have seasons.
   You would hardly notice the seasons on Jupiter – the angle of tilt of Jupiter is so small.
   Seasons are longer for planets further from the Sun because it takes longer for the planet to orbit the Sun.
   Uranus has an angle of tilt of nearly 90 degrees, so rolls like a barrel on its axis as it moves around the Sun – seasons would last about 6 months.
   Venus has very little difference between the seasons because the angle is very small – it is just spinning the other way.

## Answer guide for Big Write

| Developing | Secure | Extending |
|---|---|---|
| 1–2 marks | 3–4 marks | 5–6 marks |
| • Student picks out obvious points from the table given (e.g., year length is shorter, day length is longer) but little or no comparisons to other planets in the Solar System. | • Student shows comprehension that conditions probably too hot for life and that the same side would always face the star.<br>• Some basic comparison with other planets in the Solar system. | • Student connects the idea that temperatures not suitable for liquid water so unlikely to have life.<br>• Compares with other planets in the Solar System, e.g., rolls like Uranus. |

### kerboodle

P1 Chapter 4 Checkpoint assessment (automarked)
P1 Chapter 4 Checkpoint: Revision
P1 Chapter 4 Checkpoint: Extension
P1 Chapter 4 Progress task (Maths)

# Physics 2

| National curriculum links for this unit | |
|---|---|
| **Chapter** | **National Curriculum topic** |
| Chapter 1: Electricity and magnetism | Current electricity<br>Static electricity<br>Magnetism |
| Chapter 2: Energy | Calculation of fuel uses and costs in the domestic context<br>Energy changes and transfers<br>Changes in systems |
| Chapter 3: Speed and motion | Describing motion<br>Forces<br>Pressure in fluids<br>Forces and motion |

## Preparing for Key Stage 4 Success

**Knowledge**
Underpinning knowledge is covered in this unit for KS4 study of:
- Current, potential difference
- Resistance
- Series and parallel circuits
- Static electricity – forces and electric fields
- Permanent and induced magnetism
- Conservation of energy
- National and global energy sources
- Work done and energy transfer
- Speed, velocity, and acceleration
- Distance-time and velocity-time graphs
- Pressure

**Maths**
Skills developed in this unit.
(Topic number)
- Quantitative problem solving (1.3, 3.5, 3.6).
- Extract and interpret information from charts, graphs, and tables (1.4, 1.7, 2.3, 2.5, 3.2, 3.6).
- Calculate arithmetic means (2.4, 2.5, end-of-chapter 2).
- Plot and draw graphs selecting appropriate scales for the axes (1.5, 2.3, 3.2).
- Understand and use direct proportion and simple ratios. (2.4, 2.7, 3.3).
- Understand number size and scale and the quantitative relationship between units. (2.1, 2.7).
- Understand when and how to use estimation (2.1, 3.4, 3.6).
- Substitute numerical values into simple formulae and equations using appropriate units (1.2, 1.3, 1.5, 2.7, 2.8, 3.1, 3.5, 3.6).
- Carry out calculations involving $+, -, \times, \div$, either singly or in combination (2.2, 2.4, 2.7, 2.8, 3.1, 3.5, 3.6).

**Literacy**
Skills developed in this unit.
(Topic number)
- Select, synthesise, and compare information from a variety of sources (2.2, 2.7, 3.3, 3.4, 3.5).
- Use scientific terms confidently and correctly in discussions and writing (all spreads).
- Organisation of ideas and evidence (1.6, 1.8, 2.4, 3.1, 3.2, 3.4).
- Identify ideas and supporting evidence in text (1.7, 3.2, 3.3).
- Use correct forms of writing styles and include information relevant to the audience (1.8, 2.1, 2.5, 3.2).
- Ideas are organised into well-developed, linked paragraphs (1.8, 2.6, end-of-chapter 2 Big Write, 3.4, end-of-chapter 3 Big Write).

**Assessment Skills**
- QWC questions (1.1, 1.2, 1.3, 1.4, 1.5, 1.7, 1.8, 2.1, 2.2, 2.3, 2.4, 2.7, 2.8, 3.1, 3.2, 3.3, 3.4, 3.5, 3.6) (end-of-chapter 1 Q8, Q10, end-of-chapter 2 Q10, end-of-chapter 3 Q8, Q11).
- Quantitative problem solving (1.4, 1.5, 2.1, 2.5, 2.7, 2.8, 3.1, 3.2, 3.5, 3.6) (end-of-chapter 1 Maths Challenge, Q6, end-of-chapter 2 Q3, Q7, Q8, end-of-chapter 3 Q3, Q6, Q10).
- Application of Working Scientifically (1.3, 1.6, 1.8, 2.4, 3.3) (end-of-chapter 1 Maths Challenge, Q5, end-of-chapter 2 Q3, end-of-chapter 3 Q7).

| KS2 Link | Check before: | Checkpoint | Catch-up |
|---|---|---|---|
| Names of the basic parts in simple series circuits, for example, bulb, cell, and switch. | P2 1.2 Circuits and current | Show circuit components and their symbols for students to name and match up. | Provide names of components for students to label on a circuit diagram. |
| A complete loop is required for a circuit to work. | P2 1.2 Circuits and current | Show students a range of circuits with bulbs. Ask them to explain whether the bulbs will light up in each case. | Demonstrate building a simple series circuit with a bulb. Show students that the bulb does not light until the circuit is complete. |
| A switch opens and closes a circuit. | P2 1.2 Circuits and current | Students explain why bulbs light up depending on the position of the switch. | Students build a simple series circuit with a switch, a cell, and a bulb. |
| The brightness of a lamp depends on the number and voltage of cells used in a circuit. | P2 1.3 Potential difference | Students predict the brightness of bulbs in difference circuits. | Demonstrate a simple circuit making changes to the number of bulbs, cells, or potential difference of cells. |
| Metals are good conductors of electricity. | P2 1.5 Resistance | Ask students what sorts of materials they would use to make wires. | Demonstrate a simple series circuit, adding conductors and insulators to the circuit to show the effect on a bulb in the circuit. |
| Magnets have two poles. | P2 1.6 Magnets and magnetic fields | Students label a bar magnet. | Demonstrate labelled magnets. |
| Magnets will attract or repel each other, depending on which poles are facing. | P2 1.6 Magnets and magnetic fields | Students predict if magnets will attract or repel. | Suspend magnets from a clamp stand. Students bring other magnets close and explain what happens. |
| Some changes result in the formation of new materials | P2 2.1 Food and fuels | Students describe what happens to fuels that are burned. | Students watch a candle burn. They describe what happens by choosing from a list of products. |
| There are three states of matter: solid, liquid, and gas. | P2 2.3 Energy and temperature | Students label a diagram showing particles arranges as solids liquids and gases. | Students categorise different objects as solids, liquids, and gases. |
| Light travels in a straight line. | P2 2.5 Energy transfer: radiation | Students predict the path of a light beam reflecting off a mirror. | Students shine a torch on a mirror and predict which object will light up based on relative positions. |
| Friction slows down moving objects. | P2 3.1 Speed | Students describe motion of objects shown to them in a video clip. | Students label a force diagram of a moving object, explaining the effect of resultant forces. |
| Unsupported objects fall towards Earth because of the force of gravity. | P2 3.2 Motion graphs | Students explain why a ball falls towards Earth when thrown in the air. | Use force arrows to label forces acting on supported and unsupported objects. |
| Some mechanisms, including levers, pulleys, and gears, are force multipliers. | P2 3.6 Turning forces | Students predict what happens when a force is applied to a simple machine. | Students lift objects with and without simple machines and use labels to show where the force is being transmitted and in which direction. |

### kerboodle

- P2 Unit pre-test
- P2 Big practical project (foundation)
- P2 Big practical project (higher)
- P2 Big practical project teacher notes
- P2 Practical project hints: graph plotting
- P2 Practical project hints: planning
- P2 Practical project hints: writing frame
- P2 End-of-unit test (foundation)
- P2 End-of-unit test (foundation) mark scheme
- P2 End-of-unit test (higher)
- P2 End-of-unit test (higher) mark scheme

### Answers to Picture Puzzler
**Key Words**
Everest, newtonmeter, Earth, remote, gear, yellow
The key word is **energy**.
**Close Up**
copper wires

# 1.1 Charging up

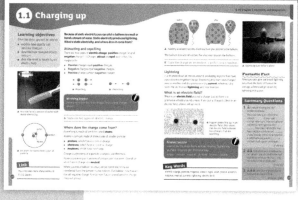

**Physics KS3 NC link:**
- separation of positive or negative charges when objects are rubbed together: transfer of electrons, forces between charged objects
- the idea of electric field, forces acting across the space between objects not in contact
- non-contact forces: forces due to static electricity
- using physical processes and mechanisms, rather than energy, to explain the intermediate steps that bring about changes in systems.

**Working Scientifically NC link:**
- interpret observations and data, including identifying patterns and using observations, measurements, and data to draw conclusions.

| Band | Outcome | Checkpoint | |
|---|---|---|---|
| | | Question | Activity |
| **Developing** | Describe how to charge insulators (Level 4). | 1 | Starter 1, Plenary 1 |
| | State the two types of charge (Level 4). | A, 1 | Lit, Main |
| | State what surrounds charged objects (Level 4). | | Main |
| | Explain simply observations linked to charge (Level 4). | | Main |
| **Secure** | Explain how objects can become charged (Level 5). | 1 | Main, Starter 1, Plenary 1 |
| | Describe how charged objects interact (Level 5). | 1 | Main, Starter 1, Plenary 1, Plenary 2 |
| | Describe what is meant by an electric field (Level 5). | 3 | Main |
| | Interpret observations, identifying patterns linked to charge (Level 5). | | Main |
| **Extending** | Explain, in terms of electrons, why something becomes charged (Level 7). | 1, 2 | Main, Starter 1, Plenary 1, Plenary 2 |
| | Predict how charged objects will interact (Level 7). | 2 | Main |
| | Compare a gravitational field and an electric field (Level 7). | 3 | |
| | Use observations to make predictions (Level 7). | | Main |

**Maths**
Students use the relative positions of materials in the triboelectric series to predict whether friction will cause an object to become positively or negatively charged.

**Literacy**
In the student-book activity students must unscramble anagrams of key words, pair them up, and explain why they have done so.

**APP**
Students use abstract ideas when describing processes in static electricity (AF1).
They use existing ideas about electrostatics to inform further predictions (AF5).

**Key Words**
electric charge, positive, negative, attract, repel, atom, proton, electron, neutron, neutral, current, lightning, electric field

## Answers from the student book

| In-text questions | **A** positive, negative | **B** electron: negative; proton: positive; neutron: no charge |
|---|---|---|
| Activity | **Atomic puzzle** proton: positive; neutron: neutral; electron: negative; These are the charges on the particles. | |

# P2 Chapter 1: Electricity and magnetism

| Summary Questions | 1 positive, negative, electrons, repel, attract (5 marks) |
|---|---|
| | 2 Electrons are transferred between the balloon and the jumper. The balloon is charged, but the wall is neutral. The charge of the balloon repels like charges from the surface of the wall. (3 marks) |
| | 3 QWC question (6 marks). Example answers: Gravitational and electric fields produce forces. You cannot see or feel a gravitational or electric field. They produce non-contact forces. Gravitational fields are produced by masses. Electric fields are produced by charges. Gravitational fields produce forces that only attract. Electric fields produce forces that attract and repel. |

**kerboodle**

| Starter | Support/Extension | Resources |
|---|---|---|
| **Charges on a balloon** (15 min) Rub a balloon (or a plastic straw) on cloth and hold it near some hair. For the best results, hair should be clean, fine, and not too long. Ask students to describe what they observe (the hairs are attracted to the balloon; when the balloon is removed, the hair strands remain repelling each other). Discuss why this is happening as a class. | **Extension**: Demonstrate the effect of a charged object on a stream of water. Students should apply their existing ideas. | |
| **Non-contact forces** (10 min) Students list as many non-contact forces as possible, describing their effects in terms of attraction/repulsion (gravitational, magnetic, electrostatic). Discuss their ideas and explain that electrostatic forces are between charged objects, and they will be investigating these forces during this lesson. | **Support**: Give examples that students group by the non-contact force they experience. Note that some objects experience more than one non-contact force. **Extension**: Students identify common features of non-contact forces. | |

| Main | Support/Extension | Resources |
|---|---|---|
| **Electrostatics** (35 min) Demonstrate several effects of electrostatics, for example, repulsion between charged balloons and the attraction between scraps of paper and a charged balloon. Students should see that a non-contact force exists between charged objects. Explain why the balloon becomes charged (electric charge moves from hair to the balloon in the example in Starter 1) and use the idea of an electric field creating forces to explain each demonstration. Ask students for their own suggestions of effects they have already seen. Students then complete the tasks on the activity sheet. | **Support**: A support sheet is available with a partially filled table for observations. **Extension**: Introduce the triboelectric series. This lists materials and their tendency to lose or gain charge. It can be used to predict which becomes negatively charged, which becomes positively charged, and which will not gain a charge. | **Activity**: Electrostatics **Skill sheet**: Recording results |

| Plenary | Support/Extension | Resources |
|---|---|---|
| **What happens with the balloon?** (5 min) Students use the interactive resource to re-order sentences to explain the effect of a charged balloon on hair. | | **Interactive**: What happens with the balloon? |
| **Draw it** (10 min) Students make labelled drawings showing what they think happens when something is charged. Use their drawings to explain any remaining misconceptions. | **Support**: Students should focus on illustrating key words from this lesson. **Extension**: This activity can be extended to electric fields. | |

| Homework |
|---|
| Students research the uses of static electricity, at home or in industry, and write a short summary paragraph. |

# 1.2 Circuits and current

**Physics KS3 NC link:**
- electric current, measured in amperes in circuits
- current as a flow of charge
- using physical processes and mechanisms, rather than energy, to explain the intermediate steps that bring about changes in systems.

**Working Scientifically NC link:**
- use appropriate techniques, apparatus, and materials during fieldwork and laboratory work, paying attention to health and safety.

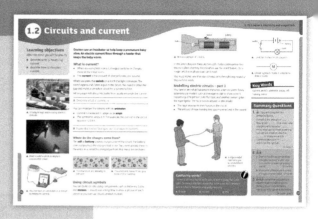

| Band | Outcome | Checkpoint | |
|---|---|---|---|
| | | Question | Activity |
| **Developing** | Name what flows in a circuit (Level 3). | 1 | Lit, Main, Plenary 1 |
| | Name the equipment used to measure current (Level 3). | B, 1 | Main, Plenary 2 |
| | Use an ammeter to measure current (Level 4). | | Main |
| **Secure** | Describe what is meant by current (Level 5). | A, 1 | Lit, Main, Plenary 1 |
| | Describe how to measure current (Level 5). | B, 1 | Main, Plenary 2 |
| | Set up a circuit including an ammeter to measure current (Level 5). | | Main |
| **Extending** | Use a model to explain how current flows in a circuit (Level 7). | 3 | Plenary 1 |
| | Predict the current in different circuits (Level 8). | | Main |
| | Measure current accurately in a number of places in a series circuit (Level 7). | | Main |

**Maths**
Students must demonstrate their understanding of the number scale if reading current in a circuit using an analogue ammeter.
Students will also use the appropriate units for current values.

**Literacy**
In the student-book activity students must explain key words using scientific understanding, and relate this to how the key words may be used differently in everyday life.

**APP**
Students apply the rope model and the water pipe analogy to understand current (AF1).
Students select the appropriate combination of equipment when carrying out the practical to investigate current (AF4).

**Key Words**
current, switch, ammeter, amps, cell, battery, motor

## Answers from the student book

| In-text questions | **A** charge flowing per second<br>**B** ammeter |
|---|---|
| Activity | **Confusing words**<br>charge: the electron has a negative charge; there is a charge to go into a theme park<br>current: current is the amount of charge flowing per second; there can be a strong current in the river<br>cell: component that pushes charge around a circuit; the smallest functional unit in an organism/American term for a mobile phone; a police or prison cell |

● P2 Chapter 1: Electricity and magnetism

| Summary Questions | 1 charge, second, electrons, ammeter, amps, A (6 marks) |
|---|---|
| | 2a Series circuit with battery of cells, motor, and switch. Students should annotate the switch, and explain how this can be switched on and off to control the circuit. (2 marks) |
| | b The electrons move/a current flows. (1 mark) |
| | 3 QWC question (6 marks). Example answers: Start with a small series circuit with a switch, lamp, and cell. Show that the light comes on as soon as you press the switch. Make the leads longer, and show that this has no effect. Make a really big circuit, and show that the lamp comes on straight away. Use the rope model to show that the bulb comes on straight away if the charges are already in the wires. It does not matter how long the wire is, the bulb still comes on straight away. If the charges were in the battery, there would be a time delay. |

**kerboodle**

| Starter | Support/Extension | Resources |
|---|---|---|
| **Drawing circuits** (5 min) Review circuit symbols from KS2. Check students can draw circuit symbols when given a names component, and vice versa. If the existing knowledge is good, they can draw simple series circuits using the correct circuit symbols. Remind them that most connecting leads are drawn with straight lines. | **Support**: Cards can be used for students to match circuit symbols to the name of the component. | |
| **Comparing currents** (10 min) Introduce current and that some appliances use larger currents than others. Explain that larger currents flow in more powerful equipment and equipment that heats things. List appliances that plug into the mains. Students to rank these in order of the current they use. If a current meter is available, the current drawn by different appliances can be demonstrated. | **Support**: Group equipment as mains and battery-operated. **Extension**: Students explain their rank order in terms of the function of the appliance. | |

| Main | Support/Extension | Resources |
|---|---|---|
| **Investigating current** (40 min) Introduce students to the idea that current is a flow of charge. The water pipe analogy can be used to facilitate understanding. Explain the use of an ammeter, introduce the unit of charge (the ampere), and demonstrate how to set up a simple series circuit (including the ammeter). Students carry out a practical to measure current using simple series circuits and answer the questions that follow on the practical sheet. Ensure that at the end of the experiment, students are aware of the conclusion. There is only one path in the (series) circuit so the current must be the same in all places. If more cells are used the current increases, and if more components are placed in the circuit for the same number of cells, the current will decrease but will still be the same in all places. | **Support**: Draw circuits on a sheet of paper. Students place components in the correct positions and link them up using wires. A partially filled results table is available on the support sheet that gives combinations students should test in their series circuit. **Extension**: Students predict changes in current if the number of components in a circuit is changed. This links to resistance, which is covered later. | **Practical**: Investigating current |

| Plenary | Support/Extension | Resources |
|---|---|---|
| **Rope model** (10 min) Explain that charge is spread throughout the circuit, and as soon as it turns on, the charge moves at the same time, transferring energy. Use the rope model, as described in the student book, to show this phenomenon. Students should discuss what each part of the model represents in a circuit. | **Extension**: Students should suggest limitations and improvements to this model. | |
| **Function of circuit components** (5 min) This interactive resource can be used as a quick recap of the functions of five circuit components. In this activity, students match the names of circuit components with their functions. | **Extension**: Students should draw the symbol for each circuit component on a mini-whiteboard. | **Interactive**: Function of circuit components |

| Homework | | |
|---|---|---|
| Students draw the circuit diagrams for simple pieces of equipment, for example, a torch, a handheld fan, or a hairdryer. | | |

# 1.3 Potential difference

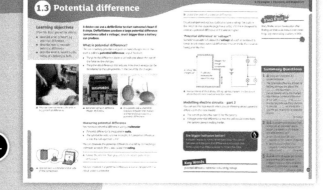

**Physics KS3 NC link:**
- potential difference, measured in volts
- battery and bulb ratings.

**Working Scientifically NC link:**
- use appropriate techniques, apparatus, and materials during fieldwork and laboratory work, paying attention to health and safety.

| Band | Outcome | Checkpoint | |
|---|---|---|---|
| | | Question | Activity |
| **Developing** | State the unit of potential difference (Level 4). | B | Main, Plenary 1 |
| | Name the equipment used to measure potential difference (Level 3). | A, 1 | Main, Plenary 1 |
| | Describe the effect of a larger potential difference (Level 4). | 1 | |
| | Use appropriate equipment to measure potential difference (Level 4). | | Main |
| **Secure** | Describe what is meant by potential difference (Level 5). | B, 1 | Starter 1, Starter 2, Plenary 1 |
| | Describe how to measure potential difference (Level 5). | A, 1 | Main |
| | Describe what is meant by the rating of a battery or bulb (Level 6). | 1 | |
| | Set up a simple circuit and use appropriate equipment to measure potential difference (Level 6). | | Main |
| **Extending** | Explain the difference between potential difference and current (Level 7). | 3 | Plenary 2 |
| | Explain why potential difference is measured in parallel (Level 7). | | Starter 1, Starter 2, Main, Plenary 1 |
| | Predict the effect of changing the rating of a battery or bulb in a circuit (Level 7). | 2 | Plenary 1 |
| | Set up and measure potential difference across various components in a circuit (Level 7). | | Main |

**Maths**
Students show understanding of number scales and relative sizes when ranking items in order of p.d. and when recording voltage readings on analogue voltmeters.

They use the correct units when measuring in the practical activity.

**Literacy**
Students use scientific key terms in the discussions of analogies, models, and their practical results.

**APP**
Students plan an experiment to investigate the relationship between battery size and p.d. in the student-book activity (AF4).

**Key Words**
potential difference, voltmeter, volts, rating, voltage

## Answers from the student book

| In-text questions | A voltmeter    B volt |
|---|---|
| Activity | **Are bigger batteries better?** Plan should include how to measure the size of the batteries, decision on diameter/weight/volume, use of voltmeter to measure the potential, difference across the battery, collect a selection of different batteries, measure the 'size' and potential difference, record results in a table, plot the correct graph type. |

## P2 Chapter 1: Electricity and magnetism

| Summary Questions | 1 push, energy, voltmeter, rating, rating (5 marks) <br> 2a The potential difference is bigger because the extra cell supplies more energy. (2 marks) <br>   b The buzzer would not work, the cells cancel out. (2 marks) <br> 3 QWC question (6 marks). Example answers: <br>    Charges flow when you connect a cell or battery. The charges are already in the wires/component. The battery pushes the charges. The size of the push is related to the potential difference. The charges flowing per second are the current. You measure the current with an ammeter. You measure the potential difference with a voltmeter. |
|---|---|

| Starter | Support/Extension | Resources |
|---|---|---|
| **Comparing potential difference** (10 min) Hand round five to six battery-powered items, and show images of appliances, including their operating potential difference (p.d.). Explain that p.d. indicates energy used by the equipment, and is measured in volts. Group items as battery operated (mainly low p.d.) or mains operated (mainly high p.d.), and rank all items from the lowest to the highest p.d. It is useful at this stage to use only the term potential difference, and not voltage, to avoid confusing students with additional terminology. <br><br> **Looking at potential difference** (10 min) Introduce sources of p.d. (e.g., lightning, power lines, railway lines). Explain that in each case a different amount of energy is used, which is linked to p.d. The interactive resource can then be used to link the operating p.d. with objects. | **Support**: Provide cards with the p.d. written on the back of each item. Students place the images on a number line. <br><br> **Extension**: Students suggest dangers of high p.d., and understand that high current is the cause of fatalities. | **Interactive**: Looking at potential difference |

| Main | Support/Extension | Resources |
|---|---|---|
| **Investigating potential difference** (40 min) Set up a simple circuit to demonstrate the position of the voltmeter in a circuit. Emphasise the difference between an ammeter (connected in series) and a voltmeter (connected in parallel). It is important to refer to p.d. **across** components, rather than inside each component. Students set up simple circuits to investigate p.d. in a range of different circuits, and answer the questions on their activity sheet. At the end of the experiment, ensure students understand the conclusions: p.d. is shared between components (depending on the component's resistance). The p.d. across the battery is the same as the sum of the p.d. across all the components in a series circuit. | **Support**: Provide enlarged circuit diagrams on A3 or A4 paper for students to place components on before linking them with wires. A support sheet is also available with suggested combinations of components to investigate in a results table. | **Activity**: Investigating potential difference <br> **Skill sheet**: Recording results |

| Plenary | Support/Extension | Resources |
|---|---|---|
| **Rope model for potential difference** (10 min) Explain that energy is transferred through the circuit from cells to components. As soon as the circuit is complete, energy is transferred in all parts of the circuit at the same time, by charge. Revisit the rope model for current, and change the analogy to that for p.d. Details can be found in the student book. <br><br> **Comparing current and voltage** (5 min) Students list similarities and differences between current and voltage, for example, how they are measured, their value in different parts of a series circuit, and what they are. | **Extension**: Students can explain the effect of changing things in this circuit, offering limitations and improvements to this model. <br><br> **Support**: Give students a list of statements describing current or p.d. for them to group. | |

| Homework | Support/Extension | |
|---|---|---|
| Students prepare a list of at least 10 pieces of electrical equipment used at home and the voltage supplied, either from batteries or the mains (230 V). Students should get parental permission to move/unplug equipment. | **Extension**: Students should rank these in order of p.d., and suggest why this is the case. | |

# 1.4 Series and parallel

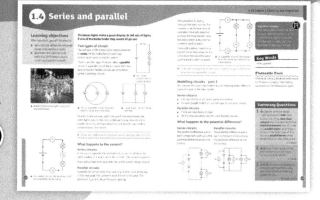

**Physics KS3 NC link:**
- series and parallel circuits, currents add where branches meet.

**Working Scientifically NC link:**
- interpret observations and data, including identifying patterns and using observations, measurements, and data to draw conclusions.

| Band | Outcome | Checkpoint | |
|---|---|---|---|
| | | Question | Activity |
| Developing | State one difference between series and parallel circuits (Level 4). | A, 1 | Starter 2, Plenary 2 |
| | State how current varies in series and parallel circuits (Level 4). | B, 2 | Maths, Main |
| | Identify the pattern of current in series and parallel circuits (Level 4). | | Main |
| Secure | Describe the difference between series and parallel circuits (Level 5). | A, 1 | Starter 2, Plenary 2 |
| | Describe how current and potential difference vary in series and parallel circuits (Level 6). | B, 2 | Maths, Main, Plenary 1 |
| | Identify the pattern of current and potential difference in series and parallel circuits (Level 6). | | Main |
| Extending | Explain the most suitable type of circuit for the domestic ring main (Level 7). | | Starter 2, Main, Homework |
| | Explain why current and potential difference vary in series and parallel circuits (Level 7). | | Maths, Main, Plenary 1 |
| | Explain the pattern in current and potential difference readings for series and parallel circuits, drawing conclusions (Level 7). | | Main |

**Maths**
Students should identify numerical patterns in the data obtained for current and p.d. from their experiment.

**Literacy**
Students should apply existing knowledge to explain the numerical patterns observed in their experiment using scientific key words.

**APP**
Students should use the rope model to compare similarities and differences between series and parallel circuits (AF1).

Students identify patterns in their data for current and p.d. to draw conclusions (AF5).

**Key Words**
series, parallel

## Answers from the student book

| In-text questions | **A** Two from: in a parallel circuit if one bulb breaks the others stay on; components can be turned on and off independently; parallel circuits have more than one loop or branch.<br>**B** increases |
|---|---|
| Activity | **Current issues**<br>0.2 ÷ 2 = 0.1 A<br>This is because current is shared between components in a series circuit. |

## P2 Chapter 1: Electricity and magnetism

| Summary Questions | 1 one, more than one, parallel, series (4 marks) |
|---|---|
| | 2 The current increases. (1 mark) |
| | 3 QWC question (6 marks). Example answers (three for each type of circuit): |
| | Series circuit: current is the same around the whole circuit, ammeter reading stays the same, p.d. is shared between components, voltmeter readings for components will add up to the p.d. of the power supply (cell/battery). Parallel circuit: current is split for each branch, the sum of the ammeter readings in the branches will add up to the ammeter reading from the main branch (by the power supply), p.d. is the same for each branch of the parallel circuit, voltmeter readings will be the same on each branch of the parallel circuit. |

**kerboodle**

| Starter | Support/Extension | Resources |
|---|---|---|
| **What do you know?** (10 min) Students write down what they already know about circuits, and then share their ideas. Identify misconceptions and correct mistakes at this stage. | **Support**: Prepare a short list of true/false statements about series circuits for students to categorise. **Extension**: Students should include explanations as well as descriptions. | |
| **Series or parallel?** (10 min) Ask students to list circuits where equipment or components can be controlled separately or together. For example, lighting circuits in the home or car, controls on a music system, cooker, or hairdryer. Explain how this can be done using series and parallel circuits. Students then apply this knowledge to group items into two categories: those that use series circuits, and those that use parallel circuits. | **Support**: Concentrate on if components require separate controls. Introduce key words in the main activity. **Extension**: Students justify why a series or parallel circuit is required in each case. | **Interactive**: Series or parallel? |

| Main | Support/Extension | Resources |
|---|---|---|
| **Series and parallel circuits** (35 min) Explain to students that the circuits they have been working with so far are series circuits, and introduce the idea of parallel circuits. Large diagrams of each type of circuit can be used to highlight similarities and differences, and will facilitate the tracing of electron paths around the circuits. Students then investigate circuit rules regarding current and p.d. in series and parallel circuits, by carrying out mini-experiments as part of an activity circus. Students must visit each station, each with a different circuit, and note down their observations. They then answer the questions that follow using their results. | **Support**: Diagrams of experimental setup are provided for students to add observations, current, and p.d. readings. **Extension**: Students should look for readings that are nearly the same, or that add up to roughly the same amount as another reading in the circuit. | **Practical**: Series and parallel circuits |

| Plenary | Support/Extension | Resources |
|---|---|---|
| **Making predictions** (10 min) Present students with circuit diagrams of simple series and parallel circuits. Each circuit will have partially filled data for current. Students must predict and complete the missing value for current in each case. | **Support**: Provide multiple-choice answers for predictions. **Extension**: Repeat the exercise for p.d. readings. | |
| **Rope model revisited** (10 min) Revisit the rope model to demonstrate current and p.d. in a series circuit. Ask students to contribute ideas as to how this model can be used to demonstrate parallel circuits. This model shows that adding more loops increases the current, that p.d. is supplied in all places of the circuit at the same time, and the same p.d. is supplied by the battery to both loops. | **Extension**: Once again, students can identify limitations and improvements to this model. | |

| Homework | Support/Extension | |
|---|---|---|
| Students consider what they have learned about series and parallel circuits, and use these ideas to draw a circuit for lighting in the home. This can be for several rooms in the home or for a staircase, for which the set-up for (two-way) switches should also be included. | **Support**: Students decide whether lights can be controlled independently or not, and draw a simple circuit diagram to explain their choice of circuit. | |

# 1.5 Resistance

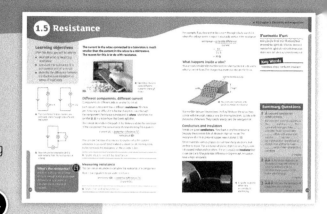

**Physics KS3 NC link:**
- resistance, measured in ohms, as the ratio of potential difference (p.d.) to current
- differences in resistance between conducting and insulating components (quantitative).

**Working Scientifically NC link:**
- select, plan, and carry out the most appropriate types of scientific enquiries to test predictions, including identifying independent, dependent, and control variables, where appropriate.

| Band | Outcome | Checkpoint | |
|---|---|---|---|
| | | Question | Activity |
| **Developing** | State the unit of resistance (Level 4). | B | Main |
| | Compare simply the resistance of conductors and insulators (Level 4). | 1 | Main |
| | List examples of conductors and insulators (Level 3). | | Main |
| | Identify some of the variables in the investigation (Level 4). | | Main |
| **Secure** | Describe what is meant by resistance (Level 5). | 1 | Main |
| | Calculate resistance of a component and of a circuit (Level 6). | 2 | Maths, Plenary 1, Homework |
| | Describe the difference between conductors and insulators in terms of resistance (Level 5). | 1, 3 | Main |
| | Identify independent, dependent, and control variables (Level 5). | | Main |
| **Extending** | Explain the causes of resistance (Level 7). | 1 | Main |
| | Explain what factors affect the resistance of a resistor (Level 7). | | Starter 2, Main |
| | Compare the effect of resistance in different materials (Level 7). | 3 | Starter 2, Main |
| | Independently select and control all the variables in the investigation, considering accuracy and precision (Level 7). | | Main |

**Maths**
Students calculate resistance using simple equations, giving units for their answers. Higher-ability students will be required to rearrange this equation.
They plot a graph of resistance against length of wire using experimental results.

**Literacy**
Students use key words correctly when suggesting a conclusion for their experiment, and when discussing aspects of working scientifically.

**APP**
Students identify key variables in their experiment (AF4), present experimental results using appropriate tables and graphs (AF3), and suggest reasons for the trends observed between variables (AF5).

**Key Words**
resistance, ohms, conductor, insulator

## Answers from the student book

| In-text questions | **A** How easy or difficult it is for the charges to pass through a component in a circuit. **B** ohms |
|---|---|
| Activity | **What's the resistance?** $\text{resistance} = \dfrac{\text{voltage}}{\text{current}} = \dfrac{12\ \text{V}}{0.6\ \text{A}} = 20\ \Omega$ |

## P2 Chapter 1: Electricity and magnetism

| Summary Questions | |
|---|---|
| 1 | potential difference, resistance, resistance, electrons, energy, conductors, insulators (7 marks) |
| 2 | lamp resistance = $\dfrac{\text{voltage}}{\text{current}}$     motor resistance = $\dfrac{\text{voltage}}{\text{current}}$ <br>                 = $\dfrac{3\text{ V}}{0.4\text{ A}}$                   = $\dfrac{3\text{ V}}{0.1\text{ A}}$ <br>                 = 7.5 Ω                    = 30 Ω        (4 marks) |
| 3 | QWC question (6 marks). Example answers: <br> Both conductors and insulators have resistance. <br> Conductors have many charges that can move readily. <br> Conductors have low resistance. <br> Insulators do not contain many charges that are free to move. <br> Insulators have high resistance. <br> Most conductors are metals that have electrons that are free to move. <br> Current in an insulator would be smaller than the current through a conductor (for the same potential difference). |

**kerboodle**

| Starter | Support/Extension | Resources |
|---|---|---|
| **What do you know already?** (5 min) This interactive resource asks students to match circuit components to their functions. This can be used as a consolidation task, before introducing students to the more abstract concept of resistance. <br><br> **What affects resistance?** (10 min) Explain what resistance is in general, for example, resistance makes it harder for something to happen. Remind students that current is the flow of charge, so electrical resistance makes it harder for charge to flow. Discuss changes you could make in a circuit to increase resistance. This is a useful activity to highlight student misconceptions. | **Extension**: Students draw circuit symbols or diagrams to illustrate each key word or phrase. <br><br> **Support**: Use the analogy of water flowing in a hosepipe. How can water flow be reduced? For example, it is harder for water to flow if the hosepipe is narrower. | **Interactive**: What do you know already? |

| Main | Support/Extension | Resources |
|---|---|---|
| **Investigating the resistance of a wire** (40 min) Introduce the idea of electrical resistance, including the equation to calculate resistance, and the difference in resistance between conductors and insulators. <br> Students will investigate how changes in a wire affect its resistance. They should list the factors they can change, for example, length, diameter, material, and temperature. It is important at this point to remind students of independent, dependent, and control variables. <br> Students will then carry out an experiment to investigate the relationship between resistance and the length of a wire. The practical sheets provided can easily be adapted to investigate other independent variables as described above. | **Support**: The support sheet contains a partially filled results table. <br> **Extension**: Students can use ammeters and voltmeters instead of a multimeter, in order to use their readings to calculate resistance for each length of wire. | **Practical**: Investigating the resistance of a wire <br> **Skill sheet**: Recording results <br> **Skill sheet**: Choosing scales |

| Plenary | Support/Extension | Resources |
|---|---|---|
| **Calculating resistance** (5 min) Draw a circuit diagram including an ammeter and voltmeter. Add sample readings for students to calculate the correct value of resistance. This can be a quiz dividing the class into three teams, and giving marks for correct calculations. <br><br> **Evaluating my experiment** (10 min) Students individually list two things that went well, and two things they would change if they repeated their experiment. They then compare these choices in their practical groups, and decide overall which factors had the greatest effect on the experiment. | **Support**: Provide a multiple-choice selection of resistance values. <br> **Extension**: Provide circuit diagrams with resistance values but current or potential difference readings missing. Students should calculate the missing information. | **Skill sheet**: Evaluation |

| Homework | Support/Extension | |
|---|---|---|
| Provide students with further examples of resistance calculations, for them to complete at home. | **Support**: Provide multiple-choice answers. <br> **Extension**: Include calculations involving rearrangements. | |

# 1.6 Magnets and magnetic fields

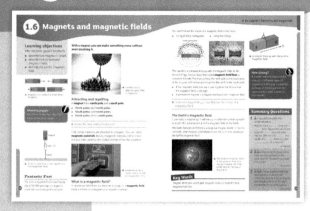

**Physics KS3 NC link:**
- magnetic poles, attraction and repulsion
- magnetic fields by plotting with compass, representation by field lines
- Earth's magnetism, compass, and navigation
- non-contact forces: forces between magnets
- using physical processes and mechanisms, rather than energy, to explain the intermediate steps that bring about changes in systems.

**Working Scientifically NC link:**
- make and record observations and measurements using a range of methods for different investigations; and evaluate the reliability of methods and suggest possible improvements.

| Band | Outcome | Checkpoint | |
|---|---|---|---|
| | | Question | Activity |
| **Developing** | Describe features of a magnet (Level 3). | A, 1 | Starter 2, Main |
| | Draw the magnetic field lines around a bar magnet (Level 4). | | Starter 2, Main |
| | State the Earth has a magnetic field (Level 4). | 2 | Main, Plenary 1 |
| | Record the shape of field lines round a magnet (Level 4). | | Main |
| **Secure** | Describe how magnets interact (Level 5). | 1, 3 | Starter 2 |
| | Describe how to represent magnetic fields (Level 6). | B, 1 | Starter 2, Main |
| | Describe the Earth's magnetic field (Level 5). | 2 | Main, Plenary 1 |
| | Draw field lines round a magnet in detail (Level 6). | | Main |
| **Extending** | Explain how magnets can be used (Level 7). | 1, 4 | Homework |
| | Compare magnetic field lines and a magnetic field (Level 7). | 2 | Starter 1, Main |
| | Explain how a compass works (Level 7). | 1, 2 | Main, Plenary 1, Plenary 2 |
| | Suggest improvements to an experiment to observe field lines around a magnet (Level 7). | | Main |

**Literacy**
Students use scientific terminology correctly when describing magnetic fields and materials.

**APP**
Students use models when explaining the abstract concept of magnetism (AF1), and communicate observations relating magnetic fields using appropriate diagrams (AF3).

**Key Words**
magnet, north pole, south pole, magnetic material, magnetic field, magnetic field lines

## Answers from the student book

| In-text questions | A north and south | B use a compass/iron filings | |
|---|---|---|---|
| Activity | **How strong?** | | |
| | Type of magnet | Distance between paperclip and magnet to get it to float (cm) | |
| | | | |

● P2 Chapter 1: Electricity and magnetism

| Summary Questions | 1 north, south, repel, attract, compass, magnetic field (6 marks) |
|---|---|
| | 2 A compass needle always points in a north–south direction. The compass needle lines up in the Earth's magnetic field (which does not change). (2 marks) |
| | 3 The game instructions and scoring system should include (6 marks): |
| | Clear list of instructions. |
| | Using magnets to pick up or guide things. |
| | Correct use of north/south poles in the game. |
| | Scoring system linked to completion/difficulty. |
| | Linking scoring system to magnetic field strength/attraction/repulsion. |
| | Correct use of magnetic field strength/attraction/repulsion in scoring system. |

**kerboodle**

| Starter | Support/Extension | Resources |
|---|---|---|
| **Changing fields** (15 min) Attach a paperclip to thread and fix the thread firmly to the bench using sticky tape. Use a clamp stand to hold a magnet above the paperclip so it levitates with 3–5 cm between the paperclip and magnet. Students predict the effect of sliding different materials between the paperclip and magnet. Show that sliding non-magnetic materials between the paperclip and magnet has no effect, but magnetic materials disrupt the field so the paperclip falls. | **Extension**: Students suggest reasons for their observations using scientific terminology. | |
| **What is a magnet?** (15 min) Snowballing activity where students describe magnets in two or three sentences individually, then share ideas in small groups to come up with one description. Demonstrate field lines around a magnet using iron filings. This can be shown in 3-D if enough iron filings are used. (Ferrofluids can be used to show the 3-D nature of magnetic fields, if available.) Use students' ideas and the demonstration to identify the main features of a magnet (e.g., it attracts certain materials, it attracts/repels other magnets). | **Support**: Provide a list of true/false statements about magnets and magnetic fields. **Extension**: Make certain key words taboo in their description, for example, magnetic, north, and south. | |

| Main | Support/Extension | Resources |
|---|---|---|
| **Drawing magnetic fields** (30 min) Students are generally familiar with the concept of magnets and magnetic fields, but a short recap will aid students in their understanding of more abstract concepts. Demonstrate the difference between a magnet and a magnetic material, and their effect on a compass. Discuss the nature of the Earth's magnetic field, and explain that most magnets held close to an object have stronger fields than Earth, which is why compasses point towards a nearby magnet. Students can suggest the properties of the materials used to make a compass needle (magnetic, magnet, or non-magnetic) and the outer casing. Students then carry out a short practical where they use a compass to plot field lines around a bar magnet, and investigate field lines for magnets of different shapes. They then answer the questions that follow. | **Support**: The support sheet provides students with a step-by-step guide on drawing field lines around a bar magnet using a compass. **Extension**: Students predict the shapes of magnetic fields for different-shaped magnets. | **Practical**: Drawing magnetic fields |

| Plenary | Support/Extension | Resources |
|---|---|---|
| **Which way does it point?** (10 min) Students choose the correct words to explain how a compass works when filling in the gaps on the interactive resource. | **Extension**: Students should compare the strength of the Earth's magnetic field with a bar magnet. | **Interactive**: Which way does it point? |
| **Navigating with magnets** (10 min) Show a video clip from the Internet of migrating birds or homing pigeons. Students suggest how they can navigate. Discuss different theories (bird brains have sensors that respond to the Earth's magnetic field or their eyes respond to directional sunlight). Suggest why people need to use a compass to navigate. | **Extension**: Students suggest other ways to navigate if a compass is not available, or factors that can disrupt a bird's navigational system. | |

| Homework | | |
|---|---|---|
| Students investigate magnets at home, finding as many uses as possible for permanent magnets and identifying magnetic materials around the home. Then write a paragraph explaining why magnets are used in these cases. | | |

# 1.7 Electromagnets

**Physics KS3 NC link:**
- the magnetic effect of a current, electromagnets, D.C. motors (principles only).

**Working Scientifically NC link:**
- make predictions using scientific knowledge and understanding.

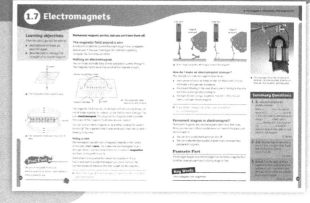

| Band | Outcome | Checkpoint | |
|---|---|---|---|
| | | Question | Activity |
| Developing | State the main features of an electromagnet (Level 4). | 1 | Starter 1 |
| | State one difference between permanent magnets and electromagnets (Level 4). | 1 | Starter 1 |
| | Test the effect of changing an electromagnet (Level 4). | | Starter 2, Main |
| Secure | Describe how to make an electromagnet (Level 5). | 1, 2 | Starter 2 |
| | Describe how to change the strength of an electromagnet (Level 6). | B, 3 | Starter 2, Main |
| | Predict and test the effect of changes to an electromagnet (Level 6). | | Main, Plenary 1 |
| Extending | Explain how an electromagnet works (Level 7). | 3 | Homework |
| | Predict the effect of changes on the strength of different electromagnets (Level 7). | | Main, Plenary 1, Homework |
| | Predict the effect of changes made to an electromagnet, using scientific knowledge to justify the claim (Level 8). | | Main, Plenary 1 |

**Maths**
Students calculate the quantitative relationship between changes made to an electromagnet and the increase in its strength, demonstrating an understanding of simple ratios.

**Literacy**
Students use scientific terminology correctly when discussing observations and conclusions from their experiment.

**APP**
Students identify quantitative relationships between variables in an experiment (AF5).

**Key Words**
electromagnet, core, magnetise

## Answers from the student book

| In-text questions | A magnetic |
| --- | --- |
| | B type of core, number of turns, current |
| Summary Questions | 1 current, magnetic field, coil, current, magnetic field (5 marks) |
| | 2 Wind a wire around the nail. |
| | Attach the ends of the wires to the battery using the leads and crocodile clips. (2 marks) |
| | 3 QWC question (6 marks). Example answers: |
| | There is a magnetic field around a wire carrying a current. |
| | The field is stronger if there are more loops of wire. |
| | This is because the fields add together. |
| | A bigger current produces a stronger magnetic field. |
| | The magnetic material inside the coil becomes magnetised when you put it in a magnetic field. |
| | This increases the strength of the electromagnet. |

# P2 Chapter 1: Electricity and magnetism

| Starter | Support/Extension | Resources |
|---|---|---|
| An alternative question-led lesson is also available. | | **Question-led lesson**: Electromagnets |
| **What is an electromagnet?** (10 min) Demonstrate an electromagnet in the laboratory or using a video clip. Show that it can be switched on and off, and that it can be adjusted in strength. Students prepare a list that compares features of an electromagnet with a magnet. | **Support**: Provide a list of statements for students to match to magnets or electromagnets. | |
| **Changing the strength** (10 min) Introduce the idea of an electromagnet using a diagram. Discuss as a class the factors affecting the strength of an electromagnet, encouraging students' ideas in the meantime. Students then recap what they have learnt using a gap-fill summary on the interactive resource. | **Support**: Prepare a list of variables from the interactive resource. Students can decide if any of these variables apply to a permanent magnet. **Extension**: Students evaluate the factors given, stating those that will cause the biggest change in strength. | **Interactive**: Changing the strength |

| Main | Support/Extension | Resources |
|---|---|---|
| **Changing the strength of electromagnets** (35 min) Students carry out a practical to investigate the effects on the strength of electromagnets of changing different variables, by taking part in a circus activity. Students will change the current, the number of turns on the coil, and the material used as the core of the electromagnet in their experiments.<br><br>Students form their own predictions before carrying out the experiment, compare results to their predictions, and answer questions that follow on the practical sheet. | **Support**: A support sheet is available that includes partially filled results tables. **Extension**: Students should be encouraged to suggest quantitative predictions based on scientific understanding. | **Practical**: Changing the strength of electromagnets **Skill sheet**: Recording results |

| Plenary | Support/Extension | Resources |
|---|---|---|
| **Testing predictions** (10 min) Students compare their original prediction with what actually happened during their experiment. They identify the factors that had the biggest effect on the strength of an electromagnet and list features of a really strong electromagnet on a mini-whiteboard. | **Support**: Students focus on general trends. **Extension**: Students should offer quantitative examples when explaining the trends observed. | |
| **What have I learned?** (10 min) Students list three things they learnt in this lesson, including the three factors that affect the strength of an electromagnet. Use this as a chance to check and correct misconceptions. | | |

| Homework |
|---|
| Provide students with information regarding costs of materials to make an electromagnet (e.g., copper costs 10p per metre; 1 m = 20 turns in the coil). Ask students to make the strongest but cheapest electromagnet possible based on prices provided. |

# 1.8 Using electromagnets

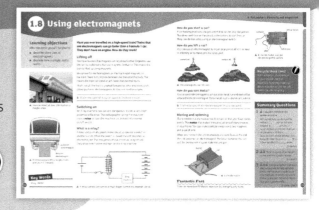

**Physics KS3 NC link:**
- the magnetic effect of a current, electromagnets, D.C. motors (principles only).

**Working Scientifically NC link:**
- identify further questions arising from their results.

| Band | Outcome | Checkpoint | |
|------|---------|------------|---|
| | | Question | Activity |
| **Developing** | State some uses of electromagnets (Level 4). | A, B, 1 | Starter 2, Lit, Plenary 2 |
| | State the main parts of a motor (Level 4). | 2 | Main |
| | Ask simple questions about motors (Level 4). | | Main |
| **Secure** | Describe some uses of electromagnets (Level 5). | 2, 3 | Lit, Starter 2, Plenary 2 |
| | Describe how a simple motor works (Level 5). | 2 | Main, Homework |
| | From your experiment, pose scientific questions to be investigated (Level 6). | | Main |
| **Extending** | Apply existing knowledge about electromagnets to design a circuit (Level 7). | 3 | Lit |
| | Suggest ways to make a motor turn faster (Level 7). | | Main, Homework |
| | Suggest investigations about electromagnets used in different applications (Level 7). | | Main |

**Literacy**
Students use scientific terms correctly when explaining observations in their experiment, when explaining the uses of motors for their homework, and when writing a letter in the student-book activity to persuade the use of electromagnets to sort soft-drinks cans for recycling.

**APP**
Students make further predictions on electromagnets and motors, based on experimental results (AF5).

**Key Words**
relay, motor

## Answers from the student book

| In-text questions | **A** electromagnets |
| | **B** To lift cars/sort metals. |
| Activity | **Recycle those cans!** The letter should explain the basic construction of an electromagnet, and that the electromagnet will attract steel cans but not aluminium. |
| Summary Questions | 1 trains, relay, current, spins, motor (5 marks) |
| | 2 A simple motor contains a coil of wire and two permanent magnets. |
| | A current flows in the coil of wire. |
| | The coil becomes an electromagnet. |
| | The forces between the coil and the permanent magnets make it spin. (4 marks) |

# P2 Chapter 1: Electricity and magnetism

| | |
|---|---|
| | **3** QWC question (6 marks). Example answers:<br>Electromagnet is on the two walls.<br>A magnetic material is on the doors.<br>When a current flows in the electromagnet there is a magnetic field around it.<br>The magnetic material on the doors is attracted to it.<br>The doors stay open while a current flows.<br>When the fire alarm sounds, the current to the electromagnet is cut.<br>There is no longer a magnetic field around the electromagnet.<br>The magnetic material on the doors is no longer attracted to it.<br>The doors close. |

| Starter | Support/Extension | Resources |
|---|---|---|
| **Introducing motors** (10 min) Explain that a motor uses electricity to make something spin. Students list as many pieces of equipment that use motors in the home as possible. This can be done as a competition in small groups. | **Extension**: Students rank their list of equipment by their prediction of the strength of the motor they use. | |
| **Uses of electromagnets** (10 min) Students sort uses of electromagnets into three categories (electromagnets that turn on and off, those that vibrate, and those that are very strong) using the interactive resources. | **Support**: Allow students to work in groups to discuss possible answers before a class discussion. | **Interactive**: Uses of electromagnets |
| **Main** | **Support/Extension** | **Resources** |
| **Using electromagnets** (35 min) Compare properties of permanent magnets and electromagnets, and introduce the different uses of electromagnets, leading to motors. Demonstrate equipment that uses a motor, and explain that motors need magnets and an electric current to spin. Students should be able to spot that both a permanent magnet and an electromagnet are required in a motor.<br><br>Students then carry out a simple practical to make a motor of their own, answering questions that follow on the practical sheet. Students may choose to use different thicknesses of wire, different batteries, or different magnets if time permits. Students should explain their observations and try to relate their results to their work from previous lesson on electromagnets. | **Support**: The support sheet contains hints for students when writing further questions they can investigate in this practical.<br>**Extension**: Students may be able to repeat the experiment, changing one variable in a methodical way, in the same time it takes the rest of the class to carry out the practical once. | **Practical**: Using electromagnets |
| **Plenary** | **Support/Extension** | **Resources** |
| **Your questions** (10 min) Students share their questions from the practical sheet with a partner, and decide in groups/pairs if they can suggest answers to these questions. If there is time, demonstrate the effect of some of their changes and see if they were right. | **Extension**: Students share their hypothesis for each change suggested. | |
| **Uses of electromagnets revisited** (10 min) Students should work independently to name as many uses of electromagnets as possible. They then join up in small groups to add to their existing ideas. Groups can then compete with each other in a competition for the longest list. | **Extension**: Students may earn bonus points if they list uses of electromagnets by category (e.g., transport: car engine and levitating train; kitchen: microwave turntable and electric whisk). | |
| **Homework** | | |
| Students find out about one application of motors in detail. They write a paragraph explaining how the motor works, explaining the roles of the permanent and electromagnet in the motor, and how to make the motor stronger. Students can decorate their work using an image of a motor. | | |
| An alternative WebQuest homework activity is also available on Kerboodle where students research the use of electromagnets in metal-recycling. | | **WebQuest**: Metal-recycling and electromagnets |

# P2 Chapter 1 Checkpoint

## Checkpoint lesson routes

The route through this lesson can be determined using the Checkpoint assessment. Percentage pass marks are supplied in the Checkpoint teacher notes.

**Route A (support)**
Resource: P2 Chapter 1 Checkpoint: Revision
Students work through a series of tasks that allows them to gradually revisit and consolidate their understanding of electricity and magnetism. Students can keep this as a summary of the topic, and use this when revising for future assessments.

**Route B (extension)**
Resource: P2 Chapter 1 Checkpoint: Extension
Students prepare a leaflet describing some of the different household circuits to a primary-school audience. Students are required to draw labelled diagrams of series and parallel circuits, explaining current and potential difference rules.

## Progression to *secure*

| No. | Developing outcome | Secure outcome | Making progress |
|---|---|---|---|
| 1 | State the two types of charge. | Describe how charged objects interact. | In Task 1 students fill in a table to show whether two charges will attract or repel. |
| 2 | Describe how to charge insulators. | Explain how objects can become charged. | In Task 1 students reorder sentences to explain how hair becomes charged when it is combed. |
| 3 | State what surrounds charged objects. | Describe what is meant by an electric field. | In Task 5 students describe the difference between a magnetic and an electric field. |
| 4 | State what flows in a circuit. | Describe what is meant by current. | In Task 2 students fill in a table to give the definitions of current and potential difference, as well as naming the circuit components that measure these. |
| 5 | Describe the effect of a larger potential difference. | Describe what is meant by the rating of a battery or bulb. | In Task 4 students predict what would happen to a bulb rated 6 V in a circuit of 10 V. |
| 6 | State one difference between series and parallel circuits. | Describe the difference between series and parallel circuits. | In Task 3 students decide if the circuit diagrams given show series or parallel circuits, explaining their answers. |
| 7 | State how current varies in series and parallel circuits. | Describe how current and potential difference vary in series and parallel circuits. | In Task 4 students use their knowledge of series and parallel circuit rules to a calculation on resistance and complete the missing values on a circuit diagram. |
| 8 | State the unit of resistance. | Describe what is meant by resistance. | In Task 4 students complete the missing words in a paragraph describing resistance. |
| 9 | List examples of conductors and insulators, comparing simply their difference in resistance. | Calculate resistance of a component in a circuit and describe the difference between conductors and insulators. | In Task 4 students explain whether wires in an electric circuit are made from conductors or insulators using the idea of resistance. |
| 10 | Describe features of a magnet. | Describe how magnets interact. | In Task 5 students explain whether a given arrangement of two magnets will attract or repel, giving reasons for their answer. |
| 11 | Draw the magnetic field lines around a bar magnet and the Earth. | Describe how to represent magnetic fields. | In Task 5 students draw the magnetic field around a bar magnet and around the Earth. |
| 12 | State the main features of an electromagnet and give some examples of their uses. | Describe how to make an electromagnet and describe some of its uses. | In Task 5 students describe two uses of electromagnets, using the main features of an electromagnet in their description. |

● P2 Chapter 1: Electricity and magnetism

| 13 | State one difference between permanent magnets and electromagnets. | Describe how to change the strength of an electromagnet. | In Task 5 students are required to describe two ways to make an electromagnet stronger. |
|---|---|---|---|
| 14 | State the main parts of a motor. | Describe how a simple motor works. | In Task 6 students reorder sentences to explain how a motor works. |

## Answers to end-of-chapter questions

**1a** B (1 mark)

**b** Circuit A: connect a lead from the bulb to the battery.
Circuit C: turn one of the cells around. (2 marks)

**2a** Diagram as in page 133 of student book. (2 marks)   **b** A: attract B: repel (2 marks)

**c** You can turn an electromagnet on and off but you cannot turn a permanent magnet on and off.

**3** A current flows in a coil of wire, the coil of wire spins in a magnetic field. (1 mark)

**4a** Credit suitable parallel circuits with two cells on one branch, with a bulb and a switch on two other branches. (2 marks)

**b** parallel (1 mark)   **c** X, Y, X and Y   **d** Attach an ammeter between the bulbs and the switches. (2 marks)

**5a** Circuit diagram as described. (2 marks)

**b** The push of the battery/energy transferred in a component. (1 mark)

**c** The potential difference that the lamp is designed to work at. (1 mark)

**d** resistance = $\dfrac{\text{voltage}}{\text{current}}$

$= \dfrac{12\text{ V}}{0.4\text{ A}}$

$= 30\ \Omega$         (2 marks)

**6a** Reading on the ammeter is halved, because there is twice the resistance. (2 marks)

**b** The voltmeter reading is halved, there is less energy transferred to the lamp because the current is less. (2 marks)

**7** This is a QWC question. Students should be marked on the use of good English, organisation of information, spelling and grammar, and correct use of specialist scientific terms. The best answers will explain in detail how the rod becomes charged and is able to attract the small pieces of paper (maximum of 6 marks).

Examples of correct scientific points:

Both the rod and cloth contain atoms.
Atoms contain electrons, protons, and neutrons.
Electrons are negatively charged.
Protons are positively charged.
When you rub the rod, electrons move from the cloth to the rod (or vice versa).

The rod becomes negatively charged/cloth becomes positively charged (or vice versa, as above)
The rod repels the electrons on the top of the pieces of paper.
The top of the pieces of paper become positively charged.
The paper is attracted to the rod.

## Answer guide for Maths Challenge

| Developing | Secure | Extending |
|---|---|---|
| 1–2 marks | 3–4 marks | 5–6 marks |
| • Identifies at least one of the variables. | • Identifies most of the variables. | • Identifies all of the variables. |
| • Draws one table but with some or all units missing from the headers. | • Draws at least one table with some units in the headers. | • Draws all the relevant tables with the correct units in the headers. |
| • Draws one bar chart but with labels on the axes missing. | • Draws at least one bar chart or line graph with correctly labelled axes. | • Draws appropriate line graphs and bar charts with correctly labelled axes, including units. |
|  | • States that tungsten has the biggest resistance because the electromagnet is weaker. | • Explains why tungsten has the biggest resistance in terms of current. |

### kerboodle

P2 Chapter 1 Checkpoint assessment (automarked)
P2 Chapter 1 Checkpoint: Revision
P2 Chapter 1 Checkpoint: Extension
P2 Chapter 1 Progress task (Literacy)

# 2.1 Food and fuels

**Physics NC link:**
- comparing energy values of different foods (from labels) (kJ)
- fuels and energy resources.

**Working Scientifically NC link:**
- present reasoned explanations, including explaining data in relation to predictions and hypotheses.

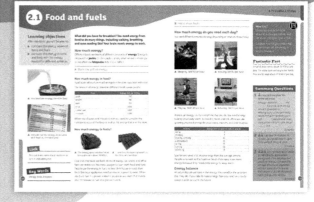

| Band | Outcome | Checkpoint | |
|---|---|---|---|
| | | Question | Activity |
| **Developing** | Identify energy values for food and fuels (Level 3). | A, 1 | Main |
| | Describe energy requirements in different situations (Level 4). | 1, 2 | Maths, Starter 2, Main, Plenary 1 |
| | Interpret data on food intake for some activities (Level 4). | | Main |
| **Secure** | Compare the energy values of food and fuels (Level 5). | 2 | Starter 1, Main, Plenary 2 |
| | Compare the energy in food and fuels with the energy needed for different activities (Level 5). | 2, 3 | Maths, Starter 2, Main, Plenary 1, Plenary 2 |
| | Explain data on food intake and energy requirements for a range of activities (Level 6). | | Main |
| **Extending** | Calculate energy requirements for various situations, considering diet and exercise (Level 7). | 2, 3 | Maths, Starter 2, Main, Plenary 1 |
| | Suggest different foods needed in unusual situations, for example, training for the Olympics (Level 7). | 3 | Starter 2, Main |
| | Explain why an athlete needs more energy from food using data provided (Level 7). | | Main |

**Maths**
In the student-book activity students carry out simple calculations involving multiplication and division to deduce the energy expenditure per minute for different activities.

Students are also required to convert between joules and kilojoules in this lesson.

**Literacy**
Students extract and use information from different resources to describe situations where food and activities need to be matched.

**APP**
Student present data from secondary sources using tables (AF3).

**Key Words**
energy, joule, kilojoule

## Answers from the student book

| In-text questions | **A** joules |
| | **B** Three from: wood, oil, coal, gas |
| Activity | **How far?** |
| | 50 g of chocolate contains: 0.5 × 1500 = 750 kJ |
| | You would need to run for: 750 ÷ 60 = 12.5 minutes |
| | This means you will need to run: 12.5 × 150 = 1875 m |

P2 Chapter 2: Energy

| Summary Questions | 1 food, fuels, joules, breathing, bones, muscles, brains (6 marks) |
| --- | --- |
| | 2 20 minutes (2 marks) |
| | 3 Example answers (6 marks): |
| |    Identifies a range of activities. |
| |    Identifies the time that he/she spends doing each activity. |
| |    Identifies the energy used per minute for the activities using the table. |
| |    Calculates the energy for each activity by multiplying the time by the energy per minute. |
| |    Identifies the energy stored in bananas, peas, chips, and chocolate from the table. |
| |    Works out the mass of each that would be needed for the daily activities. |
| |    Comments on the contrast in mass between fruit and chips/chocolate. |

**kerboodle**

| Starter | Support/Extension | Resources |
| --- | --- | --- |
| **Energy stored in foods** (5 min) A list of statements relating to the energy stored in foods is given on the interactive resource. Students must categorise these statements according to whether they are true or false. | **Extension**: Students correct the statements that are false, and prepare three more statements (true or false) to share with the class. | **Interactive**: Energy stored in foods |
| **Food and activity** (10 min) Students consider how the food requirements change for different people engaged in different activities. These can be ranked in order of energy used. | **Extension**: Students suggest how energy requirements change for different people or activity levels. They predict the effect of keeping the amount of food eaten constant. | |

| Main | Support/Extension | Resources |
| --- | --- | --- |
| **Food and fuels** (35 min) This activity uses props to demonstrate the size of a joule to students. Students extract information from food labels about energy intake per portion, suggest foods that could be eaten to provide their daily amount of energy, and rank energy requirements for carrying out different activities in order. | **Support**: The accompanying access sheet has simplified questions.<br>**Extension**: Students can suggest similar activities that use the same amount of energy (or 10 times the amount of energy). | **Activity**: Food and fuels<br>**Skill sheet**: Converting units |

| Plenary | Support/Extension | Resources |
| --- | --- | --- |
| **What used the most energy today?** (10 min) Students decide which activity they do during a typical school day has the greatest energy requirement, and give a justification for their answer. Students compare their choices. Ask students 'Do you adjust your food intake to allow for an active school day?'. | **Support**: Provide a data sheet listing approximate energy requirements by activity for a fixed duration, which students can refer to. | |
| **Energy in fuel** (10 min) Provide students with information about the energy supplied by burning fuels. Students compare the amount of energy supplied by fuel with the energy supplied by food. Explain that fuels are often a more concentrated form of energy than food. | **Extension**: Students compare reasons for using fuels in different situations (e.g., coal is not used in cars because it leaves ash). | |

| Homework | Support/Extension | |
| --- | --- | --- |
| Students keep track of what they do during a 24-hour period (activity and duration), and estimate their energy requirements for that day. | **Support**: Provide a table listing approximate energy requirements by activity and duration, which students can complete based on their own activity. | |

# 2.2 Energy adds up

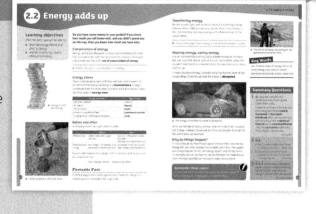

**Physics NC link:**
- energy as a quantity that can be quantified and calculated; the total energy has the same value before and after a change
- comparing the starting with the final conditions of a system and describing increases and decreases in the amounts of energy associated with movements, temperature, changes in positions in a field, in elastic distortions and in chemical compositions
- other processes that involve energy transfer: changing motion, dropping an object, completing an electrical circuit, stretching a spring, metabolism of food, burning fuels
- energy changes on deformation.

**Working Scientifically NC link:**
- make and record observations and measurements using a range of methods for different investigations.

| Band | Outcome | Checkpoint | |
|---|---|---|---|
| | | Question | Activity |
| **Developing** | State the definition of the conservation of energy (Level 4). | A, 1 | Starter 2, Main |
| | State how energy is transferred (Level 4). | B | Starter 2, Main, Plenary 2 |
| | Present simple observations of energy transfers (Level 4). | | Main |
| **Secure** | Describe energy before and after a change (Level 6). | 2, 3 | Starter 1, Main, Plenary 2 |
| | Explain what brings about transfers in energy (Level 6). | 2, 3 | Starter 2, Main, Plenary 2 |
| | Present observations of energy transfers in a table (Level 6). | | Main |
| **Extending** | Account for energy dissipation during transfers (Level 7). | 2, 3 | Starter 2, Main, Plenary 2 |
| | Compare energy transfers to energy conservation (Level 7). | 3 | Starter 2, Main, Plenary 2 |
| | Present detailed observations of energy transfers in a table, including useful and non-useful transfers (Level 8). | | Main |

**Literacy**
Students use scientific terminology to explain the Law of conservation of energy, describing energy transfers in different situations.
Students are also required to create their own mnemonics for remembering the names of energy stores in the student-book activity.

**APP**
Students present practical observations in a table (AF3).

**Key Words**
law of conservation of energy, chemical store, energy store, thermal, kinetic, gravitational potential, elastic, dissipated

## Answers from the student book

| In-text questions | **A** Energy cannot be created or destroyed. It can only be transferred. |
| | **B** light, sound, electricity |
| Activity | **Remember those stores!** Credit suitable mnemonics using the letters C, T, K, G, and E. |

82

| Summary Questions | 1 created, destroyed, chemical, thermal, cannot (5 marks) |
|---|---|
| | **2a** The battery has chemical energy. (2 marks) |
| | **b** Chemical energy transferred to thermal energy by electricity and light. (2 marks) |
| | 3 QWC question (6 marks). Example answers. |
| | There is a chemical store associated with the wood (and oxygen). |
| | The wood burns in the oxygen. |
| | Energy is transferred to the sausages. |
| | Because the fire heats the sausages. |
| | There is more energy in the thermal store associated with the sausages. |
| | There is more energy in the thermal store associated with the air. |
| | There is less energy in the chemical store associated with the wood. |

| Starter | Support/Extend | Resources |
|---|---|---|
| **Energy stores** (10 min) Introduce energy stores (chemical, thermal, kinetic, gravitational potential, and elastic) to students giving examples of each type. Students, suggest another example of each type of energy store by trying to use examples in the room. | **Support**: Provide sort cards with named energy sources to match against types of energy stores. **Extension**: Students suggest reasons for differences between electricity, light, sound, and energy stores. | |
| **Energy changes** (10 min) Show some examples of energy changes and ask students to describe in words what is happening, for example, an antacid rocket, burning an indoor sparkler, and dropping a ball. Introduce the idea of energy stores and that energy is transferred from a store when anything happens. Explain that all energy must be accounted for (law of conservation of energy). | **Extension**: Students should point out unwanted energy transfers during each activity, and discuss the differences between electricity, light, sound, and energy stores. | |

| Main | Support/Extend | Resources |
|---|---|---|
| **The conservation of energy** (35 min) It is extremely important to introduce/recap the types of energy store and transfer, as well as the law of conservation of energy before the practical. Students will then carry out a circus activity where they identify energy stores before and after an energy transfer, in addition to the energy transfers taking place during the experiment. Students then answer questions that follow to consolidate their knowledge and understanding. | **Support**: The support sheet allows students to record their observations in words, choosing the type of energy store each time from two possible answers. **Extension**: Students start to write out energy transfers in words as equations, filling in details of the transfer between energy stores. | **Practical**: The conservation of energy |

| Plenary | Support/Extend | Resources |
|---|---|---|
| **Energy stores and transfers** (10 min) Students sort a list of items and scenarios into energy stores or energy transfers using the interactive resource. **Is it conserved?** (10 min) Ask students to write the law of conservation of energy on their mini-whiteboards. Students should then use an example from the practical and account for all the energy during the transfer. | **Extension**: Students should match each energy store to a corresponding energy transfer, offering the energy transfer in full for each example. | **Interactive**: Energy stores and transfers |

| Homework | | |
|---|---|---|
| Students describe five energy changes that take place during a normal school day and the changes in the energy content of corresponding energy stores. For example, eating breakfast increases the chemical store of energy, while climbing stairs increases the gravitational (potential) energy. | | |

# 2.3 Energy and temperature

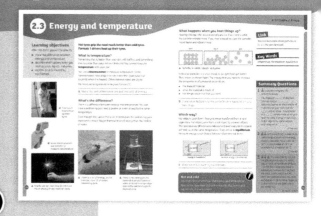

**Physics NC link:**
- heating and thermal equilibrium: temperature difference between two objects leading to energy transfer from the hotter to the cooler one
- changes with temperature in motion and spacing of particles.

**Working Scientifically NC link:**
- evaluate data, showing awareness of potential sources of random and systematic error.

| Band | Outcome | Checkpoint | |
|---|---|---|---|
| | | Question | Activity |
| **Developing** | State how energy and temperature are measured (Level 4). | A, 1 | Starter 2 |
| | Describe how energy is transferred through solids, liquids, and in air (Level 4). | B, 3 | Lit, Main |
| | State what is meant by the term 'equilibrium' (Level 4). | C, 1 | Main |
| | Identify a source of error (Level 4). | | Main, Plenary 2 |
| **Secure** | State the difference between energy and temperature (Level 6). | A, 1 | Starter 2 |
| | Describe what happens when you heat up solids, liquids, and gases (Level 6). | B, 1, 3 | Main |
| | Explain what is meant by equilibrium (Level 6). | 1, 3 | Main |
| | Describe how to reduce error in experimental apparatus (Level 6). | | Main, Plenary 2 |
| **Extending** | Give an example to show that energy and temperature are different (Level 7). | 2 | Starter 2 |
| | Explain, in terms of particles, how energy is transferred (Level 7). | B, 3 | Lit, Main, Plenary 1 |
| | Give examples of equilibrium (Level 7). | 3 | Main |
| | Describe sources of error as systemic or random, and suggest ways to minimise these (Level 7). | | Main, Plenary 2 |

**Maths**
Students use estimation for temperatures in familiar situations, and compare these to temperatures in unfamiliar situations.

**Literacy**
Students use scientific terminology when forming hypotheses and analysing and evaluating data from the experiment.
In the student-book activity students correct a scientifically incorrect phrase and justify this change.

**APP**
Students use abstract ideas and models when explaining heating and cooling (AF1).
Students collect experimental data (AF4), and suggest improvements to the experiment based on their observations (AF5).

**Key Words**
temperature, thermometer, equilibrium

## Answers from the student book

| In-text questions | **A** temperature: degrees Celsius (°C); energy: joules (J)    **B** They move/vibrate faster. **C** When objects end up at the same temperature after energy transfer. |
|---|---|
| Activity | **Hot and cold** <br> Shut the door, you will let the warm air out. (Energy moves from hot places to cold places.) |

# P2 Chapter 2: Energy

| Summary Questions | 1 temperature, thermometer, temperature, energy, solids, equilibrium (6 marks)<br>2 a cup of water at 30 °C, a saucepan of water at 30 °C, a saucepan of water at 50 °C (1 mark)<br>3 QWC question (6 marks). Example answers:<br>The particles in the metal tray vibrate. The hotter the tray the more they vibrate. When the tray goes into the oven the metal heats up. The particles on the outside of the tray vibrate more. They pass the vibrations on. The tray reaches the same temperature as the inside of the oven. The tray is in equilibrium. When you take the tray out of the oven it cools down. The energy moves from the thermal store of the tray to the thermal store of the air. The air heats up. The tray reaches the same temperature as the air. The particles in the tray vibrate less. |
|---|---|

**kerboodle**

| Starter | Support/Extension | Resources |
|---|---|---|
| **Matching temperatures** (10 min) Hand students different items to estimate the temperature of each object, and list them in rank order. For example, a warm filled hot water bottle, an ice pack, a metal spoon, a wooden spoon, and a beaker of tap water. Use the interactive resource to match examples of different objects to their temperatures.<br><br>**Energy and temperature** (10 min) Light a match and explain it burns at about 250 °C. Ask students to estimate how much it could heat a beaker of water. Dip the burning match in the water and show, using a thermometer, that the temperature rise is negligible. Explain that energy (J) stored in the match depends on temperature (°C), as well as mass and material. | **Support**: Simpler objects can be suggested in an alternative matching exercise, using boiling water, body temperature, and freezing point of water.<br><br>**Extension**: Students can apply this idea to the difference in water temperature after heating 100 ml of water for 10 minutes, compared with heating 1 litre of water for 10 minutes. | **Interactive**: Matching temperatures |

| Main | Support/Extension | Resources |
|---|---|---|
| **Energy and temperature** (35 min) Explain the difference between temperature (°C) and energy in a thermal store (J). The energy stored in something hot depends on its temperature, its size, and the material it is made from. Demonstrate how to use a thermometer, describing sources of error. Explain that the thermometer is in equilibrium (the same temperature as) with its surroundings when its reading stops changing. Review the particle model of solids, liquids, and gases briefly. Explain that changes of state change the particle arrangement. The particles themselves do not change but the spacing between them does.<br><br>Students then carry out short experiments as part of an activity circus, recording their observations, and answering questions that follow. | **Support**: A support sheet is available with a partially filled results table and a list of possible observations students should look out for during their experiments. | **Practical**: Energy and temperature<br>**Skill sheet**: Recording results |

| Plenary | Support/Extension | Resources |
|---|---|---|
| **Extreme temperatures** (10 min) Explain why objects warm up (particles vibrate more, storing more energy). Explain that absolute zero is the temperature at which particles stop moving and nothing can get colder. This is −273 °C. There is no limit on the hottest temperature. Discuss where we may find extreme temperatures (e.g., in stars).<br><br>**Types of thermometer** (10 min) Students compare different thermometers used to make measurements, ranking them in order of ease of use, accuracy of measurements, and range of temperatures measured. Then have a class discussion. | **Support**: Students may find particle diagrams of the three states of matter useful for this exercise.<br><br>**Support**: Allow groups of students to work together.<br>**Extension**: Students offer their evaluation based on different uses of each thermometer. | |

| Homework | | |
|---|---|---|
| Students investigate the temperature of different items in the home, making a list. Students should use a thermometer to make measurements if possible, or compare the temperature of some items with known temperatures. | | |

# 2.4 Energy transfer: particles

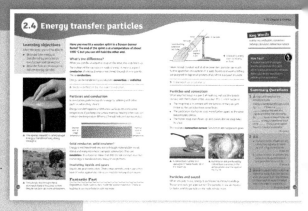

**Physics NC link:**
- heating and thermal equilibrium: temperature difference between two objects leading to energy transfer from the hotter to the cooler one, through contact (conduction); such transfers tending to reduce the temperature difference; use of insulators.

**Working Scientifically NC link:**
- interpret observations and data, including identifying patterns and using observations, measurements, and data to draw conclusions.

| Band | Outcome | Checkpoint | |
|---|---|---|---|
| | | Question | Activity |
| **Developing** | Describe simply what happens in conduction and convection (Level 4). | 1, 2 | Starter 2, Plenary 1 |
| | State that insulators reduce heat loss compared to conductors (Level 4). | 1 | Main, Plenary 1, Homework |
| | State the pattern in conduction shown in results (Level 4). | | Main |
| **Secure** | Describe how energy is transferred by particles in conduction and convection (Level 6). | 1, 2 | Starter 2, Plenary 1, Plenary 2 |
| | Describe how an insulator can reduce energy transfer (Level 6). | | Starter 1, Main, Plenary 1, Homework |
| | Describe the pattern in conduction shown by results, using numerical data to inform a conclusion (Level 5). | | Main |
| **Extending** | Explain in detail the processes involved during heat transfers (Level 7). | 3 | Starter 2, Main, Plenary 1, Plenary 2 |
| | Explain why certain materials are good insulators (Level 7). | 2 | Starter 1, Main, Plenary 1, Homework |
| | Explain the pattern in conduction shown by experimental results (Level 7). | | Main |

**Maths**
Students record numerical data in tables and calculate means, before interpreting this data to identify patterns and draw conclusions.

**Literacy**
Students explain observations and conclusions using scientific terminology.

**APP**
Students record observations in suitable tables (AF3), and draw conclusions from patterns in their experimental data (AF5).

**Key Words**
conductor, conduction, convection, radiation, insulator, convection current

## Answers from the student book

| In-text questions | **A** A material that transfers energy quickly. <br> **B** A material that does not transfer energy quickly. |
|---|---|
| Activity | **How fast?** <br> The plan should include timing how long it takes for water at a certain temperature to cool down, the need for repeat measurements, how variables are controlled, and a range of measurements of temperature. <br> Risk assessment should include sensible suggestions to avoid damage/injury from hot water. |

## P2 Chapter 2: Energy

| Summary Questions | 1 conduction, temperature difference, convection, move, slowly (6 marks) |
|---|---|
| | 2a The particles in a solid are close together, so can pass on the vibration; the particles in a gas or in a liquid are too far apart. (2 marks) |
| | b The particles in a gas or in a liquid can move; the particles in a solid cannot. Convection involves the movement of particles to transfer energy. (2 marks) |
| | 3 QWC question (6 marks). Example answers: |
| | The metal element gets hot. The particles in the metal vibrate more. Energy moves from the element to the water in contact with the element. The hot water molecules move faster. The hot water becomes less dense. Hot water floats up. Cooler (denser) water sinks to replace it. A convection current forms. The water circulates until all the water is hot. |

**kerboodle**

| Starter | Support/Extension | Resources |
|---|---|---|
| **Keeping warm** (10 min) Briefly introduce the difference between conduction and convection. Ask students to describe how they dress to keep warm. Use their suggestions to identify features reducing heat loss by conduction (e.g., insulators or trapped layers of air) and by convection (e.g., elasticated cuffs or using scarves to block gaps). | **Support**: Use items of clothing as examples, and point out the main insulating features.<br>**Extension**: Encourage students to use the terms conductor and insulator in their ideas. | |
| **Conduction and convection** (15 min) Demonstrate and explain convection (including the concept of density) using potassium permanganate crystals. Students then apply their knowledge to reorder sentences on the interactive resource to explain what happens to soup when it is heated. A common misconception is that particles themselves change in size. | **Support**: Use diagrams or simulations to aid understanding when explaining the concept of density. These are readily available on the Internet. | **Interactive**: Conduction and convection |

| Main | Support/Extension | Resources |
|---|---|---|
| **Investigating conduction** (35 min) At this stage it is important to remind students of the particle models of solids, liquids, and gases. Mini-whiteboards can be used for students to draw these particle models on, to check for retention of previous knowledge. Explain how metals have delocalised electrons that help not only to conduct electricity but also to conduct thermal energy. Introduce the concepts of conduction and convection, and demonstrate how this can be done using a thermistor and resistor, a thermometer, or thermofilm (if available).<br>Students then carry out a short investigation on different materials to determine whether they are conductors or insulators, and answer the questions that follow. | **Support**: Use the support sheet for a partially filled table of results. Students may need reminding how to calculate means. | **Activity**: Investigating conduction<br>**Skill sheet**: Recording results<br>**Skill sheet**: Calculating means |

| Plenary | Support/Extension | Resources |
|---|---|---|
| **Comparing conduction** (10 min) Ask students to offer the definitions of conduction and convection. Then demonstrate a short practical by placing two 30 cm rulers (one plastic and the other metal) in a beaker of hot water. Both rulers should have thermofilm attached to them, approximately 3 cm above the base (thermofilm should be above the water level at all times). The colour of the thermofilm attached to the metal ruler should change very quickly. | **Support**: Students describe observations, and explain using definitions of conduction and convection which concept the experiment shows.<br>**Extension**: Students should offer explanations for their observations using delocalised electrons. | |
| **Conduction versus convection** (5 min) Students compare conduction and convection by listing similarities (e.g., involving particles, transferring energy down a gradient), and differences (e.g., ability for particles to move or not, currents set up or not). | **Support**: Provide a list of true/false statements on conduction and convection for students to work through. | |

| Homework | Support/Extension |
|---|---|
| Students describe situations at home where energy is transferred by conduction or convection, and explain how the heat transfer is either helped (using good conductors and a large surface area) or reduced (using insulation). | **Extension**: Students research the meaning of radiation, and include sources around the home. |

# 2.5 Energy transfer: radiation

**Physics NC link:**
- temperature difference between two objects leading to energy transfer from the hotter to the cooler one, through radiation.

**Working Scientifically NC link:**
- evaluate risks.

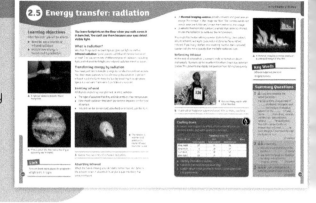

| Band | Outcome | Checkpoint | |
|---|---|---|---|
| | | Question | Activity |
| **Developing** | State some sources of infrared radiation (Level 4). | A, 1 | Main, Plenary 1 |
| | State some properties of infrared radiation (Level 4). | B, 1 | Main, Plenary 1 |
| | Identify some risks in an experiment (Level 4). | | Starter 1, Main |
| **Secure** | Describe some sources of infrared radiation (Level 5). | 1 | Main, Plenary 1 |
| | Explain how energy is transferred by radiation (Level 6). | B, 1–3 | Main, Plenary 1 |
| | Identify risks and explain why it is important to reduce them (Level 5). | | Starter 1, Main |
| **Extending** | Explain how thermal equilibrium can be established (Level 7). | 3 | Main |
| | Explain why some objects radiate more energy (Level 7). | 2, 3 | Main, Plenary 1 |
| | Explain in detail how to reduce risks (Level 7). | | Starter 1, Main |

**Maths**
Students interpret a table of results in the student-book activity and use the data to calculate means.
Students use a thermometer to accurately record temperature during their experiment.

**Literacy**
Students use scientific terminology when explaining insulating measures around the home, for their homework.

**APP**
Students identify risks in their experiments and suggest ways to reduce them (AF4).

**Key Words**
infrared radiation, thermal imaging camera

## Answers from the student book

| In-text questions | **A** two from: Sun, fire, light bulb<br>**B** It is reflected. |
|---|---|
| Activity | **Cooling down**<br>**a** first measurement for shiny white; first measurement for shiny black<br>**b** 14, 16, 13, 12.5<br>**c** The ranges overlap. |
| Summary Questions | **1** sources, radiation, temperature, reflected, absorb, medium, vacuum (7 marks)<br>**2a** White surfaces reflect infrared radiation so the houses will absorb less and stay cooler. (1 mark)<br>  **b** The fire emits infrared radiation so the camera cannot distinguish between the infrared radiation from the people and the infrared radiation from the fire. (2 marks)<br>**3** Visual summary example answers (6 marks):<br>   All objects emit infrared radiation. This is commonly referred to as thermal radiation or heat. Infrared is a type of wave. Can travel through a vacuum. Can be reflected. Can be absorbed. Transfers energy. Cannot be seen by eye. |

● P2 Chapter 2: Energy

| Starter | Support/Extension | Resources |
|---|---|---|
| An alternative question-led lesson is also available. | | **Question-led lesson**: Energy transfer: radiation |
| **Hot or cold?** (15 min) Set up a simple demonstration using three large beakers: one with hot water, one with cold water, and a third at room temperature. Ask a student to place one hand in the cold water and the other in the hot water for one minute, before placing both hands in the water at room temperature. What does each hand feel? A risk assessment is required for this demonstration. Invite students to suggest risks in this demonstration. | **Extension**: Students suggest ways to reduce risks involved with hot drinks. How can we find out how hot something is if we don't touch it? | |
| **What is radiation?** (10 min) Ask students how they can tell if something is hot or cold? What do they think the word radiation means? Discuss as a class before giving the definition (energy spreading from a source), and ask for examples. | **Support**: Give students a list of events to classify into radiation and non-radiation (e.g., light from a bulb, sound from a speaker, a magnet attracting nearby objects, and a balloon repelling another balloon). | |

| Main | Support/Extension | Resources |
|---|---|---|
| **Radiation** (35 min) Explain that infrared radiation is often called 'heat', and can be detected by our skin cells. All objects emit infrared, but cooler objects emit less. Discuss the difference between absorption and emission of infrared radiation, as well as how thermal equilibrium can be established. | **Support**: A partially filled results table is available in the corresponding support sheet. | **Practical**: Radiation **Skill sheet**: Recording results |
| If an infrared thermometer is available, a good demonstration compares the temperature of energy-efficient light bulbs, and incandescent light bulbs with the same light output. Incandescent light bulbs are hotter as they dissipate more energy. | **Extension**: Students are required to explore the idea of thermal equilibrium during their experiment. | |
| Students carry out a simple experiment to find a simple relationship between how hot or cold something feels, its temperature, its colour, and its texture. Students should decide what hot, warm, and cold feel like to them, before recording results. Encourage students to discuss the risks in this experiment and ways to reduce these risks during the practical. Students answer the questions that follow on their practical sheet. | | |

| Plenary | Support/Extension | Resources |
|---|---|---|
| **Infrared energy transfers** (5 min) Students use the interactive resource to summarise some important concepts on infrared in a gap-fill activity. This resource can be used to eliminate any outstanding misconceptions from the lesson. | **Extension**: Students give more information about each sentence by giving examples or by adding details. | **Interactive**: Infrared energy transfers |
| **Keep a tin cool** (10 min) Students use ideas from the last two lessons to compare soft-drink cans and bottles using images from the Internet. They then discuss factors affecting the length of time a drink will stay cool. | **Extension**: Students give the relative significance of each factor, and give simple ways to test these ideas. | |

| Homework | Support/Extension | |
|---|---|---|
| Students use their ideas from the lesson to identify ways to reduce heat losses at home. They should state what is used and describe how it works (e.g., curtains stop warm air reaching the window). | **Extension**: Students give examples involving conduction (materials), convection (air movement), and radiation (colour). | |
| An alternative WebQuest homework activity is also available on Kerboodle where students research how to reduce energy bills. | | **WebQuest**: Saving on heating bills |

# 2.6 Energy resources

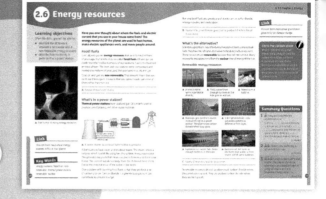

**Physics NC link:**
- domestic fuel bills, fuel use, and costs
- fuels and energy resources.

**Working Scientifically NC link:**
- interpret observations and data, including identifying patterns and using observations, measurements, and data to draw conclusions.

| Band | Outcome | Checkpoint | |
|---|---|---|---|
| | | Questions | Activities |
| **Developing** | Name renewable and non-renewable energy resources (Level 3). | A, C, 1 | Main, Plenary 1 |
| | State one advantage and one disadvantage of fossil fuels (Level 4). | B, 1 | Main, Plenary 1 |
| | Use one source of information (Level 3). | | Main |
| **Secure** | Describe the difference between a renewable and a non-renewable energy resource (Level 5). | 1, 2 | Main, Plenary 1 |
| | Describe how electricity is generated in a power station (Level 6). | 2 | Lit, Main |
| | Choose an appropriate source of secondary information (Level 5). | | Main |
| **Extending** | Compare the advantages and disadvantages of using renewable and non-renewable energy resources (Level 7). | 3 | Main, Homework |
| | Explain how a range of resources generate electricity, drawing on scientific concepts (Level 7). | 2 | Lit, Main, Homework |
| | Justify your choice of secondary information (Level 7). | | Main |

**Literacy**
In the student-book activity, students apply scientific knowledge and terminology to synthesise a children's story about the part of the carbon cycle relating to electricity generation.

Students collate information from a number of different sources to prepare a poster or leaflet to summarise information appropriately to their target audience.

**APP**
Students explain the processes involved in electricity generation (AF1), and present arguments for and against the building of different types of power stations (AF3).

**Key Words**
energy resource, fossil fuel, non-renewable, thermal power station, renewable, nuclear

## Answers from the student book

| In-text questions | **A** coal, oil, and gas |
| | **B** carbon dioxide |
| | **C** Any three from: solar, wind, wave, geothermal, hydroelectricity, tidal, or biomass. |
| Activity | **Chris the carbon atom** Story to include: tree dies, buried, over millions of years turns to coal, burnt, combines with oxygen to make carbon dioxide. |

# P2 Chapter 2: Energy

| Summary Questions | 1 non-renewable, fossil fuel, renewable, power station (4 marks)<br>2 Burning coal produces steam. Steam drives a turbine. The turbine drives a generator. The generator generates electricity. (4 marks)<br>3 Credit any suitable board game, for example, snakes and ladders or collecting cards/tokens relating to different types.<br>Points/board relates to ways fuels are formed or ways electricity is generated.<br>Point system includes ideas about climate change/pollution.<br>Board game must have a suitable scoring method relating to advantages and disadvantages of each method of electricity generation. (6 marks) |
|---|---|

| Starter | Support/Extension | Resources |
|---|---|---|
| **Sorting fuels** (10 min) Provide samples of fuels (e.g., wood, coal, oil, ethanol, and candle) for students to put into two groups. Students should justify how they have categorised their fuels during the class discussion. Introduce the idea of energy release during combustion of fuels, and the difference between renewable and non-renewable energy resources. | **Support**: Offer suggestions on how fuels can be grouped.<br>**Extension**: Students compare different ways of categorising fuels. | |
| **Life without electricity** (5 min) Students describe how their lives would be different without electricity, identifying activities that rely on electricity and activities that use other fuel sources. | **Support**: Students identify activities in everyday life that rely on electricity.<br>**Extension**: Students suggest alternatives to electricity, for example, using gas stoves and oil lamps. | |

| Main | Support/Extension | Resources |
|---|---|---|
| **Energy resources** (40 min) Provide a range of research stations, including various levels of textbooks, information posters, and leaflets, and if possible, computers with Internet access. Students carry out research in groups or independently, using the research methods provided, in order to cover the topics posed in the research activity regarding the generation of electricity.<br><br>Students must then produce a poster or leaflet to answer these questions, and if students work in small groups, they should present their findings to each other.<br><br>An animation to show how electricity is generated in thermal power stations can be shown at the end of student presentations for recap. These animations are readily available on the Internet. | **Support**: A support sheet is available that gives students a much more structured approach to their research task.<br>**Extension**: Students identify the advantages and disadvantages of using different energy resources, linking waste products from burning fossil fuels to risks. | **Activity**: Energy resources |

| Plenary | Support/Extension | Resources |
|---|---|---|
| **Fossil fuels** (5 min) Students complete the gaps on the interactive resource to explain the formation and uses of fossil fuels, including the advantages and disadvantages of using fossil fuels to generate electricity. | **Extension**: Students should offer a similar summary for renewable energy sources. | **Interactive**: Fossil fuels |
| **Ranking key points** (10 min) List the most important ways of electricity generation of this lesson on the board with help from students. Students should diamond rank these ways in order of importance, and justify their answers in small groups. | **Extension**: Students should rank the factors involved in electricity generation according to a given category, for example, impact on the environment. | |

| Homework | Support/Extension | |
|---|---|---|
| Students write a short newspaper article explaining the opening of a thermal power station in their neighbourhood. This should explain how the power station benefits the community, include some effects it has on local surroundings, and discuss the views of locals regarding this new power station. | **Extension**: Students should include a labelled diagram to illustrate how a power plant generates electricity. | |

# 2.7 Energy and power

**Physics NC link:**
- comparing power ratings of appliances in watts (W, kW)
- comparing amounts of energy transferred (J, kJ, kWh)
- domestic fuel bills, fuel use, and costs.

**Working Scientifically NC link:**
- make predictions using scientific knowledge and understanding.

| Band | Outcome | Checkpoint | |
|---|---|---|---|
| | | Question | Activities |
| **Developing** | State the definitions of energy and power (Level 4). | 1 | Main |
| | State that power, fuel used, and cost are linked (Level 4). | 1 | Main, Plenary 1, Homework |
| | Predict which equipment is more powerful when given a selection of appliances (Level 4). | | Starter 1, Starter 2, Main |
| **Secure** | Explain the difference between energy and power (Level 6). | | Main |
| | Describe the link between power, fuel use, and cost of using domestic appliances (Level 6). | 3 | Main, Plenary 1, Homework |
| | Predict the power requirements of different equipment and how much it costs to use (Level 6). | | Starter 2, Main, Plenary 1 |
| **Extending** | Compare the power consumption of different activities (Level 7). | | Starter 1, Main, Plenary 2, Homework |
| | Calculate and compare energy costs in different scenarios (Level 8). | 3 | Main, Homework |
| | Predict the effect on energy bills of changing the power of equipment (Level 7). | | Main, Plenary 1 |

**Maths**
Students carry out simple calculations for energy, power, and energy costs.

Students also demonstrate their understanding of the number scale and an appreciation of J, kJ, W, kW, and kWh in their calculations.

**Literacy**
Students use scientific terminology when explaining the link between power, energy, and cost.

**APP**
Students apply scientific knowledge to make further predictions about the power rating of appliances (AF5).

**Key Words**
power rating, watt, kilowatt, kilowatt hour

## Answers from the student book

| In-text questions | **A** watt (W) |
| | **B** kilowatt hour (kWh) |
| Activity | **What's the cost?** |
| | **a** energy = 10 kW × 1 h × 7 days = 70 kWh |
| | **b** cost = 70 kWh × 10 p ÷ 100 = £7 |

### P2 Chapter 2: Energy

| Summary Questions | 1 joules, watts, second, kWh, lower, less (6 marks) |
|---|---|
| | **2a** power = potential difference × current = 3 V × 0.2 A = 0.6 W (2 marks) |
| | **b** energy = 0.6 × 10 = 6 Ws (2 marks) |
| | **3** QWC question (6 marks). Example answers: |
| | The power rating tells you the energy that each kettle can transfer per second. |
| | The higher the power, the quicker the element will transfer energy to the water. |
| | The higher the power, the quicker the temperature of the water will rise. |
| | A power of 1200 W is the same as 1.2 kW (or 2 kW is the same as 2000 W). |
| | The 2 kW kettle will heat water faster than the 1.2 kW kettle. |
| | The energy that you pay for is measured in kilowatt hours (kWh). |
| | The energy that you pay for depends on the power and the time that you use it for. |

| Starter | Support/Extension | Resources |
|---|---|---|
| **What's the power?** (10 min) Show students a range of light bulbs of different power ratings (including energy-saving and incandescent light bulbs), and ask students to choose from everyday observations the bulb that will produce the brightest light, before offering the definition of power (amount of energy transferred per second). | **Extension**: Students link power to the energy transferred from a chemical store to a thermal store via electricity. | |
| **Power appliances** (10 min) Explain what is meant by power. Students list 10 appliances they used yesterday, and rank these according to power. Keep the list to reassess at the end of the lesson. | **Support**: Allow students to work in small groups. **Extension**: Students justify why they have ranked the appliances this way. | |

| Main | Support/Extension | Resources |
|---|---|---|
| **Power** (35 min) Introduce the difference between energy and power, and check students know the units for each. Demonstrate an energy monitor or joulemeter to show that the energy transferred depends on the power and time that the equipment is used. Compare the power of two light bulbs (an energy-saving and an incandescent light bulb), leave them on for a minute and compare their temperature. The traditional bulb is hotter and adds more to the electricity bill as it is more powerful. Students carry out the task on the activity sheet, examining different items around the home, and answer the questions that follow. | **Support**: Remind students that power is measured in watts (W) or kilowatts (kW), and that these are the only letters they should look for when reading appliance labels. **Extension**: Introduce kilowatt hours (kWh) in general terms, and allow students to read the corresponding section in the student book. | **Activity**: Power **Skill sheet:** Converting units |

| Plenary | Support/Extension | Resources |
|---|---|---|
| **Reducing energy bills** (10 min) Students use ideas gained from this lesson to summarise ways to reduce energy bills. They choose the correct words to complete sentences in the interactive resource. A common misconception is to confuse wasted money with wasted energy. Energy is conserved, but some of the energy we pay for is not used efficiently. | **Extension**: Students suggest the relative importance of each energy-saving measure. **Support**: Allow students to work in small groups. | **Interactive**: Reducing energy bills |
| **Power appliances (revisited)** (10 min) Students check their order of the 10 appliances from the start of the lesson, and decide if they still agree with their original ranking based on what they have learnt this lesson. Ask students to justify any changes made. | **Extension**: Students justify their order based on their scientific understanding. | |

| Homework | Support/Extension | |
|---|---|---|
| Students check appliances at home to find out the power rating of each. Students **must** check with their parents before unplugging or moving appliances, or else carry out this task under adult supervision. They then list these appliances in order of power, starting from the lowest power rating, and stating the relevance power rating has on an energy bill. | **Extension**: Students should provide an additional list in order of energy used (and therefore the amount of time each appliance is used per day and the cost of running each appliance). | |

# 2.8 Work, energy, and machines

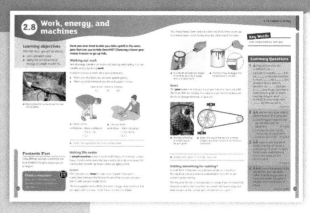

**Physics NC link:**
- work done
- examples of processes that cause change with forces (work = force × distance) levers and gears reducing force by increasing distance simple machines give bigger force but at the expense of smaller movement (and vice versa): product of force and displacement unchanged.

**Working Scientifically NC link:**
- evaluate data, showing awareness of potential sources of random and systematic error.

| Band | Outcome | Checkpoint | |
|---|---|---|---|
| | | Question | Activity |
| **Developing** | State how work is calculated (Level 4). | A, 1 | Main |
| | State machines conserve energy (Level 4). | 1 | Main |
| | State one way the experiment can be improved (Level 4). | | Main |
| **Secure** | Calculate work done (Level 6). | 2, 3 | Main |
| | Apply the conservation of energy to simple machines (Level 6). | 4 | Starter 2, Main, Plenary 1, Plenary 2 |
| | Evaluate results from the practical (Level 6). | | Main |
| **Extending** | Compare the work done in different scenarios and by different machines (Level 7). | 3, 4 | Plenary 2 |
| | Explain how conservation of energy applies in one example (Level 7). | 4 | Main, Plenary 1, Plenary 2 |
| | Evaluate results (including random and systematic errors) and suggest how the experiment can be improved (Level 8). | | Main |

**Maths**
Students carry out simple calculations for work done in different scenarios, including balancing forces (moments), and use the concept of ratios in their practical activity.

**Literacy**
Students use scientific terminology when explaining the role of levers, pulleys, and gears in simple machines, applying their knowledge to other appliances around the home.

**APP**
Students evaluate the method used in their experiment and suggest possible improvements (AF5).

**Key Words**
work, simple machine, lever, gear

## Answers from the student book

| In-text questions | **A** work (J) = force (N) × distance (m) <br> **B** levers, gears |
|---|---|
| Summary Questions | **1** force, distance, machine, lever, force, gear, conservation, energy (8 marks) <br> **2 a** lever (1 mark) <br>   **b** work done = force × distance = 200 N × 0.25 m = 50 J (2 marks) <br> **3** Climbing Mount Everest: Work done = force × distance = 600 N × 10 000 m = 6 000 000 J <br>   Climbing upstairs to bed: Work done = force × distance = 600 N × 2.5 m = 1500 J <br>   Comparing the two: 6 000 000 J ÷ 1500 J = 4000 <br>   so climbing Mount Everest requires 4000 times the work. (4 marks) |

# P2 Chapter 2: Energy

> **4** QWC question (6 marks). Example answers:
> A small force acting over a big distance produces a big force.
> The big force cannot move a large distance because this would mean a larger output of energy than input.
> Law of conservation of energy applies in gears as well.
> Gears work on rotational movement.
> work done = force × distance
> You do work when you apply a force over a distance on the pedal.
> The law of conservation of energy says that energy cannot be created, so you cannot get more energy out than you put in.

| Starter | Support/Extension | Resources |
|---|---|---|
| **What machines do you use?** (5 min) Ask students to list machines they have used today. Invite some suggestions before explaining that levers, pulleys, and gears are simple machines. Give students a further minute to add some simple machines to their existing list. | **Extension**: Students should suggest why levers, pulleys, and gears are considered as simple machines. | |
| **Can a rabbit lift an elephant?** (10 min) Students may not realise how levers work at this stage. Start with a simple example that students may have experienced before, by asking them if an adult and a child can use a see-saw together. Students should realise that the adult must sit much closer to the pivot. Extend to an example using a rabbit and an elephant. | **Extension**: Introduce numerical values to the discussion, for example, a rabbit (mass 3 kg) could lift an elephant (3000 kg) if the rabbit was 1000 times further from the pivot. | |

| Main | Support/Extension | Resources |
|---|---|---|
| **Work** (40 min) Introduce the use of levers, pulleys, and gears as simple machines that change the size, direction, or distance a force moves. Using an example such as a screwdriver to open a paint can, introduce the terms effort, load, and pivot. Students then carry out four short experiments investigating the effect on movement of using simple machines, and answer the questions that follow on the practical sheet. | **Support**: An access sheet is available where students are given further guidance to use their results in forming a conclusion. **Extension**: Students should be encouraged to use numerical data to support their answers on the practical sheet. | **Practical**: Work |

| Plenary | Support/Extension | Resources |
|---|---|---|
| **Types of machine** (5 min) Students group a list of machines according to whether they use levers, pulleys, or gears using the interactive resource. | **Extension**: Students should explain the job of each type of machine in the examples given, and how energy is conserved. | **Interactive**: Types of machines |
| **Why do we use machines?** (10 min) Students use their ideas from the experiment to describe advantages of using machines (to reduce the force needed, to increase the distance an object can move, to send a force around corners, and so on). | **Extension**: Students should include examples of machines used for each advantage given, and explain how energy is conserved. | |

| Homework | Support/Extension | |
|---|---|---|
| Students describe five machines that have made their lives easier or more interesting, from transport to roller coasters. Students should give the application of each machine and state whether the machines use levers, pulleys, gears, or a mixture of these. | **Extension**: Students may choose to research exactly how one of these machines works, using a labelled diagram. | |

# P2 Chapter 2 Checkpoint

## Checkpoint lesson routes

The route through this lesson can be determined using the Checkpoint assessment. Percentage pass marks are supplied in the Checkpoint teacher notes.

### Route A (support)
Resource: P2 Chapter 2 Checkpoint: Revision

Students work through a series of tasks that allows them to gradually revisit and consolidate their understanding of energy resources, energy stores, and energy transfers. Students can keep this as a summary of the topic, and use this when revising for future assessments.

### Route B (extension)
Resource: P2 Chapter 2 Checkpoint: Extension

Students act as consultants for an energy provider and prepare reports on the most suitable energy resource to use for electricity generation in three different areas. Students are required to discuss common methods of electricity generation, including advantages and disadvantages of each method.

## Progression to *secure*

| No. | Developing outcome | Secure outcome | Making progress |
|---|---|---|---|
| 1 | Identify energy values for food and fuels, describing energy requirements in different situations. | Compare the energy values of different food and fuels with the energy needed for different activities. | In Task 1 students use a table of secondary data to answer questions based on energy requirements in different situations. |
| 2 | Define the conservation of energy, and relate this to simple machines. | Describe energy before and after a change, applying the conservation of energy to simple machines. | In Task 2 students state the law of conservation of energy before describing the changes in energy when burning a coal fire and apply the conservation of energy to levers. |
| 3 | State how energy is transferred. | Explain what brings about transfers in energy. | In Task 3 students explain what brings about the energy transfer between two objects that are in contact. |
| 4 | State how energy and temperature are measured. | State the difference between energy and temperature. | In Task 3 students link the correct definition to the key words energy and temperature. |
| 5 | Describe how energy is transferred through solids, liquids, and in air. | Describe what happens when you heat up solids, liquids, and gases. | In Task 3 students complete a diagram to describe how energy is transferred during changes of state. |
| 6 | State what is meant by equilibrium. | Explain what is meant by equilibrium. | In Task 3 students explain the transfer of energy between two objects in contact with each other using the term equilibrium. |
| 7 | Describe simply what happens in conduction and convection. | Describe how energy is transferred by particles in conduction and convection. | In Task 3 students answer questions to describe how energy is transferred by conduction and convection in the context of coffee cup. |
| 8 | State that insulators reduce heat loss compared to conductors. | Describe how an insulator can reduce energy transfer. | In Task 3 students suggest the best material to manufacture coffee cups based on their knowledge of conductors and insulators. |
| 9 | State some properties and sources of infrared radiation. | Describe some sources of infrared radiation and explain how energy is transferred by radiation. | In Task 3 students describe what all sources of infrared radiation have in common and explain how energy is transferred by infrared radiation. |
| 10 | Name renewable and non-renewable resources. | Describe the difference between a renewable and a non-renewable energy resource. | In Task 4 students describe the difference between wood and coal in terms of renewable and non-renewable sources of energy. |
| 11 | State one advantage and one disadvantage of fossil fuels. | Describe how electricity is generated in a power station. | In Task 4 students fill in a table to describe the functions of different parts of the power station in sequence of how electricity is generated. |

# P2 Chapter 2: Energy

| 12 | State the definitions of energy and power. | Explain the difference between energy and power. | In Task 5 students fills in a table to show the difference between energy and power in terms of units and whether the value changes depending on how long the circuit component is left running. |
|---|---|---|---|
| 13 | State that power, fuel used, and cost are linked. | Describe the link between power, fuel use, and cost of using domestic appliances. | In Task 5 students compare the cost of running two lightbulbs of different power, linking this to how much fuel is used in each case. |
| 14 | State how work is calculated. | Calculate work done. | In Task 5 students complete a calculation of work done using the equation provided. |

## Answers to end-of-chapter questions

**1** wind, solar, geothermal (1 mark)  **2a** C (1 mark)  **b** kW, watts, kilowatts, W (1 mark)

**3a** Purple solid dissolves, the Bunsen burner heats the water around the solid, and the purple colour diffuses throughout the water in a convection current. (3 marks)

**b** Any three from:
Water is heated by the Bunsen burner.
The water molecules move faster.
This is replaced by cold water, forming a convection current.
The water expands/becomes less dense.
Hot water floats.

**4a** coal/oil/gas. (1 mark)  **b** Fossil fuels are formed from the remains of plants and animals that died millions of years ago. (1 mark)

**c** When all fossil fuels are burnt there will not be any more as they take millions of years to form. (2 marks)

**5a** gravitational potential (1 mark)

**b i** Energy is conserved/cannot be lost. (1 mark)  **ii** Some energy is transferred/dissipated to the thermal store as the ball falls through the air. (1 mark)  **c** There is a force (of gravity) acting on the ball. (2 marks)

**6a** work done = force × distance = 500 N × 200 m = 100 000 J (2 marks)  **b** work done = force × distance = 50 N × 1.5 m = 75 J (2 marks)

**7a** power = energy ÷ time = 6000 J ÷ 60 s = 100 W (2 marks)  **b** power = current × p.d. = 0.05 A × 240 V = 12 W (2 marks)

**c** 12 W bulb, since kWh is lower and therefore it is cheaper to use this lightbulb. (2 marks)

**8a** Energy is transferred by conduction through the inner pane of glass/passed on by vibrations from the hot room.
Air inside the gap heats up/conduct occurs very slowly through the air. Energy is transferred by conduction through the outer pane of glass/passed on by vibration to the cold air outside. (3 marks)

**b** The rate of transfer would decrease. There is no air to transfer the energy between the panes.
Conduction will not occur/energy would be transferred very slowly by radiation. (3 marks)

**9** This is a QWC question. Students should be marked on the use of good English, organisation of information, spelling and grammar, and correct use of specialist scientific terms. The best answers will explain in detail how insulation reduces energy bills (maximum of 6 marks).
Examples of correct scientific points:
Energy is transferred from a warm house to the cold air outside.
Energy is transferred by conduction, convection, and radiation.
To keep a house at the same temperature it needs to be heated.
A lot of insulators trap air.
Air is a poor conductor.
Insulators reduce the rate of transfer of energy to the surroundings.
The rate at which you need to heat the house to maintain the temperature decreases.
A lower power heater is needed/heating is required for less time.
This reduces the number of kWh of energy used.
This will cost less money.

## Answer guide for Big Write

| Developing | Secure | Extending |
|---|---|---|
| 1–2 marks | 3–4 marks | 5–6 marks |
| • Design a simple diary that students could use to log what they eat/the activities that they do. | • Describe some foods and their energy content.<br>• Describe the energy used in some activities.<br>• Design a diary that students could use to log what they eat/the activities that they do. | • Describe in detail foods and their energy content.<br>• Describe the energy used in many activities.<br>• Design a detailed diary that students could use to log what they eat/the activities that they do. |

| P2 Chapter 2 Checkpoint assessment (automarked) | P2 Chapter 2 Checkpoint: Extension |
|---|---|
| P2 Chapter 2 Checkpoint: Revision | P2 Chapter 2 Progress task (Handling information) |

# 3.1 Speed

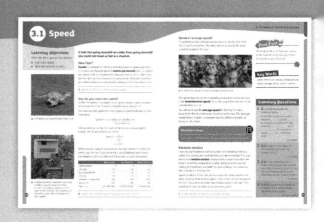

**Physics NC link:**
- speed and the quantitative relationship between average speed, distance, and time (speed = distance ÷ time)
- relative motion: trains and cars passing one another
- using physical processes and mechanisms, rather than energy, to explain the intermediate steps that bring about changes in systems.

**Working Scientifically NC link:**
- use appropriate techniques, apparatus, and materials during fieldwork and laboratory work, paying attention to health and safety.

| Band | Outcome | Checkpoint | |
|---|---|---|---|
| | | Question | Activity |
| **Developing** | State the equation for speed (Level 4). | B | Maths, Main |
| | Define relative motion (Level 4). | C | Plenary 1 |
| | Use appropriate techniques and equipment to measure times and distances (Level 4). | | Main |
| **Secure** | Calculate speed using the speed equation (Level 6). | 2 | Maths, Starter 2, Main |
| | Describe relative motion (Level 5). | 3 | Plenary 1 |
| | Choose equipment to make appropriate measurements for time and distance to calculate speed (Level 6). | | Main |
| **Extending** | Use the speed equation to explain unfamiliar situations (Level 7). | | Main, Homework |
| | Explain what is meant by relative motion and how it can be calculated (Level 7). | 4 | Plenary 1 |
| | Choose equipment to obtain data for speed calculations, justifying their choice based on accuracy and precision (Level 7). | | Main |

**Maths**
Students carry out simple calculations to work out the average speed of objects given total distance and time taken.

Students must also use the correct units in their calculations, converting between various units of time and distance.

**Literacy**
Students explain the concept of speed in their practical using scientific terminology, explaining how different factors affect reaction times, and in turn suggest why motorists should slow down at different places, for their homework.

**APP**
Students collect data, choosing appropriate ranges of numbers and values for measurements and observations to calculate speeds of various moving objects, justifying their choice of apparatus used (AF4).

**Key Words**
speed, metres per second, instantaneous speed, average speed, relative motion

## Answers from the student book

| In-text questions | **A** How far something travels in a particular time. **B** metres per second (m/s) **C** The movement of a body compared to another. |
|---|---|
| Activity | **Marathon times** distance in a marathon = 42.2 km time taken to run marathon = 2.5 h average speed = distance ÷ time = 42.2 ÷ 2.5 = 16.88 km/h |

● P2 Chapter 3: Motion and pressure

| Summary Questions | 1 distance, time, total distance, total time, relative (5 marks)<br>2 Average speed = total distance ÷ total time = 100 m ÷ 12.5 s = 8 m/s (2 marks)<br>3 Their relative motion is 70 km/h either towards each other, if they haven't passed yet, or away from each other if they have already passed. (2 marks)<br>4 QWC question (6 marks). Example answers:<br>Lines are painted on the road a set distance apart. The camera takes a photograph of the car on the road. The camera takes a photograph of the car a short time later. From the position of the car the camera can work out how far the car has travelled. The camera can use the time between the photographs to find the time using the equation speed = distance ÷ time. The speed camera uses the information obtained from the two photographs to calculate the speed of the car. If the car is travelling faster than the speed limit it will travel too far in the time between the photographs. |
|---|---|

**kerboodle**

| Starter | Support/Extension | Resources |
|---|---|---|
| **How fast?** (10 min) Students estimate speeds in different situations, for example, walking, running, driving, flying, speed of sound, and speed of light. Use tangible examples to begin with, for example, with speed limits on roads. | **Extension**: Students discuss the importance of units when considering numerical values. Ask students how they would convert a speed from kilometres per hour (km/h) to metres per second (m/s). | |
| **How quick was the ball?** (10 min) Students measure the time taken for a ball to fall from a vertical height of one metre. This can be done as a demonstration. Discuss where the ball travelled slowest and fastest in order to introduce the difference between average and instantaneous speed. Introduce the speed equation and calculate the average speed of the ball. | **Extension**: Ask students to consider whether the average speed of the ball would change if the ball was dropped from a greater height. | |

| Main | Support/Extension | Resources |
|---|---|---|
| **What's the speed?** (35 min) Introduce students to the speed equation and the difference between average and instantaneous speed. Students may require practice with using the correct units in the speed equation before working independently to answer questions on the experiment.<br><br>Students carry out two short experiments and answer the questions that follow. The first experiment is to obtain data to calculate the speeds of different moving objects, while the second experiment focuses on reaction times, and hence the effect of reaction times on the readings obtained in the first experiment. | **Support**: The accompanying support sheet includes a partially filled results table, with suggestions for moving objects that students can use around the classroom.<br>**Extension**: Challenge students to record all their speeds in metres per second (m/s) in order to practise the conversion of units. | **Practical**: What's the speed?<br>**Skill sheet:** Recording results |

| Plenary | Support/Extension | Resources |
|---|---|---|
| **Talking about relative speed** (10 min) Students choose the correct words on the interactive resource to summarise relative motion. This resource covers the definition, description, and an example of relative speed and motion.<br><br>**What affects your reaction time?** (10 min) Students discuss who had the quickest reaction time, and factors that affect it. Discuss why a quick reaction time is important for athletes and drivers. This discussion can include drink driving, use of mobile phones while driving, and reasons why motorists should take regular breaks when driving long distances. | | **Interactive**: Talking about relative speed |

| Homework | Support/Extension | |
|---|---|---|
| Produce a safety leaflet explaining when drivers should slow down (in built-up areas, during periods of poor visibility, and so on) and explain the physics behind this. An explanation of the speed equation should be included. | **Extension**: Students should be encouraged to give examples using the speed equation with numerical values. | |

# 3.2 Motion graphs

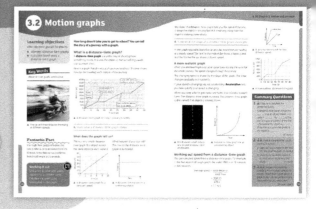

**Physics NC link:**
- the representation of a journey on a distance–time graph.

**Working Scientifically NC link:**
- present observations and data using appropriate methods, including tables and graphs.

| Band | Outcome | Checkpoint | |
|---|---|---|---|
| | | Question | Activity |
| **Developing** | Describe simply what a distance–time graph shows (Level 4). | | Starter 2, Plenary 1 |
| | Use a distance–time graph to describe a journey qualitatively (Level 4). | | Starter 1, Starter 2, Main, Plenary 2 |
| | Present data given on a distance–time graph with support (Level 4). | | Main |
| **Secure** | Interpret distance–time graphs (Level 6). | A, B, 1, 2 | Starter 1, Starter 2, Main, Plenary 1, Plenary 2 |
| | Calculate speed from a distance–time graph (Level 5). | 2 | Maths, Main, Homework |
| | Plot data on a distance–time graph accurately (Level 6). | | Main |
| **Extending** | Draw distance–time graphs for a range of journeys (Level 7). | 3 | Main, Plenary 2, Homework |
| | Analyse journeys using distance–time graphs (Level 7). | 3 | Starter 1, Starter 2, Main, Plenary 2 |
| | Manipulate data appropriately to present in a distance–time graph (Level 7). | | Main |

**Maths**
Students interpret and manipulate data from tables in order to draw and analyse distance–time graphs.
Students calculate speeds of moving objects using distance–time graphs.

**Literacy**
Students describe journeys shown on distance–time graphs using scientific terminology, prepare a presentation to explain a distance–time graph they have drawn, and write a short story to accompany a new distance–time graph.

**APP**
Students transfer numerical data from tables and present these in distance–time graphs (AF3).

**Key Words**
distance–time graph, acceleration

## Answers from the student book

| In-text questions | A  The distance that something travels in a certain time |
| | B  The speed of an object. |
| Activity | **Working it out**<br>speed = distance ÷ time = 60 ÷ 10 = 6 m/s |

## P2 Chapter 3: Motion and pressure

| Summary Questions | |
|---|---|
| | 1 distance, time, slope, stationary, changing (5 marks) |
| | 2a distance = 3900 m − 2400 m = 1500 m |
| |     time = 45 min − 35 min = 10 min = 10 × 60 = 600 s |
| |     speed = distance ÷ time = 1500 m ÷ 600 s = 2.5 m/s (4 marks) |
| | b 0 m/s (1 mark) |
| | 3 QWC question (6 marks). Example answers: |
| | Both graphs start at a distance of zero and finish at a distance of 3 km. The graph for the car reaches 3 km faster than the graph for walking. Both graphs might have horizontal sections. If the graph is horizontal the car or person has stopped. The slope of the graph for the car is much steeper. Cars travel faster than people. The car reaches school in a shorter time. The average speed of a car is much higher than that of a person. Both graphs should include curved lines. Curved lines show periods of changing speed. |

| Starter | Support/Extension | Resources |
|---|---|---|
| **Using graphs** (5 min) Sketch a distance–time graph on the board, explain what it shows, and demonstrate it to students by acting out each section of the graph. Draw a second graph for students to describe to one another in pairs. | **Support**: Label each section of the graph before acting it out. **Extension**: Students draw and interpret their own graphs. | |
| **Comparing speeds** (10 min) List typical speeds for different activities, for example, walking quickly (2 m/s) or running slowly (4 m/s). Students work out how long it will take to travel 10 m. Explain how a distance–time graph is used to compare speeds. Sketch a distance–time graph showing the three people travelling the same distance and point out the different slopes and times despite covering the same distance. | **Support**: Remind students of the speed equation. **Extension**: Students sketch and interpret their own graph. | |

| Main | Support/Extension | Resources |
|---|---|---|
| **Using distance–time graphs** (40 min) Introduce the idea of distance–time graphs, and explain how graphs can be used to interpret movement in detail. Demonstrate how the speed of a section of a journey can be found from the slope, and demonstrate this with two examples, in order to show that a steeper line shows the movement of a faster object. Students then interpret data on the activity sheet to plot a distance–time graph for a migrating bird, the Tour de France, or a sled dog race, and prepare a short summary of the graph they have drawn to present to the rest of the class. | **Support**: A support sheet is available where the breakdown of the times and distances during the ten-day sled dog race has been filled in for them to plot the information. **Extension**: Students carry out the extension task where they must write a short story and plot the graph of the journey described. | **Activity**: Using distance–time graphs |

| Plenary | Support/Extension | Resources |
|---|---|---|
| **What can you tell from a distance–time graph?** (5 min) Students match halves of sentences using the interactive resource to explain how distance–time graphs can be interpreted. | **Support**: Allow students to work in small groups. | **Interactive**: What can you tell from a distance–time graph? |
| **Drawing distance–time graphs** (10 min) Each pair of students should draw a distance–time graph on a mini-whiteboard. If a double-sided whiteboard is used, the other side can be used to write down the correct description of the sketch-graph drawn. Choose one side of the whiteboard to display, and allow students to walk around the classroom to find other whiteboards, giving descriptions of graphs shown, or imagining the shape of a graph if the description is shown. | **Support**: Choose pairs of students so that students in need of support are supported by extending students. | |

| Homework | | |
|---|---|---|
| Students note down typical times and distances for their journey to or from school, a friend's house, or an after-school club. They produce a labelled distance–time graph, calculating the speed at different stages of the journey and explain what is shown on each section of the graph. | | |

# 3.3 Pressure in gases

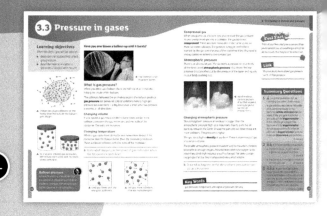

**Physics NC link:**
- atmospheric pressure, decreases with increase of height as weight of air above decreases with height.

**Working Scientifically NC link:**
- interpret observations and data, including identifying patterns and using observations, measurements, and data to draw conclusions.

| Band | Outcome | Checkpoint | |
|---|---|---|---|
| | | Question | Activity |
| **Developing** | State two things that can affect gas pressure (Level 4). | 1 | Main, Plenary 1 |
| | State the cause of atmospheric pressure (Level 4). | | Main |
| | Describe the effects of atmospheric pressure (Level 4). | | Main |
| **Secure** | Describe the factors that affect gas pressure (Level 6). | 1 | Starter 1, Main, Plenary 2 |
| | Describe how atmospheric pressure changes with height (Level 5). | B, 1, 2 | Main, Plenary 2 |
| | Interpret observations of atmospheric pressure (Level 6). | | Main, Plenary 1 |
| **Extending** | Explain gas pressure in different situations (Level 7). | 1–3 | Starter 1, Main, Homework |
| | Compare some effects of atmospheric pressure (Level 7). | 2, 3 | Main, Homework |
| | Predict the changes to the effects of atmospheric pressure at different altitudes or temperatures (Level 8). | | Main |

**Maths**
Understand and use direct proportion between pressure, volume, and temperature.

**Literacy**
Students explain the effect of gas pressure in different situations using scientific terminology.
Students also plan an investigation to see how the volume of a fixed amount of air changes with temperature, in the student-book activity.

**APP**
Students use abstract ideas and models to explain atmospheric pressure, applying these principles to different scenarios (AF1).

**Key Words**
gas pressure, compressed, atmospheric pressure, density

## Answers from the student book

| In-text questions | A They move more slowly. |
| --- | --- |
| | B Atmospheric pressure decreases. |
| Activity | **Balloon pressure** |
| | The plan should include: a method of changing temperature – by location or changing temperature of water, method of measuring volume – by circumference of balloon, variables to control, range of temperature, the need to repeat measurements, and a risk assessment. |
| Summary Questions | 1 collide with, bigger, smaller, less, fewer (4 marks) |
| | 2a There is less oxygen as you go up a mountain because gas pressure is reduced. The density of oxygen is low. (2 marks) |
| | b It would take up too much space if it were not compressed. The oxygen pressure will be very high if the gas is compressed. (2 marks) |

## P2 Chapter 3: Motion and pressure

| | **3** QWC question (6 marks). Example answers:<br>The temperature inside the can is much higher. The temperature of the water around the can is lower. The density of water and air molecules inside the can is much lower. The density of water outside the can is higher. The atmospheric (water) pressure outside the can is higher than the pressure inside. The atmospheric pressure from the outside pushes in on all sides of the can. The pressure on the inside of the can is less, so the can collapses. |
|---|---|

| Starter | Support/Extension | Resources |
|---|---|---|
| **Balloons** (10 min) Inflate two balloons, one fully and the other partially. Use these balloons to introduce gas pressure and explain that gas pressure is caused by particles colliding with the walls of the balloon. This means there is more pressure in the fully inflated balloon because there are more particles and more collisions. Students will have met gas pressure in C1. | **Extension**: Students should predict the effect of temperature on gas pressure, giving reasons. | |
| **Gases under pressure** (10 min) Display objects under pressure, for example, fizzy-drink bottles, aerosol cans, and bicycle tyres. Ask students to suggest what these objects have in common. Introduce the origin of gas pressure and demonstrate what happens when gas pressure is released (e.g., by unscrewing the bottle lid). Ask students to explain what is happening in terms of particles. | **Extension**: Discuss the similarities and differences between a still- and a fizzy-drink bottle in terms of gas pressure exerted by the drink, and the strength of material required in manufacturing the bottles. | |

| Main | Support/Extension | Resources |
|---|---|---|
| **Investigating gas pressure** (40 min) Demonstrate the collapsing bottle experiment to the class by adding a small amount of boiling water (about 15 cm³ from the kettle) into a non-reinforced plastic bottle. Swirl the hot water around the bottle, pour the hot water out, and immediately secure the bottle lid. The bottle should collapse with a loud bang. Ask students to suggest what has happened to the bottle in terms of pressure, before offering the answer.<br><br>An additional demonstration is to show the difficulty in pulling out the plunger of an empty but sealed syringe, since atmospheric pressure is pushing the syringe in, with no pressure pushing out from the inside.<br><br>Students note down their observations to these two demonstrations on their activity sheets and answer the questions that follow. | **Support**: An access sheet is available with multiple-choice answers for students to choose from when explaining the scientific concept behind each demonstration.<br><br>**Extension**: Students should suggest differences in observations if these demonstrations were carried out under different temperatures and pressures. | **Activity**: Investigating gas pressure |

| Plenary | Support/Extension | Resources |
|---|---|---|
| **The collapsing bottle** (10 min) Show a video clip from the Internet of the collapsing bottle experiment as a visual recap before asking students to reorder phrases on the interactive resource to explain what happens during this experiment. | **Support**: Allow students to refer to their access sheets during this activity. | **Interactive**: The collapsing bottle |
| **Traffic-lighting atmospheric pressure** (10 min) Summarise lesson outcomes as questions with multiple-choice answers. Students should write their choice clearly on a mini-whiteboard (1, 2, or 3; A, B, or C) to ensure whole-class participation. | **Extension**: Students can write their own questions and answers for the rest of the class to answer. | |

| Homework | Support/Extension | Resources |
|---|---|---|
| Students research effects of atmospheric pressure and write a paragraph on 'Atmospheric pressure at work'. For example, the need for pressurised cabins on planes, why fizzy drinks aren't as fizzy in winter, or how changes in atmospheric pressure affect the weather (high pressure produces clear skies but low pressure produces unsettled weather). | **Extension**: Students should include detailed explanations of atmospheric pressure in terms of particles in their summary. | |
| An alternative WebQuest homework activity is also available on Kerboodle where students research atmospheric pressure and mountain climbing. | | **WebQuest**: Pressure and altitude |

# 3.4 Pressure in liquids

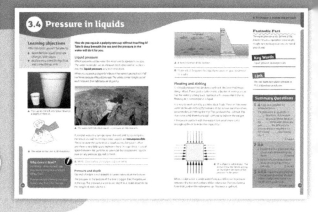

**Physics NC link:**
- pressure in liquids, increasing with depth; upthrust effects, floating and sinking.

**Working Scientifically NC link:**
- make predictions using scientific knowledge and understanding.

| Band | Outcome | Checkpoint | |
|---|---|---|---|
| | | Question | Activity |
| Developing | State simply what happens to pressure with depth (Level 4). | 1 | Plenary 2 |
| | Describe characteristics of some objects that float and some that sink (Level 4). | 2 | Lit, Starter 1, Main 2 |
| | Predict if water pressure will increase, decrease, or stay the same in a familiar context (Level 4). | | Main 2 |
| Secure | Describe how liquid pressure changes with depth (Level 5). | B, 1 | Starter 2, Plenary 2 |
| | Explain why some things float and some things sink, using force diagrams (Level 6). | 2, 3 | Lit, Main 2, Plenary 1, Homework |
| | Predict how water pressure changes in a familiar context, using scientific knowledge and understanding (Level 6). | | Main 2 |
| Extending | Explain why liquid pressure changes with depth (Level 7). | | Main 2, Plenary 2 |
| | Explain why an object will float or sink in terms of forces or density (Level 7). | 2, 3 | Lit, Starter 1, Main 2, Plenary 1, Homework |
| | Predict how water pressure changes in an unfamiliar context, using detailed scientific knowledge and understanding (Level 7). | | Main 2 |

**Literacy**
Students use scientific terminology when explaining water pressure and floating and sinking in the main activity and in the student-book activity.

**APP**
Students use abstract ideas to explain water pressure (AF1), display observations appropriately in results tables (AF3), and draw conclusions based on scientific knowledge and data obtained through experiment (AF5).

**Key Words**
liquid pressure, incompressible

## Answers from the student book

| In-text questions | **A** It cannot be compressed into a smaller space.   **B** It gets bigger. |
|---|---|
| Activity | **Why does it float?**<br>The bottom of the ferry is in contact with the water. The top of the ferry is in contact with the air.<br>The water molecules and air molecules collide with the ferry.<br>There are more water molecules hitting the bottom of the ferry than there are air molecules hitting the top.<br>The water pressure is higher than the air pressure.<br>The difference in pressure between the top and the bottom produces upthrust that keeps the ferry afloat if the area is big enough.<br>The ferry floats when upthrust is the same as the weight of the ferry. |

# P2 Chapter 3: Motion and pressure

| Summary Questions | 1 all, increases, weight, bigger, upthrust (5 marks) |
|---|---|
| | 2a Water pressure from the bottom creates the force upthrust. The clay boat floats because the upthrust balances out the weight of the boat. (2 marks) |
| | b The area is much smaller, the difference between the force pushing down and the force pushing up is not enough for the upthrust to balance the weight. (2 marks) |
| | 3 QWC question (6 marks). Example answers: |
| | The ping pong ball has a small weight. |
| | When it is held at the bottom of the bucket there is the force of your hand pushing down. |
| | The force from your hand is bigger than the upthrust due to the difference in pressure. |
| | When you let the ball go the upthrust is bigger than its weight. |
| | When the ball reaches the surface it floats. |
| | The pressure on the bottom of the ball produces a (upthrust) force that depends on the area of the ball in contact with the water. |
| | The ball will sink until there is enough water in contact with the ball to produce enough upthrust. |

| Starter | Support/Extension | Resources |
|---|---|---|
| **Mass versus weight** (10 min) Ask if a kilogram of feathers or a kilogram of iron weighs more. Use student responses to correct student misconceptions and remind students of the difference between mass and weight. Introduce the idea of water pressure and how this relates to floating and sinking. Students predict whether a plastic bag of feathers or lead is more likely to float in water. | **Extension**: Students should apply newly-acquired knowledge of water pressure to explain their prediction. | |
| **Water pressure** (5 min) Students discuss, with reasons, how water pressure changes moving down to the bottom of a swimming pool. Many students will have experienced the increased pressure on their body at the bottom of the pool or sea. | **Extension**: Students should suggest why this is the case. | |

| Main | Support/Extension | Resources |
|---|---|---|
| **Floating and sinking** (15 min) Introduce the idea of water pressure. Explain how floating and sinking are related to the difference in pressure at the bottom and top of an object in a fluid (liquid or gas), causing an upthrust force. Objects float when the upthrust is the same size as weight. Students should then practise drawing force diagrams using upthrust and weight arrows to illustrate floating and sinking. | **Extension**: Students should illustrate floating and sinking using relative sizes of upthrust and weight arrows on force diagrams. | |
| **Liquids at work** (25 min) Display a range of objects for students to predict whether they will float or sink in water. Show students the drinks bottle with holes at various heights, and explain that the bottle will be filled with water to show water pressure at work. Students should fill in the prediction section of the activity sheet, watch the demonstrations, and answer the questions that follow. | **Support**: The accompanying support sheet gives students further prompts to spot patterns in their observations. | **Activity**: Liquids at work |

| Plenary | Support/Extension | Resources |
|---|---|---|
| **The floating orange** (10 min) Students predict if an orange floats when it is unpeeled (yes) and peeled (no). Demonstrate this experiment and ask students to explain their observations. The orange floats if upthrust equals weight. Peeling the orange reduces its weight and also its volume, but its volume decreases more than its weight. Upthrust becomes smaller than weight so the orange sinks. | **Support**: Allow students to work in small groups when explaining their observations. | |
| **Water pressure** (5 min) Students fill in the missing words on the interactive resource to explain water pressure in different scenarios. | **Support**: Allow students to look back at their activity sheets. | **Interactive**: Water pressure |

| Homework | Support/Extension | |
|---|---|---|
| Students answer simple questions about the effects of pressure in liquids, for example, why does a block of iron sink but an iron boat float? Why does some fruit float and some fruit sink? How does a life jacket keep a person from sinking? Why do air bubbles rise in water? | **Extension**: Students should be encouraged to use as many scientific terms as possible. | |

# 3.5 Pressure on solids

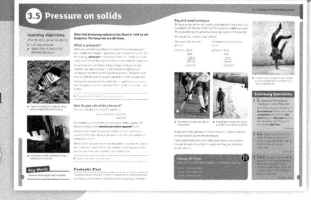

**Physics NC link:**
- pressure measured by ratio of force over area – acting normal to any surface.

**Working Scientifically NC link:**
- make predictions using scientific knowledge and understanding.

| Band | Outcome | Checkpoint | |
|---|---|---|---|
| | | Question | Activity |
| Developing | State the equation of pressure (Level 4). | 1 | Main |
| | Use ideas of pressure to describe familiar situations qualitatively (Level 4). | | Starter 1, Starter 2, Plenary 1, Plenary 2 |
| | Predict qualitatively the effect of changing area and/or force on pressure (Level 4). | | Main, Plenary 2 |
| Secure | Calculate pressure (Level 6). | 2 | Main, Plenary 2 |
| | Apply ideas of pressure to different situations (Level 6). | | Starter 1, Starter 2, Main, Plenary 1, Plenary 2, Homework |
| | Predict quantitatively the effect of changing area and/or force on pressure (Level 6). | 3 | Main, Plenary 2 |
| Extending | Calculate pressure in multistep problems (Level 8). | 3 | Main |
| | Compare pressure in different situations, explaining the differences in pressure using scientific knowledge (Level 8). | 3 | Starter 1, Starter 2, Main, Plenary 1, Plenary 2, Homework |
| | Predict quantitatively the effect of changing area and/or force on pressure in a range of situations (Level 7). | 3 | Main, Plenary 2 |

**Maths**
Students carry out simple calculations using the pressure equation, manipulating numbers and compound units.

In the student-book activity students rearrange the pressure equation to find the correct equation to calculate force.

**Literacy**
Students describe the effects of pressure in different scenarios, explaining their answers using scientific terminology.

**APP**
Students choose appropriate range and intervals of measurements during their experiment (AF4), display observations in tables (AF3), and draw conclusions from patterns in their findings (AF5).

**Key Words**
pressure, newtons per metre squared

## Answers from the student book

| In-text questions | **A** At 90°, or normal to the surface. |
| | **B** N/m² or N/cm² |
| Activity | **Finding the force** |
| | B force = pressure × area |

● P2 Chapter 3: Motion and pressure

| Summary Questions | 1 force, area, big, small, N/m (5 marks) |
|---|---|
| | 2 area of two hands = 150 cm² × 2 = 300 cm² |
| | pressure = force ÷ area = 600 N ÷ 300 cm² = 2 N/cm² (3 marks) |
| | 3 QWC question (6 marks). Example answers: |
| | pressure = force ÷ area |
| | small area = large pressure |
| | The pressure of lying on one nail = 700 N ÷ 0.25 cm² = 2800 N/cm² |
| | A bed of nails consists of 4000 nails, so the total area is bigger. |
| | And the pressure is much less. |
| | total area = 4000 × 0.25 cm² = 1000 cm² |
| | The pressure of lying on a bed of nails = 700 N ÷ 1000 cm² = 0.7 N/cm² |

**kerboodle**

| Starter | Support/Extension | Resources |
|---|---|---|
| An alternative question-led lesson is also available. | | **Question-led lesson**: Pressure on solids |
| **Rescue!** (10 min) Students suggest ways to walk through soft snow. Students discuss in pairs before offering them in a class discussion. Suggestions may include using snow shoes rather than normal shoes. Explain how these ideas reduce pressure on the snow. Introduce the idea of pressure and the pressure equation. | **Support**: Ask structured questions, for example, would you rather wear stiletto heels or snow boots when walking in snow? **Extension**: Students analyse the suggestions to synthesise the equation for pressure. | |
| **Why is it this shape?** (5 min) Students discuss why a drawing pin has a sharp point at one end and a flat head at the other. Explain the force applied is the same through the drawing pin, but the large head reduces pressure and the sharp point increases pressure. | **Support**: Prompt students by asking them to consider the effect of using the drawing pin upside-down. **Extension**: Students should be able to suggest that pressure is dependent on force and area. | |

| Main | Support/Extension | Resources |
|---|---|---|
| **Investigating pressure** (40 min) Introduce the pressure equation by demonstrating how changing the force or the area of an object affects the pressure. Try simple calculations on the board using this equation, and ask students to carry out calculations of their own, giving answers on mini-whiteboards. Students then carry out a short experiment to investigate pressure exerted by different masses, using different supports in a tray of sand. Students should look for patterns in their results and attempt the questions that follow. | **Support**: The support sheet includes a partially filled results table for students to fill in. **Extension**: Students should plot a graph of their results (depth of indentation versus weight ÷ surface area) if time, and evaluate their results. | **Practical**: Investigating pressure **Skill sheet**: Recording results |

| Plenary | Support/Extension | Resources |
|---|---|---|
| **Useful pressure** (5 min) Students categorise a list of scenarios on the interactive resource according to whether high pressure or low pressure is useful. | **Extension**: Students offer other examples of useful pressure, explaining their answer in terms of force and area. | **Interactive**: Useful pressure |
| **Comparing tracks** (10 min) Students carry out simple calculations to work out the pressure exerted by different students when wearing different types of shoes. Use the average weight of a KS3 student (500 N) for students sensitive about their weight. Answers can be shown on individual mini-whiteboards. | **Support**: Encourage students to give qualitative answers and comparisons before using a calculator for their calculations. | |

| Homework | | |
|---|---|---|
| Students find other examples of useful pressure in everyday life. Students should write about how pressure is created in these scenarios and how it is helpful, using the terms force and area. | | |

# 3.6 Turning forces

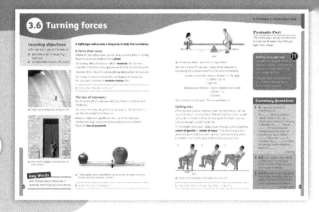

**Physics NC link:**
- moment as the turning effect of a force.

**Working Scientifically NC link:**
- identify further questions arising from their results.

| Band | Outcome | Checkpoint | |
|---|---|---|---|
| | | Question | Activity |
| **Developing** | State the law of moments (Level 4). | B | Maths, Main, Plenary 1 |
| | State the equation to calculate a turning force (Level 4). | A, 1 | Maths, Main, Plenary 2 |
| | Identify questions from results with help (Level 4). | | Main |
| **Secure** | Describe what is meant by a 'moments' (Level 6). | 1 | Main, Plenary 2 |
| | Calculate the moment of a force (Level 5). | 2 | Maths, Main |
| | Independently identify scientific questions from results (Level 6). | | Main |
| **Extending** | Apply the concept of moments to everyday situations (Level 7). | 2 | Maths, Starter 1, Starter 2, Main, Plenary 1 |
| | Use calculations to explain situations involving moments (Level 8). | 2, 3 | Maths |
| | Suggest relevant, testable questions (Level 7). | | Main |

**Maths**
Students carry out simple calculations to work out forces, or distances that objects have to be away from a pivot, in order to balance. They apply the moments equation to deduce if a system is balanced.

**Literacy**
Students explain the applications of moments using scientific terminology.

**APP**
Students use models to explain the concept of moments (AF1), draw conclusions from experimental observations and data (AF5), and form further questions that can be investigated further from their results (AF3).

**Key Words**
pivot, moment, newton metres, law of moments, centre of gravity, centre of mass

## Answers from the student book

| In-text questions | **A** newton metre (Nm) |
|---|---|
| | **B** An object is in equilibrium if the total anticlockwise moments equals the total clockwise moments. |
| | **C** The point through which all the weight of an object seems to act. |
| Activity | **Sitting on a see-saw** |
| | If the child sits on one end she is 1 m from the pivot. |
| | Clockwise moment = 150 N × 1 m = 150 N m |
| | You need the anticlockwise moment to be the same: |
| | 600 N × distance from the pivot = 150 N m |
| | Distance from the pivot = 150 N m ÷ 600 N = 0.25 m |

● P2 Chapter 3: Motion and pressure

| Summary Questions | 1 turning, force, distance, equilibrium, law, weight, gravity (7 marks)<br>2 moment = force × distance so, 5 N × 0.75 m = 3.75 Nm<br>3 QWC question (6 marks). Example answers:<br>　A ruler or beam that you hang things from, or something that can balance.<br>　A system of adding things to one side or the other.<br>　An explanation of what is meant by a 'moment'.<br>　An explanation of the law of moments.<br>　A scoring system that uses the law of moments, for example, predicting where you have to put something before you add it.<br>　An element of skill in terms of the items you can hang, or where you can put them. |
|---|---|

| Starter | Support/Extension | Resources |
|---|---|---|
| **A balancing act** (10 min) Set up a see-saw on the bench (using a plank and support). Students suggest how you can have two objects of unequal size and mass on either side of the see-saw. Remind students of the terms effort, lever, pivot, and load, and introduce the idea of moments.<br><br>**Pivots** (10 min) Pick a strong student to push a door open normally. Invite ideas from the rest of the class as to why the student's hand is placed far away from the pivot (door hinge). Then ask the same student to try pushing open the door with their hand as close to the pivot as possible. Introduce the concept of moments, and explain how a door acts as a force multiplier. | **Extension**: Students should be able to link this idea to other objects of different masses, for example, a mouse and an elephant.<br><br>**Extension**: Students should be able to offer other examples of force multipliers and explain their choices. In doing so, they may be able to synthesise the equation for calculating moments. | |

| Main | Support/Extension | Resources |
|---|---|---|
| **Just a moment!** (40 min) Introduce that the moment of a force indicates its turning effect, and is calculated as force × distance from pivot. This is a difficult concept so it might be a good idea to illustrate moments using props around the classroom.<br><br>Carry out simple moments calculations on the board to ensure that students are comfortable with the difference between clockwise and anticlockwise moments. Mini-whiteboards will be useful to ensure whole-class participation.<br><br>Students then carry out a practical where they investigate the turning force required to topple a clamp stand at different heights from the base, and answer questions that follow. | **Support**: A partially filled results table is available on the accompanying support sheet.<br>**Extension**: Students may choose to investigate moments when there is more than one force acting on the clamp stand in the same or opposite directions, if time. | **Practical**: Just a moment!<br>**Skill sheet**: Recording results |

| Plenary | Support/Extension | Resources |
|---|---|---|
| **Pouring drinks** (5 min) Pose the following question for students to solve: How can we pour drinks into two identical cups so that one cup has exactly twice the amount of the other without using scales or measuring the amount of liquid poured? (Using moments, place one cup twice as far away from the pivot as the other, and ensure that the cups are in equilibrium.)<br><br>**Moments** (5 min) Students revise key terms used in this lesson by pairing key words to their definitions using the interactive resource. | **Support**: Prompt students towards what they have learnt this lesson.<br><br><br><br>**Extension**: Students add to the key terms listed on the resource and provide their own definitions. | **Interactive**: Moments |

| Homework | | |
|---|---|---|
| Students identify five examples that use the principle of moments at home. They explain how the turning effects are balanced by comparing the distance and force either side of a pivot for each example, and research one example in detail to explain exactly how moments work in context. | | |

# P2 Chapter 3 Checkpoint

## Checkpoint lesson routes

The route through this lesson can be determined using the Checkpoint assessment. Percentage pass marks are supplied in the Checkpoint teacher notes.

**Route A (support)**
Resource: P2 Chapter 3 Checkpoint: Revision
Students work through a series of tasks that allows them to gradually revisit and consolidate their understanding of speed, distance–time graphs, pressure, and moments. Students can keep this as a summary of the topic, and use this when revising for future assessments.

**Route B (extension)**
Resource: P2 Chapter 3 Checkpoint: Extension
Students investigate the changes in density when substances undergo changes of state. Students will calculate values of density using numerical data provided and will carry out research into the role of intermolecular forces in the three states of matter.

## Progression to *secure*

| No. | Developing outcome | Secure outcome | Making progress |
|---|---|---|---|
| 1 | State the equation for speed. | Calculate speed using the speed equation. | In Task 1 students calculate speeds in three different scenarios given the speed equation. |
| 2 | Define relative motion. | Describe relative motion. | In Task 1 students describe the relative motion of two students who walk in opposite directions. |
| 3 | Use a distance–time graph to describe a journey qualitatively. | Interpret distance–time graphs, including calculating speed from the gradient. | In Task 2 students carry out a calculation and describe a journey in detail given the distance–time graph. |
| 4 | State what is meant by Brownian motion. | Describe Brownian motion. | In Task 3 students label a diagram to show the direction of pollen movement to describe Brownian motion. |
| 5 | State the cause of atmospheric pressure. | Describe how atmospheric pressure changes with height. | In Task 3 students label a diagram of a mountainous area according to regions with the highest and lowest atmospheric pressure. |
| 6 | State simply what happens to pressure with depth. | Describe how liquid pressure changes with depth. | In Task 3 students label a diagram according to regions with the highest and lowest water pressure in the ocean. |
| 7 | Describe characteristics of some objects that float and some that sink. | Explain why some things float and some things sink, using force diagrams. | In Task 3 students complete a force diagram to explain how a rubber duck floats in the water, and explain in terms of forces and pressure what causes objects to float or sink. |
| 8 | State the equation of pressure. | Calculate pressure. | In Task 4 students calculate pressure exerted on the floor by a dancer when he is standing on one foot and both feet. Students are given the pressure equation as a starting point. |
| 9 | Use ideas of pressure to describe familiar situations qualitatively. | Apply ideas of pressure to different situations. | In Task 4 students apply their knowledge of pressure to explain whether women prefer to wear heels or boots in the snow. |
| 10 | State the law of moments. | Describe what is meant by a moment. | In Task 5 students describe what is meant by a moment. |
| 11 | State the equation to calculate a turning force. | Calculate the moment of a force. | In Task 5 students calculate the moment of a person on a seesaw and use the moment calculated to deduce where another person of a different weight must sit on the opposite end of the seesaw. |

# P2 Chapter 3: Motion and pressure

## Answers to end-of-chapter questions

1. m/s, mph, km/s (3 marks)
2. B (1 mark)
3. **a** B (1 mark)
   **b** D (1 mark)
   **c** C (1 mark)
4. **a** Carrier bags have narrow handles, so the pressure on the surface of your hand is large. (2 marks)
   **b** A smaller pressure is required when riding over mud/fields, so tyres are wider. (2 marks)
5. **a** 70 mph − 50 mph = 20 mph faster/in the same direction (2 marks)
   **b** 50 mph − 50 mph = 0 mph (1 mark)
6. Any six from:
   Speed can be calculated from the slope/gradient of distance–time graphs.
   Cyril started fastest, slowed down, and sped up again.
   Gertie started at a steady speed, slowed down, then sped up.
   Harold started slowest, sped up, stayed still, then sped up again. Harold slowed down towards the end of the race.
   Cyril finished first.
   Gertie came second.
   Harold finished last.
   Cyril's average speed was 30 cm ÷ 120 s = 0.25 cm/s
   Gertie's average speed was 30 cm ÷ 160 s = 0.19 cm/s
   Harold's average speed was 30 cm ÷ 200 s = 0.15 cm/s
   Harold was the only snail to stop.
7. **a** Clockwise moment = force × distance = 1.5 N × 0.3 m = 0.45 Nm (2 marks)
   **b** anticlockwise moment = 0.45 Nm = force (exerted by muscle) × 0.03 m
   force exerted by muscle = 0.45 Nm ÷ 0.03 m = 15 N (2 marks)
   **c** The force is bigger because anticlockwise moment = clockwise moment (for the system to remain balanced). The distance from the pivot is much less. (2 marks)
8. This is a QWC question. Students should be marked on the use of good English, organisation of information, spelling and grammar, and correct use of specialist scientific terms. The best answers will explain in detail how a bag of crisps appears to expand at a higher altitude (maximum of 6 marks).
   Examples of correct scientific points:
   The bag of crisps contains air.
   Air molecules collide with the inside of the bag.
   Air molecules in the atmosphere collide with the outside of the bag
   If the pressure is the same inside and outside the bag, the bag does not get bigger.
   Atmospheric pressure decreases with height, because gravity pulls the air molecules down.
   There are fewer collisions between air molecules and objects as you go higher.
   The air pressure inside the plane is less than the air pressure on the ground (inside the crisp packet) so the bag gets bigger.

## Answer guide for Case Study

| Developing | Secure | Extending |
| --- | --- | --- |
| 1–2 marks | 3–4 marks | 5–6 marks |
| • Correct description of interaction of spacecraft with a gaseous atmosphere and an ocean of liquid.<br>• Some discussion of whether the spacecraft would float or sink on an ocean. | • Discussion of change of pressure as you near the surface of the unknown planet, and at various depths in the ocean.<br>• Explanation of what affects whether something floats or sinks in terms of liquid pressure and upthrust. | • Detailed description of how the pressure would change in a gas atmosphere, and at various depths in the ocean.<br>• Detailed explanation of why things float or sink using the ideas of pressure differences and upthrust. |

P2 Chapter 3 Checkpoint assessment (automarked)
P2 Chapter 3 Checkpoint: Revision
P2 Chapter 3 Checkpoint: Extension
P2 Chapter 3 Progress task (Maths)

# Physics 3

| National curriculum links for this unit | |
|---|---|
| **Chapter** | **KS3 National Curriculum topic** |
| Chapter 1: New technology | Calculation of fuel uses and costs in the domestic context<br>Forces and motion<br>Energy and waves |
| Chapter 2: Turning points in physics | Space physics     Forces and motion<br>Particle model     Energy and waves<br>Current electricity     Magnetism |
| Chapter 3: Detection | Light waves<br>Energy and waves<br>Forces and motion |

## Preparing for Key Stage 4 success

**Knowledge**

Underpinning knowledge is covered in this unit for KS4 study of:

- Non-contact forces and fields
- The three Newtonian laws of motion
- Electromagnetic radiation and matter
- Applications for generation and detection
- Superposition, reflection, absorption, and resonance
- Absorption and emission of ionising radiations
- Applications and effects on body tissues of radioactive materials
- Solar system, stability of orbital motions, satellites
- Red-shift, the Big Bang, and universal expansion
- Amplitude and frequency modulation to transfer information
- National and global energy sources
- Speed, velocity, and acceleration
- Contact forces, stretching, and friction
- Waste and efficiency
- Collisions and safety
- Refraction and lens action (qualitative)
- Magnetic effects of currents
- Half-lives
- Motors, induction, and dynamos
- Energy of the Sun and fusion

**Maths**

Skills developed in this unit. (Topic number)

- Quantitative problem solving (1.3, 1.5, 2.4, 3.5).
- Use geometry to solve problems (1.5, 3.5)
- Understand number size and scale and the quantitative relationship between units (2.3, 2.5).
- Plot and draw graphs selecting appropriate scales for the axes (1.4).
- Extract and interpret information from charts, graphs, and tables (1.7, 2.7)
- Understand when and how to use estimation (2.2, 2.3).
- Understand and use direct proportion and simple ratios (1.3).
- Identify patterns in data (2.2, 2.8, 2.9).
- Substitute numerical values into simple formulae and equations using appropriate units (1.3, 2.3, 3.1).
- Carry out calculations involving $+, -, \times, \div$, either singly or in combination (1.3, 3.4, 3.5).

**Literacy**

Skills developed in this unit. (Topic number)

- Planning and adapting writing style to suit audience and purpose (1.3, 1.5, 1.6, 1.7, 2.2, 2.3, 2.5).
- Accessing information to ascertain meaning, using word skills and comprehension strategies (2.1, 2.4, 3.1).
- Predicting, making inferences, and describing relationships (3.1).
- Identifying main ideas, events, and supporting details from scientific text (1.5, 2.1, 3.5).
- Take part in a debate and put forward a point of view (1.7, 2.5).
- Use of scientific terms (all spreads)
- Organisation of ideas and information (1.3, 1.5, 2.1, 2.2, 3.4, 3.5).

**Assessment Skills**

- QWC questions (1.1, 1.2, 1.3, 1.4, 1.5, 2.1, 2.4, 2.5, 2.6, 2.7, 2.8, 3.1, 3.2, 3.3, 3.4, 3.5) (end-of-chapter 1 Q10, end-of-chapter 2 Q10, end-of-chapter 3 Q11)
- Quantitative problem solving (1.1, 1.2, 1.5, 2.4, 2.6, 2.9, 3.2, 3.3, 3.4) (end-of-chapter 1 Q9, end-of-chapter 3 Q6, Q10)
- Application of Working Scientifically (end-of-chapter 1 Q5, end-of-chapter 2 Q 5)

| | Key Concept | Catch-up |
|---|---|---|
| **Chapter 1: New technology** | The uses of electromagnetic waves in communication and in medicine are discussed in this chapter, offering students a recap of the **electromagnetic spectrum**, and an introduction to **electromagnetic waves**. | P1 2.1 Waves<br>P1 2.2 Vibrations and energy transfer |
| | Circuits and circuit symbols are consolidated using sensor circuits in the home and in hospitals. These are topics that are essential when studying **electricity**. | P2 1.2–1.5: Electricity and magnetism |
| | Properties of light waves and ray diagrams are consolidated using endoscopes. These topics are essential when studying **light**, including **reflection** and **refraction**. | P1 3.1–3.4: Light |
| | Forces acting on a moving object are discussed when predicting projectile motion. This can be used as a scaffold towards further study of **forces and matter**. | P1 1.1–1.5: Forces |
| | Reaction time is revisited in this chapter, giving students further practice on the **average speed equation** and the **manipulation of mathematical equations**. | P2 3.1 Speed<br>P2 3.2 Motion graphs |
| | Fuel sources are covered when discussing methods of electricity generation, which helps students understand **electromagnetic induction**, **radioactivity**, and **the National Grid**. | P2 2.1 Food and fuels<br>P2 2.6 Energy resources |
| **Chapter 2: Turning points in physics** | Different models of the Solar System and the Universe are discussed, in context of how observations changed the way we viewed things. This serves as a foundation for understanding the **law of gravitational attraction**, **the Solar system**, and **forces**. | P1 1.1 Introduction to forces<br>P1 1.4 Forces at a distance<br>P1 4.1–4.3: Space |
| | The formation of the Universe is discussed in terms of the Big Bang. Understanding of the **Big Bang** is essential when studying **universal expansion** and **redshift**. | P1 4.1 The night sky<br>P1 4.2 The Solar System |
| | Forces on moving objects are further consolidated when discussing satellites in orbit and rockets fired into space. This topic offer students further foundations towards topics in **the Solar System**, **satellites**, and **forces and matter**. | P1 1.1–1.5: Forces<br>P1 4.2 The Solar System<br>P1 4.4 The Moon |
| | The radioactivity of materials is introduced in this chapter. Students will meet these concepts again when studying **the atomic model**, **isotopes**, **radiation**, and their **effect on body tissues**. | C1 1.1 The particle model<br>C1 2.2 Atoms |
| | Circuit diagrams are once again consolidated in the introduction of electromagnetic induction. This is one of the most important discoveries in physics and will be revisited in further study of **electricity** and **magnetism**. | P2 1.2 Circuits and current<br>P2 1.3 Potential difference<br>P2 1.6–1.8: Electricity and magnetism |
| | The generation, transmission, and detection of electromagnetic waves for communication are discussed. This is an important concept for understanding **wave modulation**. | P1 2.1 Waves |
| **Chapter 3: Detection** | The reflection and refraction of light and other electromagnetic waves are further consolidated in the context of telescopes. The drawing of ray diagrams is a necessity for all the topics in **light as rays**, including **reflection** and **refraction**. | P1 2.1 Waves<br>P1 2.2 Vibrations and energy transfer<br>P1 3.1–3.4: Light |
| | The use of electromagnetic waves in communication is consolidated in discussing AM and FM waves, as well as the detection of waves by satellites. These are important concepts towards further study of the **electromagnetic spectrum** and **wave modulation**. | P1 2.1 Waves<br>P1 2.2 Vibrations and energy transfer |
| | Atomic structure is further examined with the introduction of further subatomic particles, for example, the Higgs boson. This is important for understanding **atomic structure** and the **changes in the atomic model** over time. | C1 2.1 Elements<br>C1 2.2 Atoms |

## kerboodle

- P3 Unit pre-test
- P3 Big practical project (foundation)
- P3 Big practical project (higher)
- P3 Big practical project teacher notes
- P3 Practical project hints: graph plotting
- P3 Practical project hints: planning
- P3 Practical project hints: writing frame
- P3 End-of-unit test (foundation)
- P3 End-of-unit test (foundation) mark scheme
- P3 End-of-unit test (higher)
- P3 End-of-unit test (higher) mark scheme

## Answers to Picture Puzzler

**Key Words**

parachute, Lewis Hamilton, aerial, Neptune, Earth, turtle

The key word is **planet**.

**Close Up**

face of a phosphorescent watch

# 1.1 Your phone

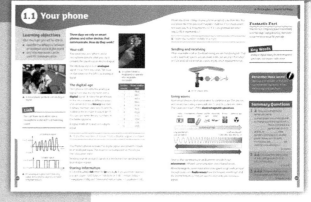

**KS3 Physics NC Link:**
- sound waves
- light waves.

**KS3 Working Scientifically NC Link:**
- apply sampling techniques.

**KS4 Physics NC Link:**
- recall that electromagnetic waves are transmitted through space where all have the same velocity
- give examples of some practical uses of electromagnetic waves.

| Band | Outcome | Checkpoint | |
|---|---|---|---|
| | | Question | Activity |
| **Developing** | Give examples of a digital and an analogue signal (Level 4). | 1, 2 | Main, Plenary 1, Plenary 2, Homework |
| | State the types of electromagnetic waves used for communication (Level 4). | 1, 2 | Starter 2, Main, Plenary 1, Homework |
| | Sample an analogue signal (Level 3). | | Main |
| **Secure** | Describe the difference between an analogue and a digital signal (Level 6). | 1, 2 | Main, Plenary 2, Homework |
| | Describe how waves can be used for communication (Level 5). | 2 | Main, Plenary 1, Homework |
| | Reproduce a wave using sampling (Level 5). | | Main |
| **Extending** | Suggest reasons to explain the difference in quality of analogue and digital signals (Level 7). | | Main, Plenary 2 |
| | Explain how electromagnetic waves transfer phone signals (Level 8). | 2 | Main, Plenary 1 |
| | Analyse the quality of digital signals when the rate of sampling is varied (Level 8). | | Main |

**Maths**
Students extract information from a graph of an analogue wave, sampling this to give a digital signal.

**Literacy**
Students create their own mnemonic to remember the order of waves in the electromagnetic spectrum in the student-book activity.

**APP**
Students interpret analogue and digital signals provided (AF5).

**Key Words**
analogue, digital, bit, electromagnetic spectrum, microwave, radio wave

## Answers from the student book

| In-text questions | **A** 2 |
| | **B** 8 |
| Activity | **Remember those waves!** |
| | Credit sensible suggestions for mnemonics, for example, Red Monkeys In Venice Use eXtra Grapes. |
| Summary Questions | 1 analogue, digital, electromagnetic, infrared (4 marks) |
| | 2 There are 1 000 000 000 bytes in 1 GB and 1 000 000 bytes in 1 MB. |
| | Therefore there are 1 000 000 000 ÷ 1 000 000 = 1000 MB in 1 GB. |
| | A 500 GB hard drive will hold 500 × 1000 = 500 000 songs (2 marks) |

# P3 Chapter 1: New technology

**3** QWC question (6 marks). Example answers:
When you speak into a microphone the sound wave is converted to an electrical signal.
The electrical signal is an analogue signal.
An analogue signal can have any value.
Your mobile phone converts the analogue signal to a digital signal.
A digital signal is made of 1s and 0s.
Each 1 or 0 is called a bit (binary digit).
The digital signal is coded into an electromagnetic wave.
The wave is transmitted through the air to another phone.
The other phone decodes the signal and converts it back to an analogue signal.
The analogue signal is sent to a loudspeaker and you hear a sound.

| Starter | Support/Extend | Resources |
|---|---|---|
| **Measuring digital and analogue** (5 min) Demonstrate the digitisation of technology using props, for example, show old style telephones, early brick-like mobile phones, phones with infrared technology, ones with Bluetooth, wifi, and finally 3G and 4G phones. Students put the devices in chronological order and discuss similarities and differences between them. | | |
| **The electromagnetic spectrum** (5 min) Introduce the electromagnetic (EM) spectrum to the class, describing how certain waves can be used in communication. Ask students to use the EM spectrum to identify the types of waves used in radio, TV, phones, remote controls, photography, and optical fibres. | **Support**: Use a mnemonic to remember the order of waves, for example, Red Monkeys In Venice Use eXtra Grapes. **Extension**: Students use their existing knowledge to justify their answers. | |

| Main | Support/Extend | Resources |
|---|---|---|
| **Digital and analogue** (40 min) Introduce analogue and digital signals in communication using a simple example such as a phone call. Discuss how the different waves in the EM spectrum are used in communication. Ensure students are confident that analogue signals take any value but digital signals have fixed values before starting the activity.<br>Show students how analogue waves can be sampled, and discuss advantages of sampling over recording continuous values. In the activity students sample analogue signals into digital data and answer questions that follow. | **Support**: Remind students of the different waves that make up the EM spectrum.<br>When sampling the analogue signal, if the signal falls in the middle of two values, students should round up to the next integer as a rule of thumb. | **Activity**: Digital and analogue |

| Plenary | Support/Extend | Resources |
|---|---|---|
| **How do mobile phones work?** (10 min) Students reorder statements provided on the interactive resource to explain how your voice is transmitted to another person via a mobile phone. | **Extension**: Students compare this to how a signal is transmitted from a broadcasting station to a digital radio. | **Interactive**: How do mobile phones work? |
| **Comparing analogue and digital signals** (5 min) Students should give examples of digital and analogue signals using mini-whiteboards, describing the similarities and differences between them. | **Support**: Provide a list of points for students to classify as similarities or differences. **Extension**: Students explain how sampling techniques affect the quality of sound in digital signals. | |

| Homework | | |
|---|---|---|
| Students find three devices at home that use analogue or digital signals. They describe how these devices process data and the EM waves used. Students use this information to explain whether the devices they have chosen use analogue or digital signals. | | |

# 1.2 Your house

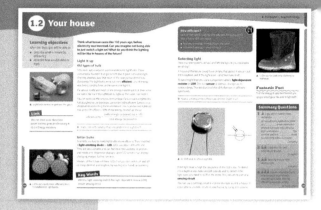

**KS3 Physics NC Link:**
- calculation of fuel uses and costs in the domestic context
- current electricity.

**KS3 Working Scientifically NC Link:**
- make and record observations and measurements using a range of methods for different investigations; and suggest possible improvements.

**KS4 Physics NC Link:**
- design and use circuits to explore changes in resistance – including for LDRs
- explain that mechanical processes become wasteful when they cause a rise in temperature so dissipating energy in heating the surroundings.

| Band | Outcome | Checkpoint | |
|---|---|---|---|
| | | Question | Activity |
| **Developing** | State the equation for efficiency (Level 3). | | Main |
| | Name the component that detects light levels (Level 3). | B, 1 | Main, Homework |
| | Record experimental observations using the results table given (Level 3). | | Main |
| **Secure** | Describe what is meant by efficiency (Level 5). | 1 | Starter 2, Main, Homework |
| | Describe how an LDR detects light (Level 6). | 3 | Main, Homework |
| | Design a suitable results table and use this to record data obtained from an investigation (Level 5). | | Main |
| **Extending** | Compare quantitatively the efficiency of a range of devices (Level 7). | 2 | Main, Plenary 1, Homework |
| | Suggest different ways to use an LDR (Level 7). | 3 | Main, Homework |
| | Record observations in a suitable results table and suggest possible improvements to the experimental procedure (Level 7). | | Main, Plenary 2 |

**Maths**
Students calculate the efficiency of appliances throughout this lesson, and use percentage efficiency to calculate energy dissipated in the student-book activity.

**Literacy**
Students organise scientific information and adapt their language to suit a general audience when writing a leaflet on increasing efficiency in the home for homework.

**APP**
Students record results from the experiment in a suitable results table (AF3), suggesting possible improvements to the method (AF5).

**Key Words**
efficient, light-emitting diode (LED), light-dependent resistor (LDR), sensor, sensing circuit

## Answers from the student book

| In-text questions | **A** 10%  **B** light-dependent resistor (LDR) |
|---|---|
| Activity | **How efficient?**  Energy used to light the room = 45% of 100 J = 0.45 × 100 = 45 J  Energy to heat the room = 100 J − 45 J = 55 J |

| | |
|---|---|
| Summary Questions | 1 lighting, heating, LDR, sensing (3 marks)<br>2 An LED is much more efficient than an incandescent light bulb because an LED lights the room more than heating it. (2 marks)<br>3 The resistance of the LDR changes in different light levels. If the light level is high, the resistance of the LDR is low. (2 marks)<br>4 QWC question (6 marks). Example answers:<br>An LDR senses light levels. It can be used to sense when it is day or night.<br>If the light level is high the resistance of the LDR is low.<br>Two LDRs can be used in a sensing circuit.<br>An LDR inside the house and one outside it can form part of a sensing circuit.<br>An LDR near a lightbulb could sense when it is on and turn it off during the day.<br>This means that the lightbulb would be on for less time.<br>The number of kWh/units of electricity used would be fewer. The cost of your electricity bill would be less. |

| Starter | Support/Extend | Resources |
|---|---|---|
| **Automatic controls** (5 min) Ask students to list devices in their home that include automatic controls, for example, automatic lights, the kettle turning off, radiators, thermostats, and chargers for mobile devices. Ask students to suggest how they think these devices work.<br><br>**The meaning of efficiency** (10 min) Explain what is meant by efficiency and ask students to suggest examples of pairs of devices that are efficient/not efficient, for example, well-maintained and badly-maintained cars or incandescent and energy-saving lightbulbs. Give the equation for efficiency and ask students to explain why machines can never be 100% efficient (due to energy dissipation). | **Extension**: Students suggest implications of using energy-efficient devices, for example, they may cost more to buy but have lower running costs due to lower fuel consumption. | |
| **Main** | **Support/Extend** | **Resources** |
| **Investigating the efficiency of lightbulbs** (40 min) Introduce how the efficiency of different appliances can be calculated before relating this to specific examples, such as lightbulbs. Students should appreciate that incandescent bulbs are extremely inefficient as a lot of the electrical energy is transferred as heat to the surroundings. Discuss ideas of increasing efficiency and reducing fuel costs by using LEDs and LDRs in sensor circuits before moving onto the practical investigation.<br>In this practical students carry out an investigation to measure the power, temperature, and light intensity of different bulbs and the resulting resistance of the LDR in the sensor circuit. Students then answer the questions that follow. | **Support**: You may wish to recap the law of conservation of energy, and the definitions for power, resistance, and light intensity before starting the practical. The accompanying support sheet contains a partially filled results table for students to use. | **Practical**: Investigating the efficiency of lightbulbs<br>**Skill sheet**: Recording results |
| **Plenary** | **Support/Extend** | **Resources** |
| **Efficiency statements** (5 min) Students choose the correct words to complete sentences provided on the interactive resource that relate to efficiency.<br><br>**The scientific method** (10 min) Students compare results with other groups in the class, explaining possible differences in results, and suggesting improvements to the experimental procedure. | **Extension**: Encourage students to offer other sentences for the rest of the class to complete.<br><br>**Support**: Structure the discussion so that students are only looking for similarities and differences in data between different groups. | **Interactive**: Efficiency statements |
| **Homework** | | |
| Students research ways to use machines/appliances efficiently in the home and design a leaflet suitable for homeowners to advise them on how they can reduce the amount of money spent on fuel with simple changes. | | |

# 1.3 Your hospital – intensive care

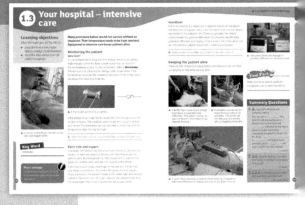

**KS3 Physics NC Link:**
- light waves
- current electricity.

**KS3 Working Scientifically NC Link:**
- evaluate data, showing awareness of potential sources of random and systematic error.

**KS4 Physics NC Link:**
- design and use circuits to explore changes in resistance – including for thermistors.

| Band | Outcome | Checkpoint | |
|---|---|---|---|
| | | Question | Activity |
| **Developing** | Give the name of the circuit component that detects changes in temperature (Level 3). | A, 1 | Lit, Plenary 1, Plenary 2, Homework |
| | State ways that sensors can be used in hospitals (Level 4). | 1 | Lit, Plenary 1, Homework |
| | Name the most accurate method of measuring temperature used in the experiment (Level 4). | | Main |
| **Secure** | Describe how a thermistor detects changes in temperature (Level 5). | 2 | Lit, Main, Plenary 1, Plenary 2, Homework |
| | Describe how sensors can be used in hospitals (Level 5). | 2 | Lit, Main, Plenary 1, Homework |
| | Compare the accuracy of the different methods of measuring temperature used in the experiment (Level 6). | | Main |
| **Extending** | Explain in basic terms how a thermistor works (Level 8). | | Main, Homework |
| | Compare two ways in which sensors are used in hospitals (Level 7). | 3 | Main, Plenary 2 |
| | Evaluate the qualitative and quantitative data obtained using different methods of measuring temperature (Level 8). | | Main |

**Literacy**
Students write a summary of how technology is used in hospital equipment for a press release in the student-book activity.

Students adapt writing style to write a leaflet for patients, reassuring them about hospital sensors, for homework.

**APP**
Students use models to mimic conditions in the hospital in order to investigate different ways of monitoring temperature (AF1). Students present results in appropriate tables (AF3) and evaluate the accuracy and precision of the methods used and of the data obtained (AF5).

**Key Words**
thermistor

## Answers from the student book

| In-text questions | **A** thermistor |
| | **B** small changes in potential difference |
| Activity | **Press release** |
| | Summary should include the following points: |
| | You can monitor temperature with a thermistor, or pulse rate using light and infrared. |
| | You can monitor heart rate by using electrodes that detect a change in potential difference. |
| | Ventilators pump air into the lungs of patients who struggle to breathe. |
| | You can use a defibrillator to start the heart of a patient when it has stopped and a pacemaker to keep it going. |

# P3 Chapter 1: New technology

| Summary Questions | 1 thermistor, infrared, potential difference, pacemaker, defibrillator (5 marks) |
|---|---|
| | 2 Connect a thermistor in a circuit with a cell and an ammeter. The resistance of the thermistor will decrease when the temperature increases. The current will increase as the temperature increases. (3 marks) |
| | 3 QWC question (6 marks). Example answers: |
| | Measuring pulse rate and heart rate both involve sensors. |
| | Electrodes are used to measure heart rate and electromagnetic waves (light and infrared) are used to measure pulse rate. |
| | As the heart beats, electrodes detect a change in potential difference, whereas for pulse rate, a sensor is placed on the end of a patient's finger. |
| | This sensor emits light and infrared. |
| | Blood with high oxygen content absorbs more infrared than visible light. |
| | The sensor detects the changes in blood oxygen content by monitoring infrared absorption and converts this change into a pulse rate. |

| Starter | Support/Extend | Resources |
|---|---|---|
| **Monitoring temperature** (5 min) Ask students for situations where it is important to monitor temperature continuously and how this could be done. Explain how sensors like thermistors are used. Students apply ideas from the previous lesson with the LDR.<br><br>**Incubators** (10 min) Students suggest requirements for newborn babies in incubators. What conditions should be monitored inside the incubator? What sorts of circuits can do this? Students then discuss requirements for helpless patients (those in intensive care) and suggest how sensors could be used to provide for their needs. Be aware that this topic may be a sensitive one for some students. | **Extension**: Students discuss which is better — a temperature monitor or an automatic control to maintain temperature between fixed limits.<br><br>**Support**: Prompt students towards requirements of these patients. Show students a thermistor, discuss its name, and ask students how it is similar to an LDR. (A thermistor is essentially a temperature-dependent resistor.) | |

| Main | Support/Extend | Resources |
|---|---|---|
| **Monitoring temperature** (40 min) Show students a thermistor and ask them what it may do. You may wish to tell students its name and say it is similar to an LDR as clues. Explain how they can be used in hospitals and introduce other common sensors.<br>Students then calibrate a thermistor using a thermometer, use the thermistor to monitor the temperature of a model incubator, and answer the questions that follow on the practical sheet. You may wish to show students a video of a baby in an incubator so they have a clearer idea of why continuous monitoring is important.<br>Students discuss other methods to monitor temperature, evaluating the accuracy and precision of each technique. | **Support**: A support sheet is available with a suggested results table.<br>**Extension**: Explain to students the basic principle of how a thermistor works (semiconductors with more delocalised electrons to carry charge at higher temperatures). Students should be encouraged to draw a calibration curve if time. | **Practical**: Monitoring temperature<br>**Skill sheet**: Recording results |

| Plenary | Support/Extend | Resources |
|---|---|---|
| **Technology in hospitals** (10 min) Students link together the different sensors used in hospitals with what they monitor. Students should then describe in full how each technique works.<br><br>**Methods for measuring temperature** (5 min) Students use what they have learnt this lesson to reconsider how best to monitor temperature continuously, justifying their answers. | **Extension**: Students compare the use of thermistors in hospitals to that of another sensor, suggesting how other sensors can also be improved. | **Interactive**: Technology in hospitals |

| Homework | | |
|---|---|---|
| Students produce a patient leaflet to describe how sensors are used around the hospital. This leaflet should be used to reassure patients about the use of technology in hospitals. | **Extension**: Students write a basic explanation of how each sensor works. | |

# 1.4 Your hospital – seeing inside

**KS3 Physics NC Link:**
- sound waves
- light waves.

**KS3 Working Scientifically NC Link:**
- interpret observations and data, including identifying patterns and using observations, measurements, and data to draw conclusions.

**KS4 Physics NC Link:**
- recall that different substances may absorb, transmit, refract, or reflect electromagnetic waves
- give examples of some practical uses of electromagnetic waves.

| Band | Outcome | Checkpoint | |
|---|---|---|---|
| | | Question | Activity |
| **Developing** | State one way in which optical fibres are used (Level 3). | 1 | Main, Homework |
| | State the types of electromagnetic wave used to see inside the human body (Level 3). | B, 1 | Main, Plenary 1, Plenary 2 |
| | Choose a suitable technique to diagnose symptoms in a given patient (Level 4). | | Main |
| **Secure** | Describe how optical fibres work (Level 5). | 1, 2 | Main, Homework |
| | Describe some techniques for seeing inside the human body (Level 5). | 3 | Main, Plenary 1, Plenary 2 |
| | Choose a suitable technique to diagnose symptoms in a given patient, justifying their answer (Level 6). | | Main |
| **Extending** | Use a ray diagram to explain how optical fibres work (Level 7). | | Main, Homework |
| | Compare the use of different waves in the EM spectrum for seeing inside the human body (Level 7). | 4 | Main, Plenary 1 |
| | Evaluate the risks and benefits of using one of the techniques discussed to diagnose symptoms, giving an overall conclusion (Level 8). | | Main |

**Maths**
Students use protractors correctly when measuring angles and drawing ray diagrams to show total internal reflection (TIR).

**Literacy**
Students write crossword clues for scientific vocabulary in the student-book activity. They summarise uses of optical fibres and TIR in a poster for homework.

**APP**
Students draw conclusions from observations given (AF5).

**Key Words**
endoscope, critical angle, total internal reflection, optical fibre, X-ray, gamma ray, magnetic resonance imaging (MRI)

## Answers from the student book

| In-text questions | **A** The angle at which the angle of refraction is 90°. |
|---|---|
| | **B** visible light, X-rays, gamma rays |
| Activity | **Crossword clues**<br>Credit sensible suggestions for crossword clues, for example:<br>visible light – used in an endoscope<br>X-rays – used to see broken bones<br>gamma rays – used to see internal organs<br>ultrasound – used to see a fetus or internal organs (the latter is done by using this wave on the end of an endoscope) |

# P3 Chapter 1: New technology

| Summary Questions | |
|---|---|
| | **1** bigger, reflected, endoscope, X-rays, gamma rays (5 marks) |
| | **2** The angle of incidence must be bigger than the critical angle. The ray of light must be hitting the boundary from inside the medium/glass. (2 marks) |
| | **3a** MRI scanners can be used to investigate how the brain works. This technique relies on the use of extremely powerful magnets to produce images. (2 marks) |
| | **b** Gamma rays can be used to check for kidney function. The patient drinks a special chemical that is taken in by the kidneys and emits gamma rays (medical tracer). A detector is then used outside the body, detecting the gamma rays emitted and producing an image. (2 marks) |
| | **4** QWC question (6 marks). Example answers: Visible light is used in endoscopes. Light is reflected within optical fibres. X-rays are used to take images of bones. Bones absorb more X-rays than soft tissues, so the X-rays that pass through a body can build an image of the bones inside. Gamma rays are used to investigate kidney function. A medical tracer is ingested and is absorbed by the kidney. Detectors detect the gamma rays emitted. Ultrasound is emitted from a transmitter. It reflects off objects and is detected by a receiver. This can be used to monitor soft tissues. MRI scanners use powerful electromagnets to see how organs like the brain work. |

| Starter | Support/Extend | Resources |
|---|---|---|
| An alternative question-led lesson is also available.<br><br>**What's wrong?** (10 min) Ask students to suggest ways that a doctor can diagnose what is wrong with a patient without operating. If appropriate, present a student as a patient with imaginary symptoms.<br><br>**Optical fibres** (10 min) Demonstrate optical fibres by shining an LED light in one end and allowing students to use the other end as a light. Ideally, the optical fibre should be over 2 m in length. Students suggest possible uses of optical fibres. They may already know some uses in communication (e.g., fibre optic broadband). | **Extension**: Students discuss advantages and disadvantages of the methods suggested, for example, ease/speed of use and reliability. | **Question-led lesson**: Your hospital – seeing inside |

| Main | Support/Extend | Resources |
|---|---|---|
| **Patient diagnosis** (40 min) Introduce the different EM waves that can be used by doctors to see inside the body without operating. Discuss the risks and benefits of these techniques.<br>It is important at this stage that students understand total internal reflection (TIR) in the use of optical fibre endoscopes. Demonstrate TIR using optical fibres or the TIR of light through a stream of water. Students then read a summary of five different diagnosis techniques and answer the questions that follow.<br>Before starting the activity, you may wish to discuss with students their experiences, for example, having X-rays taken for broken bones or at the dentist. If possible, include X-ray images or ultrasound footage to make the lesson more relevant. Be aware that this topic may be sensitive for some students. | **Support**: Recap reflection, refraction, and the EM spectrum if necessary.<br>The support sheet lists uses of the EM spectrum to help students answer the questions. | **Activity**: Patient diagnosis |

| Plenary | Support/Extend | Resources |
|---|---|---|
| **X-rays** (5 min) Students reorder sentences provided on the interactive resource to describe how X-rays can be used in hospitals to assess broken bones.<br><br><br><br>**Summary of diagnosis techniques** (10 min) Students work in groups to present a 30-second infomercial that summarises the different diagnosis techniques available in hospitals. | **Extension**: Students consider why some diagnosis methods are available in doctors' surgeries, while others are only available in hospitals (cost, risks, etc.). | **Interactive**: X-rays |

| Homework | | |
|---|---|---|
| Students produce a poster to summarise the uses of optical fibres and TIR. (This poster should not be limited to medical uses.) | **Extension**: Include a clearly labelled ray diagram of TIR. | |

# 1.5 Your sports

**KS3 Physics NC Link:**
- describing motion
- forces and motion.

**KS3 Working Scientifically NC Link:**
- evaluate data, showing awareness of potential sources of random and systematic error.

**KS4 Physics NC Link:**
- explain the vector-scalar distinction as it applies to displacement, velocity, and speed
- recall Newton's First Law and relate it to observations showing that forces can change direction of motion as well as its speed
- explain that force is rate of momentum change and explain the dangers caused by large decelerations and the forces involved.

| Band | Outcome | Checkpoint | |
|---|---|---|---|
| | | Question | Activity |
| **Developing** | State one way in which technology is used in sport (Level 3). | 1 | Starter 1, Plenary 1 |
| | State the name of the time taken for a person to react to a signal (Level 3). | B | Plenary 1 |
| ↓ | Give the definitions of random and systematic error (Level 4). | | Plenary 2 |
| **Secure** | Describe how technology is used in sport (Level 5). | 3 | Starter 1, Main |
| | Describe what is meant by reaction time (Level 5). | 2 | Main |
| ↓ | Identify sources of random and systematic errors in given scenarios (Level 5). | | |
| **Extending** | Explain the advantages of using technology in timing for sport (Level 7). | 4 | Main |
| | Explain the impact of reaction time on the timing of different sport races (Level 8). | 4 | Main |
| ↓ | Suggest ways to minimise random and systematic errors for given scenarios (Level 7). | | Plenary 2 |

**Maths**
Students demonstrate understanding of proportion when discussing effects of reaction times on sprints compared to marathons. Students quantitatively compare this in the extension task of the activity sheet.

**Literacy**
Students interpret ideas provided in scientific text and use scientific terms correctly when explaining the difference between accuracy and precision.

**APP**
Students discuss possible sources of error in using technology for timing sports events (AF4).

**Key Words**
projectile motion, reaction time, uncertainty

## Answers from the student book

| In-text questions | **A** The speed and the direction of motion. |
| | **B** reaction time |
| Summary Questions | **1** speed, reaction, time, force (4 marks) |
| | **2** Reaction time is the time taken for a signal to be sent from the ear to the brain, where it is interpreted, and then for the brain to send signals to the relevant part(s) of the body to produce a response to a given signal. (2 marks) |

# P3 Chapter 1: New technology

3 A stopwatch depends on the reaction time of the person holding it. They have to see the ball touch the ground before reacting, which takes time. A light gate does not involve reaction times. When the ball interrupts the light beam, the timer stops. The time given is therefore more accurate. (4 marks)

4 QWC question (6 marks). Example answers:
Light gates are used to time races. This occurs in a variety of sports such as athletics, swimming, and racing. These are important as they eliminate human reaction time. A beam of light is fired from one light gate to another on the other side of the track. Finishers interrupt the beam, which sends an electric signal to the timer, giving an accurate time for the race. Formula one is another sport that uses technology. Drivers wear special helmets and clothing that have been designed to absorb shock, and are fire-proof. Cars are designed to increase contact time in a collision to minimise injury (crumple zones). Cameras also take photos at high speeds (hundreds per second) to help decide photo finishes in races.

**kerboodle**

| Starter | Support/Extend | Resources |
|---|---|---|
| **Olympic timings** (10 min) Show students a video about the importance of timing in sport, for example, 'Science of the Summer Olympics – Measuring a champion' from NBC Learn is an excellent resource. Students list and describe ways of using technology for timing in different sports after watching this video. This video also discusses the importance of accuracy and precision. <br><br> **Why do champions win?** (10 min) In groups, students select a sport and write down reasons why champions win. They use their list to discuss the impact of speed and reaction times on winning. Open up to a class discussion. | **Support**: Give students a list of methods for measuring time to match against the sports in the video. <br> **Extension**: Students suggest the advantages and disadvantages of using different timing methods for different events. <br><br> **Support**: Provide a set of reasons for students to rank in a diamond nine. | |

| Main | Support/Extend | Resources |
|---|---|---|
| **Reaction times** (35 min) Introduce reaction times and their importance in timing sport events. Point out to students how athletes take time to react, and how significant reaction times are in short-distance races. You could show video clips of different sporting events to demonstrate this, in slow motion if possible. Alternatively, use an interactive reaction timer. These are readily available on the Internet. Students then read information about data obtained in 100-m races to discuss the effect of reaction time on athletes' performances, answering questions that follow. <br> If time, allow students to calculate their reaction time using a video of Usain Bolt's 100-m race and a stopwatch. Difference between official race time and stopwatch reading is roughly twice their reaction time. Good Internet connection will be necessary for this part of the activity. | **Support**: Students may require a reminder of the factors affecting reaction time before the start of this activity. | **Activity**: Reaction times |

| Plenary | Support/Extend | Resources |
|---|---|---|
| **Sport events** (10 min) Students use the clues provided on the interactive resource to complete a crossword based on the key words in this lesson. <br><br> **Accuracy versus precision** (10 min) Recap the definition of accuracy and precision. Students describe the accuracy and precision of scenarios in sports. They give the definition of random and systematic errors, identifying possible sources of these errors in the given scenarios. | **Extension**: Students add their own key words and clues. <br><br> **Extension**: Students suggest ways to minimise errors. | **Interactive**: Sport events |

| Homework | | |
|---|---|---|
| Students research another way (other than timing races in athletics) where technology is used in sport. This can be done as an information poster or leaflet. <br><br> An alternative WebQuest homework activity is also available on Kerboodle where students research technology used for timing in sport. | **Extension**: Challenge students to find out about crumple zones in cars and how this relates to safety in Formula 1. | **WebQuest**: Timing in sport |

# 1.6 Your planet

**KS3 Physics NC Link:**
- calculation of fuel uses and costs in the domestic context.

**KS3 Working Scientifically NC Link:**
- interpret observations and data, including identifying patterns and using observations, measurements, and data to draw conclusions.

**KS4 Physics NC Link:**
- list and describe the main energy sources available for use on Earth (including fossil fuels, nuclear fuel, biofuel, wind, the tides, and the Sun) and distinguish between renewable and non-renewable sources.

| Band | Outcome | Checkpoint | |
|---|---|---|---|
| | | Question | Activity |
| **Developing** | State how the demand for electricity is changing (Level 3). | 1 | Lit, Starter 1, Main |
| | State ways to meet future electricity demands (Level 4). | B, 2 | Main, Plenary 2, Homework |
| | Use graphical data to state the countries that have the highest and lowest oil use per person (Level 3). | | Main |
| **Secure** | Explain why demand for electricity is increasing (Level 5). | A, 1 | Lit, Starter 1, Main, Plenary 1 |
| | Describe how future demand for electricity could be met (Level 5). | 2 | Main, Plenary 2, Homework |
| | Describe the general relationship between oil use and average income per person (Level 5). | | Main |
| **Extending** | Suggest reasons why the demand for electricity is increasing in different countries (Level 7). | | Lit, Main, Plenary 1 |
| | Evaluate advantages and disadvantages of different methods of electricity generation (Level 8). | 3 | Main, Plenary 2, Homework |
| | Calculate and compare the oil consumption of different countries using the data provided (Level 8). | | Main |

**Maths**
Students interpret information from graphs and tables, identifying patterns given in numerical form to draw conclusions and answer questions.

**Literacy**
In the student-book activity students write a summary for 'an electricity journey' that lists everything the student uses electricity for in a day.

**APP**
Students interpret numerical data provided in graphs and tables and evaluate the different methods of electricity generation (AF5).

**Key Words**
nuclear fusion

## Answers from the student book

| In-text questions | **A** Any from: bigger population, more developed countries, or more devices that use electricity.<br>**B** Two from: wind, waves, tides, falling water (hydroelectric), geothermal.<br>**C** nuclear fusion |
|---|---|
| Activity | **How many?**<br>Students' entries should include all the devices they use or encounter in a day that require electricity, for example, electric light, phone, radio, alarm, shower, toaster, kettle, car, traffic lights, laptop/computer/tablet, MP3 player, projector, power packs, oven, and TV. |

| Summary Questions | 1 increasing, increasing, increasing, don't (4 marks) |
|---|---|
| | 2 Any two from (4 marks): |
| | Wind, wave, tidal, falling water (hydroelectric) – these turn the turbines directly. |
| | Geothermal – water is pumped underground. The Earth heats the water to steam that drives a turbine. |
| | Nuclear fusion – hydrogen atoms fuse together to make helium, releasing large amounts of energy. |
| | Solar cells – absorb light from the Sun, produce a potential difference directly. |
| | 3 Credit sensible suggestions for the rules of a snakes and ladders game. Example answers (6 marks): |
| | Ladders for: |
| | An increase of renewable fuel sources, because carbon dioxide emission is less than for fossil fuels overall, and these fuel sources will not run out. |
| | Using nuclear fusion, because a lot of energy is released in the reaction, with no greenhouse gases produced. |
| | Snakes for: |
| | Using fossil fuels, as these add to pollution and contribute to climate change. |
| | Using nuclear fusion, as this is extremely difficult to set up, and a working fusion reactor for electricity generation has yet to be achieved. |

| Starter | Support/Extend | Resources |
|---|---|---|
| **What have you used yesterday?** (10 min) Students list everything they used the day before that requires electricity to run. How does this list compare to students 30 years ago? Ask students to suggest how the demand for electricity is changing based on their answer to the previous question. | **Extension**: Students categorise equipment as necessities or luxury items. | |
| **Demand graphs** (10 min) Students sketch a graph showing demand for electricity varying during one day in their home. The graph should show peaks (morning/evening) and troughs (at night). Students should then explain the shape of the graphs they have drawn. | **Support**: Ask students if they use electricity when asleep compared to when watching TV. | |

| Main | Support/Extend | Resources |
|---|---|---|
| **The demand for electricity** (35 min) Discuss with students the general trend (increase) in the demand for electivity over the last 30 years. Explain why this is the case on a global scale. Introduce the different methods of electricity generation that can meet demand. Ask students for advantages and disadvantages of each method. Ensure students understand that nuclear fusion is in its experimental stage. You may wish to show students photographs of the 'doughnut' from the JET reactor for added context.<br>Students then use numerical data presented in graphs and tables to interpret oil usage in different countries and how this relates to other factors (climate, average annual income of population). Students use their own knowledge and the data provided to answer questions about electricity demand and generation, suggesting reasons for patterns identified in the data. | **Support**: Discuss with students what the data provided show, and how the graph can be linked to the table before allowing students to begin the activity.<br>**Extension**: The main differences between nuclear fission and fusion can be explained briefly, where appropriate. | **Activity**: The demand for electricity |

| Plenary | Support/Extend | Resources |
|---|---|---|
| **The demand for electricity** (10 min) Students categorise possible reasons for the increasing demand for electricity using the interactive resource. | **Extension**: Students think of other reasons, particularly relating to other countries. | **Interactive**: The demand for electricity |
| **Future demand** (10 min) Students write a paragraph on one method of generating electricity. Include a brief description, one advantage, one disadvantage, and a conclusion. Students peer mark their answers, and share some with the rest of the class. | **Support**: Limit methods to ones that are easy to explain, for example, fossil fuels. | |

| Homework |
|---|
| Students complete the activity sheet and write a report on how each country on the activity sheet can meet its demand for electricity, using the data provided. |

# P3 Chapter 1 Checkpoint

## Checkpoint lesson routes

The route through this lesson can be determined using the Checkpoint assessment.
Percentage pass marks are supplied in the Checkpoint teacher notes.

### Route A (revision)
Resource: P3 Chapter 1 Checkpoint: Revision
Students work through a series of tasks that allows them to revisit and consolidate their understanding of the topics within this chapter. Students can keep this as a summary of the topic, and use this when revising for future assessments.

### Route B (extension)
Resource: P3 Chapter 1 Checkpoint: Extension
Students design exam questions and an accompanying mark scheme that must include a visual summary of the key concepts covered in this topic.

## Progression to *secure*

| No. | Developing outcome | Secure outcome | Making progress |
| --- | --- | --- | --- |
| 1 | Give examples of a digital and an analogue signal. | Describe the difference between an analogue and a digital signal. | In Task 1 students label analogue and digital signals and use these to describe similarities and differences between them. |
| 2 | State the types of electromagnetic waves used for communication. | Describe how waves can be used for communication. | In Task 1 students match different electronic devices to the types of electromagnetic waves they use. |
| 3 | State the equation for efficiency. | Describe what is meant by efficiency. | In Task 2 students describe the term efficiency using the context of two lightbulbs. |
| 4 | Name the component that detects light levels. | Describe how an LDR detects light. | In Task 3 students use a resistance–light graph to describe how changing light levels affect the resistance in an LDR. |
| 5 | Give the name of the circuit component that detects changes in temperature. | Describe how a thermistor detects changes in temperature. | In Task 3 students complete a word fill to describe how a thermistor detects temperature. |
|  | State ways that sensors can be used in hospitals. | Describe how sensors can be used in hospitals. | In Task 3 students complete a table to describe how different sensors are used in hospitals. |
| 6 | State one way in which optical fibres are used. | Describe how optical fibres work. | In Task 3 students use the key terms provided to describe how optical fibres work. |
| 7 | State the types of electromagnetic wave used to see inside the human body. | Describe some techniques for seeing inside the human body. | In Task 3 students match different techniques for looking inside the human body with their descriptions. |
| 8 | State one way in which technology is used in sport. | Describe how technology is used in sport. | In Task 4 students complete a table to describe how different types of technology are used in sport. |
| 9 | State the name of the time taken for a person to react to a signal. | Describe what is meant by reaction time. | In Task 4 students describe reaction time in the context of a 100-m race. |
| 10 | State how the demand for electricity is changing. | Explain why demand for electricity is increasing. | In Task 5 students suggest three possible reasons for the increase in electricity demand. |
| 11 | State ways to meet future electricity demands. | Describe how future demand for electricity could be met. | In Task 5 students select possible ways to meet the increasing demand for electricity from statements provided. |

# P3 Chapter 1: New technology

## Answers to end-of-chapter questions

1. radio waves, visible light, X-rays, infrared (4 marks)
2. LDR – used to detect light      thermistor – used to detect temperature
   LED – an efficient lightbulb      endoscope – used to see inside people    (4 marks)
3. 0.2 seconds (1 mark)
4. a Any two from: endoscopy/X-rays/gamma rays/ultrasound/MRIs
   b Design helmets/protective clothing for the driver and having design features on the car to increase contact time during a collision. (2 marks)
5. a How does the number of layers of plastic film affect the potential difference produced by a solar cell? (1 mark)
   b Column headers: Number of layers of plastic film, Potential difference (V) (1 mark)
   c A bar chart should be drawn because the number of layers of plastic film is a discrete variable. (2 marks)
6. a The complete diagram should include the following points (4 marks):
   existing light ray continues in a straight line through the first surface
   reflected through 90° at the second surface
   continues in a straight line through the third surface
   b Waves entering a surface along the normal are not refracted. Waves approaching the second surface at an angle greater than the critical angle are totally internally reflected. (2 marks)
7. Sketch graph should show the resistance decreasing with temperature in a curve (credit $\frac{1}{x}$ or exponential decay). This is because in a thermistor, the resistance decreases with an increase in temperature. (2 marks)
8. a analogue (1 mark)    b digital (1 mark)    c digital (1 mark)    d analogue (1 mark)
9. lightbulb – 20 J, 20% (2 marks)     kettle – 1500 J, 75% (2 marks)
   television – 5000 J, 50% (2 marks)     car – 300 J, 25% (2 marks)
10. This is a QWC question. Students should be marked on the use of good English, organisation of information, spelling and grammar, and correct use of specialist scientific terms. The best answers will fully explain how thermistors and heaters can be used to keep the temperature of a greenhouse constant (maximum of 6 marks). Examples of correct scientific points:
    A heater increases the temperature inside the greenhouse.
    A thermistor detects temperature.
    Its resistance goes down as temperature increases.
    A sensing circuit can be used, containing a thermistor, to detect when the temperature inside the greenhouse is too low.
    This can then switch on the heater to warm the greenhouse.
    The thermistor can detect when the optimum temperature is reached.
    The sensing circuit can then turn off the heater.

## Answer guide for Big Write

| Developing | Secure | Extending |
|---|---|---|
| 1–2 marks | 3–4 marks | 5–6 marks |
| • Display boards include some examples of technology from two the following categories: homes, hospitals, sport, and electricity generation.<br>• Display describes briefly some of the ways technology has affected our lives. | • Display boards include some examples of technology from three of the following categories: homes, hospitals, sport, and electricity generation.<br>• Display describes the impact of the following technologies:<br>  o LEDs<br>  o endoscopes/scanning<br>  o electronic timing<br>  o renewable resources.<br>• Display describes at least one of the uses above in detail. | • Display boards include at least one example of technology from all of the following categories: homes, hospitals, sport, and electricity generation.<br>• Display describe the impact of the following technologies:<br>  o LEDs/LDRs<br>  o endoscopes/X-rays/gamma rays/MRI<br>  o electronic timing<br>  o renewable resources.<br>• Display describes at least three of the uses above in detail.<br>• Display explains how at least one of the uses above works. |

| | |
|---|---|
| P3 Chapter 1 Checkpoint assessment (automarked) | P3 Chapter 1 Checkpoint: Extension |
| P3 Chapter 1 Checkpoint: Revision | P3 Chapter 1 Progress task (Maths) |

# 2.1 Discovering the Universe 1

**KS3 Physics NC Link:**
- forces
- space physics.

**KS4 Physics NC Link:**
- give examples of forces that act without contact across an empty space, linking these to the gravity, electric, and magnetic fields involved
- explain the difference between planetary orbits and orbits of meteors
- explain for circular orbits how the force of gravity can lead to changing velocity of a planet but unchanged speed.

| Band | Outcome | Checkpoint | |
|---|---|---|---|
| | | Questions | Activities |
| **Developing** ↓ | State some ideas about the Universe that developed in different cultures (Level 4). | 1 | Lit, Starter 1, Main, Plenary 1 |
| | State what is meant by geocentric (Level 3). | 2 | Starter 2, Main, Plenary 2 |
| **Secure** ↓ | Describe some ideas about the Universe that developed in different cultures (Level 6). | 1 | Lit, Starter 1, Main, Plenary 1 |
| | Describe the geocentric model of the Solar System (Level 5). | 2 | Starter 2, Main, Plenary 2 |
| **Extending** ↓ | Compare ideas about the Universe that developed in different cultures (Level 7). | 3 | Main, Plenary 1 |
| | Suggest an observation that could not be explained by the geocentric model (Level 8). | | Main, Homework |

**Literacy**
Students extract and summarise a range of information from different sources about the beliefs of different cultures regarding the Earth and the Solar System, discussing ideas in a presentation.

**APP**
Students use models to describe the beliefs of different cultures regarding the Earth and the Solar System (AF1).

**Key Words**
evidence, prediction, model, geocentric model

## Answers from the student book

| In-text questions | A make observations, take measurements<br>B geocentric |
|---|---|
| Activity | **Strange moon**<br>Eclipses can be demonstrated using light sources and round objects.<br>Demonstrate how the shadow produced when an object blocks a light source can be cast over a celestial body, for example, the Moon.<br>There is no light for the moon to reflect, meaning that we will not see the Moon during an eclipse. |

# P3 Chapter 2: Turning points in physics

| Summary Questions | |
|---|---|
| | **1** geocentric model – Greece |
| | the Earth on the back of a tortoise – India |
| | the Sun is swallowed by a god during a solar eclipse – Thailand (3 marks) |
| | **2** The Earth is at the centre. The Sun, Moon, planets, and stars move around the Earth (on crystal spheres that allow light to be transmitted). (2 marks) |
| | **3** QWC question (6 marks). Example answers: |
| | Stories and scientific explanations both tried to explain what we see. |
| | Scientists collect evidence. |
| | Evidence can be obtained by measurements or observations. |
| | Scientists use evidence to develop the explanation. |
| | They use the explanation to make predictions about what will happen in the future. |
| | If the predictions come true then it supports the explanation. |
| | You cannot make predictions with stories. |
| | Stories do not depend on evidence. Stories are often rooted in beliefs. |

| Starter | Support/Extend | Resources |
|---|---|---|
| **Beliefs about the Universe** (10 min) Describe one theory from the corresponding student-book spread about the Universe. Ask students for ideas about what they think. If students know that the story is untrue, ask them to justify this by comparing the story with known observations/explanations today. Be aware that sensitivity is required when discussing different religious beliefs. | **Support**: Choose a belief that is far-fetched by today's standards, for example, Apollo pulling the Sun along in his chariot. | |
| **Geo- words** (5 min) Show students a list of words with the prefix 'geo-' on the board. Ask students what these words have in common, and what the prefix may mean. | **Extension**: Students should explain what the geocentric model of the Solar System is based on other words given. | |

| Main | Support/Extend | Resources |
|---|---|---|
| **The Solar System in different cultures** (40 min) Introduce different ideas about the Solar System that developed in different cultures, focusing on the geocentric model. Students then work in groups to make a model of one of these beliefs (flat Earth, world turtle, or geocentric model). Students have 30 minutes to research and create their models before giving a two-minute presentation to the rest of the class. Students should complete the grid summarising the three different beliefs during the presentations. | **Support**: You may wish to read the corresponding spread in the student book with students to support weaker readers. Further prompts may be required to help students find the relevant information. **Extension**: Encourage students to evaluate the models created by others. | **Activity**: The Solar System in different cultures |

| Plenary | Support/Extend | Resources |
|---|---|---|
| **The Solar System in other cultures** (5 min) Students match each country to how its people believed the Solar System was constructed using the interactive resource. Students should then be asked to describe each model given. | **Extension**: Students compare one model with another. | **Interactive**: The Solar System in other cultures |
| **The geocentric model** (10 min) Ask students true or false questions relating to the geocentric model. Questions may relate to the name or description of the model. Ask students to show their answers using thumbs up/thumbs down, coloured cards, or a traffic light system. | **Extension**: Students should add further questions to ask the rest of the class. | |

| Homework | | |
|---|---|---|
| Students carry out further research on the geocentric model, writing down three interesting facts that were not covered in the lesson. | **Extension**: Students focus on observations that could not be explained using the geocentric model. | |

# 2.2 Discovering the Universe 2

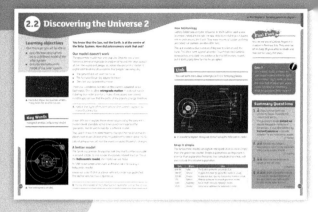

**KS3 Physics NC Link:**
- space physics.

**KS3 Working Scientifically NC Link:**
- present reasoned explanations including explaining data in relation to predictions and hypotheses.

| Band | Outcome | Checkpoint | |
|---|---|---|---|
| | | Questions | Activities |
| Developing | State some observations that led to our present model of the Solar System (Level 4). | 1, 2 | Main, Plenary 1 |
| | Name our present model of the Solar System (Level 3). | B | Main, Plenary 2 |
| Secure | Describe how observations led to a different model of the Solar System (Level 6). | 1, 2 | Main, Plenary 1 |
| | Describe the heliocentric model of the Solar System (Level 5). | 3 | Starter 2, Main, Plenary 2 |
| Extending | Compare similarities and differences between different models of the Solar System (Level 7). | | Main, Plenary 1 |
| | Explain the importance of evidence in developing the heliocentric model (Level 7). | 4 | Main, Plenary 2 |

**Maths**
Students show their understanding of number size and scale when presenting the developments of the geocentric and heliocentric models on a scaled timeline.

**Literacy**
In the student-book activity students find out about words beginning in 'geo'. Students collate scientific information from a range of sources to write a presentation about the development of the heliocentric model from the geocentric model.

**APP**
Students use the geocentric and heliocentric models of the Solar System to explain observations in the night sky (AF1). Students research these models and present their ideas to the rest of the class (AF3).

**Key Words**
retrograde motion, heliocentric model

## Answers from the student book

| In-text questions | **A** retrograde motion |
| | **B** heliocentric model |
| Activity | **Geo-?** |
| | geography – relating to maps and images of the Earth |
| | geometry – relating to measurements (of the Earth) |
| | Words beginning with 'helio-' are related to the Sun, for example, heliocentric, heliosphere. |
| Summary Questions | **1** did not, Galileo (2 marks) |
| | **2** The geocentric model has the Earth at its centre. The Sun and planets orbited the Earth. This did not explain Galileo's observation that objects (moons) orbited Jupiter. (2 marks) |
| | **3** The heliocentric model has the Sun at the centre. Planets orbit the Sun. (2 marks) |

> **4** Timeline should include (6 marks):
> Over 2000 years ago – Plato and Aristotle wrote books explaining the geocentric model. This model was hypothesised due to several observations: the ground did not seem to move, the Sun and Moon did appear to move, and the stars also appeared to move.
> Around 200 BC – Greek astronomer Aristarchus hypothesised the heliocentric model. This was ignored.
> Around 1000 years ago – an Indian mathematician and astronomer called Bhaskaracharya said there was a force between all objects called gravity.
> 140 AD – Ptolemy published his modified version of the geocentric model. This model was made to explain retrograde motion, the apparent backward motion of planets at various points throughout the year.
> 1543 – Copernicus published a book with the heliocentric model.
> Around 500 years ago – Newton published his ideas about gravity, using equations as evidence for his and Bhaskaracharya's ideas.
> 1609 – Galileo used a telescope to observe the moons of Jupiter. This provided evidence that supported the heliocentric model.

| Starter | Support/Extend | Resources |
|---|---|---|
| **How are observations about the Solar System made?** (5 min) Ask students to suggest how observations about the Solar System are made, leading the discussion towards the use of telescopes and how Galileo was the first person to use the telescope for celestial observations. Observations of the Solar System can be presented in the form of a timeline.<br><br>**Geocentric versus heliocentric** (10 min) Students recap what is meant by the geocentric model of the Universe. Ask students to discuss whether this is the model we use today. Why/why not? Encourage students to give examples (moons orbiting other planets, retrograde motion). | **Extension**: You may wish to introduce some of the different types of telescopes available (light, radio waves, etc.). | |

| Main | Support/Extend | Resources |
|---|---|---|
| **Understanding the Universe** (40 min) Review the geocentric model before introducing the heliocentric model. You may wish to use animations or ask students to volunteer in a role play depicting the two models for consolidation. Students then carry out a research task using the student book (and other available resources) on the geocentric and heliocentric models. Students answer questions posed on the activity sheet and add further information of their own in order to discuss their findings in a presentation.<br>It is important that students have covered the contents of the two corresponding spreads in the student book prior to beginning this activity. | **Support**: The accompanying support sheet gives students a writing frame to complete about the two models of our Solar System. Students may then read their completed writing frames for the presentation. | **Activity**: Understanding the Universe |

| Plenary | Support/Extend | Resources |
|---|---|---|
| **From geocentric to heliocentric** (5 min) Students reorder statements provided on the interactive resource to describe how observations led to the geocentric model being discarded in favour of the heliocentric model.<br><br>**The heliocentric model** (10 min) Students work in groups to perform a role play that describes the heliocentric model of the Solar System. There should be added commentary to the role play. | **Extension**: Students should compare similarities and differences between the different models of the Solar System.<br><br>**Extension**: Students can start by modelling the geocentric model before explaining the evidence for the shift towards the heliocentric model. | **Interactive**: From geocentric to heliocentric |

| Homework |
|---|
| Students write a short article in the school magazine explaining the meaning of retrograde motion and how this led to the change from the geocentric to heliocentric model. The article should contain a model/analogy to explain retrograde motion, as well as a description of the heliocentric model. |

# 2.3 The Big Bang

**KS3 Physics NC Link:**
- space physics.

**KS3 Working Scientifically NC Link:**
- present observations and data using appropriate methods, including tables and graphs.

**KS4 Physics NC Link:**
- explain the redshift of light from galaxies that are receding (qualitative only), that the change of speed with galaxies' distances is evidence of an expanding universe, and hence explain the link between the evidence and the Big Bang model.

| Band | Outcome | Checkpoint | |
|------|---------|------------|---|
| | | Questions | Activities |
| **Developing** | State the age of the Solar System (Level 3). | B, 2 | Main |
| | Name the theory of how the Universe started (Level 3). | A | Main, Plenary 2 |
| | Present key events following the Big Bang visually (Level 4). | | Main |
| **Secure** | Describe the timescale of the Universe (Level 6). | 1, 2, 4 | Main, Plenary 1 |
| | Describe what is meant by the Big Bang (level 5). | 3 | Main, Plenary 2, Homework |
| | Present and describe key events following the Big Bang (Level 5). | | Main |
| **Extending** | Explain why atoms could not be formed immediately after the Big Bang (Level 7). | | Main, Plenary 1 |
| | Explain ways in which the Big Bang theory is supported by evidence (Level 8). | | Main, Plenary 2, Homework |
| | Present and describe key events following the Big Bang, focusing on one event in detail (Level 7). | | Main |

**Maths**
Students convert units of time to equivalents in length, presenting major events leading from the Big Bang to the beginning of the human race on a scaled timeline.

**Literacy**
Students collate information from different sources, interpreting meaning from scientific text, and adapting their language to suit the audience when presenting a summary of this information on a poster.

**APP**
Students describe evidence to support the Big Bang theory (AF1) and present major events in the development of the Universe on a poster and on a timeline (AF3).

**Key Words**
Big Bang, analogy

## Answers from the student book

| In-text questions | **A** the Big Bang |
| | **B** 5 billion years |

● P3 Chapter 2: Turning points in physics

| Summary Questions | |
|---|---|
| | 1  Big Bang, formation of the Solar System, first living things, dinosaurs died out (4 marks) |
| | 2  Age of the Earth = 5 billion years<br>Age of the Universe = 14 billion years<br>So the Earth is $\frac{5}{14}$ of the age of the Universe. (2 marks) |
| | 3  The beginning of the Universe and expansion of space and time from something smaller than an atom. (2 marks) |
| | 4  Timeline should include the following events (measurements given assume a timeline that is 14 cm in length is drawn) (6 marks):<br>14 billion years ago (0 cm) – the Big Bang. Space and time expanded from something smaller than an atom.<br>13.85 billion years ago (0.15 cm) – the first stars began to appear<br>5 billion years ago (9 cm) – our Solar System was formed<br>4 billion years ago (10 cm) – first signs of life on Earth<br>Between 65–200 million years ago (13.8–13.935 cm) – dinosaurs on Earth<br>Half a million years ago (13.9995 cm) – start of human life<br>Students may wish to zoom in on the sections with dinosaurs and humans for clarity. |

**kerboodle**

| Starter | Support/Extend | Resources |
|---|---|---|
| **What is a billion?** (5 min) Ask students what a billion means to them. Students may have met million before but they may not have met billion. Help students appreciate the scale of a billion by writing one billion in full. You may wish to give examples of one billion, for example, one million seconds = 11.5 days but one billion seconds = 31.7 years. Take care that 1 billion = $1 \times 10^9$ and not $1 \times 10^{12}$.<br><br>**How did the universe begin?** (10 min) Ask students to discuss their ideas of how the Universe began. Allow students to pair-share their ideas before opening up as a class discussion. Some students may have learnt about the Big Bang before but others may not. | **Extension**: Encourage students to write these large numbers using standard form. | |

| Main | Support/Extend | Resources |
|---|---|---|
| **The timescale of the Universe** (40 min) Students carry out an activity where they read the information provided about the Big Bang theory and present the information in a different and eye-catching way on a poster. Other resources, for example, textbooks and the Internet, may be provided if available for students to carry out further research on one area of interest. | **Support**: You may wish to read the text provided as a group to help weaker readers access the material given. | **Activity**: The timescale of the Universe |

| Plenary | Support/Extend | Resources |
|---|---|---|
| **How the Universe began** (5 min) Students arrange the main events in the evolution of the Universe into sequence using the interactive resource.<br><br>**What is the Big Bang?** (10 min) Students line up in a traffic light system to show how confident they are at answering this question. Those that are confident (green) should explain to those who are less sure (amber and red). Ask students to line up again after five minutes. Encourage students to provide evidence to support the Big Bang theory, for example, cosmic microwave background radiation (CMBR). | **Extension**: Students explain why one event cannot happen without another before it.<br><br>**Support**: Provide students with a list of key words from this lesson that they can use to answer the question posed. | **Interactive**: How the Universe began |

| Homework | | |
|---|---|---|
| Students write a poem to describe the Big Bang. | **Extension**: Students write a poem about how CMBR or redshift supports the Big Bang theory. | |

# 2.4 Spacecraft and satellites

**KS3 Physics NC Link:**
- describing motion
- forces
- forces and motion
- balanced forces
- space physics.

**KS3 Working Scientifically NC Link:**
- make predictions using scientific knowledge and understanding.

**KS4 Physics NC Link:**
- explain that motion in a circle involves constant speed but changing velocity (qualitative only)
- relate linear motion to other relative motions, such as the Earth's relative to the Sun
- explain the concept of equilibrium and identify, for equilibrium situations, the forces that balance one another
- explain for circular orbits how the force of gravity can lead to changing velocity of a planet but unchanged speed, and relate this association to the orbits of communications satellites around the Earth.

| Band | Outcome | Checkpoint | |
|---|---|---|---|
| | | Questions | Activities |
| Developing | Name the orbits a satellite can take (Level 4). | B, 1 | Main, Plenary 2, Homework |
| | State some uses of satellites (Level 4). | 1 | Starter 1, Plenary 2, Homework |
| | Predict the orbit of a given satellite based on its use (Level 4). | | Main |
| Secure | Describe how to get a satellite into orbit (Level 6). | 2 | Main, Plenary 1 |
| | Describe some uses of satellites (Level 5). | 3 | Plenary 2, Homework |
| | Predict with justification the orbit of a given satellite based on its use (Level 6). | | Main |
| Extending | Compare the orbits of different satellites (Level 7). | 3 | Main, Homework |
| | Compare the different uses of satellites (Level 7). | 3 | Main, Homework |
| | Provide detailed explanations of the orbits of satellites given their uses (Level 7). | | Main |

**Maths**
In the student-book activity students convert between units of time to calculate the number of times the ISS orbits the Earth each day.

Students calculate the radius and circumference of different orbits, and the speed, distance, and time in orbit for satellites. These calculation require some rearrangement of the relevant equations.

**APP**
Students predict the orbit taken by different satellites based on the information given (AF5).

**Key Words**
geostationary orbit, low Earth orbit (LEO), polar orbit

# P3 Chapter 2: Turning points in physics

## Answers from the student book

| In-text questions | **A** force of the gases on the rocket, force of the Earth on the rocket (gravity) **B** geostationary |
|---|---|
| Activity | **How many?**<br>There are 24 × 60 minutes in one day = 1440 minutes    The ISS orbits 1440 ÷ 90 = 16 times a day |
| Summary Questions | **1** geostationary orbit – satellite television<br>polar orbit – mapping the Earth's surface<br>low Earth orbit – International Space Station (3 marks)<br>**2** The satellite must be launched at the right speed, to the right height. The force of gravity keeps the satellite in orbit. (2 marks)<br>**3** QWC question (6 marks). Example answers:<br>Both types of satellites orbit the Earth. Both types of satellites can be used to monitor the Earth. Geostationary orbits are always above the same place on Earth. Geostationary satellites are used for satellite television. The orbit of a geostationary satellite is much bigger than low Earth orbit (LEO) satellites. A geostationary satellite is about 36 000 km from the Earth. A LEO has an orbit below 1000 km from Earth. LEOs can be used to see the whole of the Earth's surface. The ISS is an example of a satellite in LEO. Some LEO satellites go over the North and South Poles in polar orbit. These are useful for mapping. |

| Starter | Support/Extend | Resources |
|---|---|---|
| An alternative question-led lesson is also available.<br>**Using satellites** (5 min) Students list the applications they know of that require satellite technology, for example, communication, navigation, and the gathering of information weather (forecasts, tracking, and so on).<br>**Into orbit** (10 min) Tell students a fantastic fact about sending things into orbit, for example, that fruit flies were the first living things to go into outer space. Ask students to suggest how scientists can launch objects into space. | **Support**: Prompt students in the discussion by using terms like satellite dish and GPS.<br>**Extension**: Extend discussion to include the impact of sending too many satellites into space. | **Question-led lesson**: Spacecraft and satellites |
| **Main** | **Support/Extend** | **Resources** |
| **Satellites** (40 min) Introduce students to the uses of satellites, how these can be launched into orbit, and the three different types of satellite orbits (geostationary, LEO, and polar).<br>Students then watch two short demonstrations to model a rocket launch, and how a satellite stays in orbit, before carrying out an activity where they compare different orbits of satellites before using their knowledge and the information provided to predict the orbits taken by different satellites based on their uses. | **Support**: Allow extra time to guide students through the demonstrations. Use prompt questions (e.g., What does the bung represent in this case?)<br>**Extension**: Ask students to give a quick evaluation of the demonstrations shown. | **Activity**: Satellites |
| **Plenary** | **Support/Extend** | **Resources** |
| **Launching a satellite** (10 min) Students reorder sentences provided on the interactive resource to describe how to get a satellite into orbit.<br><br>**Satellite uses and their orbits** (5 min) Issue students with mini-whiteboards on which they must write geostationary on one side and LEO on the other. Give different uses of satellites and ask students to hold up their mini-whiteboards as appropriate, as fast as they can. Pick on students randomly to describe how the satellite is used for a certain purpose. | **Extension**: Give alternative scenarios to explain, for example, what happens if the speed of the rocket when it is fired is too high or low?<br><br>**Extension**: Ask students to justify why a certain orbit must be used for a particular use of satellite, for example, why can a TV satellite not be in LEO? | **Interactive**: Launching a satellite |
| **Homework** | | |
| Students prepare two contrasting stories or comic strips about a day in the life of someone with satellite technology, and another without. This should cover different uses of satellite technology and the orbits in which the satellites are situated. | | |

# 2.5 Mission to the Moon

**KS3 Physics NC Link:**
- forces
- forces and motion
- space physics.

**KS3 Working Scientifically NC Link:**
- evaluate risks.

**KS4 Chemistry NC Link:**
- give examples of forces that act without contact across empty space, linking these to gravity, electric, and magnetic fields involved
- recall that fusion in stars involves pairs of hydrogen nuclei forming helium, emitting radiation and increasing the particle kinetic energy.

| Band | Outcome | Checkpoint | |
|---|---|---|---|
| | | Questions | Activities |
| Developing ↓ | State one risk and one benefit of the space programme (Level 4). | 1 | Starter 1, Main, Plenary 1, Plenary 2, Homework |
| | Identify risks for given hazards in a space mission (Level 4). | | Main |
| Secure ↓ | Describe some of the risks and benefits of the space programme (Level 6). | 2, 3 | Starter 1, Main, Plenary 1, Plenary 2, Homework |
| | Complete a risk assessment for a space mission (Level 6). | | Main |
| Extending ↓ | Explain risks and benefits of the space programme (Level 7). | 3 | Main, Plenary 1, Plenary 2, Homework |
| | Write a detailed risk assessment for a space mission (Level 7). | | Main |

**Literacy**
Students retrieve information from a range of sources and use the ideas identified to evaluate risks and benefits of space travel.

**APP**
Students identify risks and benefits of space travel (AF4).

**Key Words**
risk, solar flare

## Answers from the student book

| In-text questions | **A** The probability that something will happen and the consequences if it should. |
|---|---|
| Activity | **What's the risk?**<br>For example:<br>A cyclist can reduce the probability of being in an accident by watching other traffic carefully, by travelling at a safe speed, or by obeying traffic rules.<br>If a cyclist is involved in an accident, the severity of consequences can be reduced by wearing a helmet or protective clothing. |
| Summary Questions | 1 Risks: rocket exploding, radiation<br>   Benefits: smart-phone technology, baby milk (4 marks)<br>2 Credit sensible suggestions, for example, the Moon landings accelerated the development of computers, modern hospitals use computers for imaging and diagnosing disease. (2 marks) |

**3** QWC question (6 marks). Students should offer at least three risks and three benefits of the space programme. Examples answers:

Any three risks from:

During take-off the astronauts lie on top of an enormous rocket that can explode.

The spacecraft can combust as it re-enters the atmosphere due to intense friction between the body of the spacecraft and the atmosphere.

If the parachute fails to open in time the spacecraft would land on Earth at higher speeds than anticipated, causing a crash.

Solar flares can stop all on-board computers working while the spacecraft is in space.

Any three benefits from:

Without the Apollo missions and the space programme we would not have many of the technological devices that we take for granted today.

In 1963 half the computers in the world were developed for the Moon missions.

The liquid-cooled suits used by racing car drivers and fire-fighters are based on the Apollo astronauts' spacesuits.

The shock-absorbing materials used in sports shoes were developed for spacesuits.

Baby-milk formulas are based on protein-rich drinks developed for astronauts.

Computer programs for swiping credit cards use software designed for the Apollo missions.

Water filters use technology designed to recycle astronauts' urine.

| Starter | Support/Extend | Resources |
|---|---|---|
| **Space missions** (5 min) Students categorise statements about space missions provided on the interactive resource as advantages and disadvantages. This activity serves as a starting point for further discussion.<br>**Ideas on space exploration** (10 min) Show students a video clip from a film about space exploration. These are readily available on the Internet. Ask students to discuss what they know already about space exploration, and identify examples of incorrect science given in the video. (For example, many films depict sound travelling through space.) | **Extension**: Encourage students to justify their choices.<br><br>**Support**: Time should be spent correcting misconceptions as appropriate. | **Interactive**: Space missions |

| Main | Support/Extend | Resources |
|---|---|---|
| **Space travel** (40 min) Introduce students to the different risks and benefits of the space programme. This can be done using the student book. Review the definitions of the key words risk and hazard, starting from a familiar scenario, for example, travelling to school.<br>Students then carry out an activity where they read the opinions of four different people on the space programme and complete a risk assessment for a space mission. Students answer questions that follow. | **Support**: The accompanying support sheet offers students a partially completed grid for their risk assessment. | **Activity**: Space travel |

| Plenary | Support/Extend | Resources |
|---|---|---|
| **Risks and benefits of space travel** (5 min) Students pair-share ideas for a class discussion on the risks and benefits of space travel.<br>**The most important factor** (10 min) Issue students with nine cards. For each card, one side should have a benefit of space travel, and the other side, a risk. Students then sort the cards to show all the benefits of space travel and rank these in a diamond nine. Repeat for the risks of space travel. | **Extension**: Encourage students to justify their choices throughout the activity. | |

| Homework | | |
|---|---|---|
| Students find out about one space mission and present risks and benefits of this mission in a table, with a short evaluation afterwards about whether they think this mission was worth it. | | |

# 2.6 Radioactivity 1

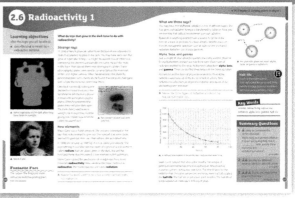

**KS4 Physics NC Link:**
- recall that some nuclei may emit alpha, beta, or neutral particles and electromagnetic radiation as gamma rays
- explain that radioactive decay is a random process, the concept of half-life, and how the hazards associated with radioactive material differ according to the half-life involved, and to the differences in the penetration properties of alpha particles, beta particles, and gamma rays.

| Band | Outcome | Checkpoint | |
|---|---|---|---|
| | | Questions | Activities |
| **Developing** ↓ | State the term given to a material that gives out radiation (Level 3). | A, 1 | Starter 1, Starter 2, Plenary 1, Plenary 2, Homework |
| **Secure** ↓ | Describe what is meant by a radioactive material (Level 6). | 1, 2 | Starter 2, Main, Plenary 1, Plenary 2, Homework |
| **Extending** ↓ | Explain how the radioactivity of a sample changes with time (Level 8). | 3 | Maths, Main, Plenary 1, Plenary 2, Homework |

**Maths**
Students draw, interpret, and carry out calculations involving half-life.

**Literacy**
Students summarise information from a range of sources about different scientists who contributed towards the discovery of radioactivity.

**APP**
Students draw graphs to show the activity of a radioactive sample and demonstrate half-life (AF3).

**Key Words**
radium, radioactivity, radioactive, radiation, alpha, beta, gamma, half-life

## Answers from the student book

| In-text questions | **A** radioactive <br> **B** alpha, beta, and gamma |
|---|---|
| Activity | **Half-life** <br> After two days: <br> radiation emitted per second = 2000 ÷ 2 = 1000 alpha particles per second <br> After four days: <br> radiation emitted per second = 1000 ÷ 2 = 500 alpha particles per second |
| Summary Questions | 1 radioactive, less (2 marks) <br> 2 radiation – waves or particles emitted by radioactive materials <br>   radioactive – (a description of) a material that gives out radiation (2 marks) <br> 3 QWC question (6 marks). Example answers: <br> The graph shows a general decrease in the number of waves/particles emitted per second. <br> For example, from 1000 waves/particles emitted per second at 0 s to 60 waves/particles emitted per second at 80 s. <br> The graph is in the shape of a downward curve. <br> This curve is known as exponential decay. <br> The decrease in the number of particles emitted is fast at first, and then slows down. <br> For example, at 20 s, 500 particles are emitted per second. <br> At 40 s, 500 ÷ 2 = 250 particles are emitted per second. <br> *Credit alternative examples given with numerical data.* |

P3 Chapter 2: Turning points in physics

| Starter | Support/Extend | Resources |
|---|---|---|
| **Existing knowledge about radioactivity** (5 min) Show students images of glowing green items. You may wish to show students video clips of glowing green items that are often found in cartoons. Ask students what they think these items are and what they know about them.<br><br>**Reviewing hazard symbols** (5 min) Ask students to draw as many hazard symbols as they can remember before displaying these on the board. Ask students to name and describe each symbol in turn. In particular, the radioactivity symbol should be covered as this will form the focus for this lesson. | | |

| Main | Support/Extend | Resources |
|---|---|---|
| **Discovering radioactivity** (40 min) Formally introduce the definitions of the key words radioactivity and radioactive material. Explain how there are three types of radiation emitted by radioactive substances – alpha, beta, and gamma, and that the radioactivity of sources decreases with time.<br>A good way to model the decrease of radioactivity in a radioactive source with time is to issue each student with a die. At the start of the demonstration, every student stands up to represent a radioactive atom. Every time that a student rolls a certain number, for example, a six, they sit down. This is an effective and visual way of showing the random nature of radioactive decay. Students then carry out an activity where they read an information sheet about Becquerel, Curie, and Rutherford. Students can carry out further research on one of these scientists if resources are available (textbooks, the Internet) and complete a fact file for one of these scientists. Students then answer the questions that follow. | **Support**: You may wish to read the information sheet as a group to help weaker readers.<br>**Extension**: GCSE textbooks can be offered to students during their research, and the concept of half-life can also be discussed. | **Activity**: Discovering radioactivity |

| Plenary | Support/Extend | Resources |
|---|---|---|
| **What is radioactivity?** (10 min) Students complete the sentences provided on the interactive resource to describe radioactivity.<br><br><br><br>**Sketch graphs** (10 min) Students draw a sketch graph on mini-whiteboards to show how the radioactivity of a radioactive material changes with time. They should use these graphs to describe radioactivity to each other. | **Extension**: Ask students to explain why the radioactivity of a material decreases with time. Students should include an explanation of half-life in their answers.<br>**Extension**: Students explain the shape of the sketch graph. | **Interactive:** What is radioactivity? |

| Homework | | |
|---|---|---|
| Students design a poster about one radioactive element of their choice, including the properties of the element, how it was discovered, who discovered it, and when it was discovered. The poster should also include a brief description of the term radioactivity.<br>The poster can be presented in the form of a fact file, ready for display. | | |

# 2.7 Radioactivity 2

**KS3 Working Scientifically NC Link:**
- evaluate risks.

**KS4 Physics NC Link:**
- give examples of practical use of alpha particles, beta particles, and gamma rays
- describe and distinguish between uses of nuclear radiations for exploration of internal organs, and to control or destroy unwanted tissue
- explain why radioactive material, whether external to the body or ingested, is hazardous because of damage to the tissue cells.

| Band | Outcome | Checkpoint | |
|---|---|---|---|
| | | Questions | Activities |
| Developing | State one risk of using radioactive materials (Level 3). | A, 1 | Main, Plenary 1, Homework |
| | State one use of radioactive materials (Level 3). | B, 1 | Lit, Main, Plenary 2, Homework |
| | Give the risks of using a radioactive technique in medicine and an everyday activity using probability (Level 4). | | Main |
| Secure | Describe the risks of using radioactive materials (Level 6). | 2 | Lit, Main, Plenary 1, Homework |
| | Describe some uses of radioactive materials (Level 5). | 3 | Main, Plenary 2, Homework |
| | Explain why radioactive techniques are used in medicine despite the associated risks (Level 6). | | Main |
| Extending | Explain how to reduce the risks of using radioactive materials (Level 8). | | Main, Plenary 1, Homework |
| | Compare different uses of radioactive materials (Level 7). | 3 | Main, Plenary 2 |
| | Evaluate the risks and benefits of using radioactive techniques to suggest appropriate treatment of patients in different scenarios (Level 8). | | Main |

**Maths**
Students calculate probability in quantitative problem solving.

**Literacy**
In the student-book activity students extract and summarise information to write clear and concise explanations linking the terms radioactive, radiation, and radiotherapy.

Students identify meaning in scientific texts and summarise the information provided by answering questions.

**APP**
Students identify evidence supporting or refuting the use of radioactivity techniques in medicine (AF1) and draw conclusions from data provided (AF5).

**Key Words**
cancer, mutation, sterilise, gamma camera, radiotherapy

## Answers from the student book

| In-text questions | **A** cancer |
|---|---|
| | **B** In sterilising medical equipment and food, and to diagnose and treat diseases. |

# P3 Chapter 2: Turning points in physics

| Activity | **Confusing?** Credit sensible suggestions, for example, doctors use radioactive materials that give out radiation in a cancer treatment called radiotherapy. |
|---|---|
| Summary Questions | **1** cure, cause, radiotherapy (3 marks) <br> **2** Long half-life means that the radioactive material remains highly radioactive for a long time. This increases the time the radioactive material has to damage body cells and cause diseases such as cancer. (2 marks) <br> **3** QWC question (6 marks). Example answers: <br> Radioactive materials emit radiation. Radiation can damage cells. It can also cause mutations in cells. This can cause cancer. <br> However, radiation can also be used to kill cells, for example, harmful bacteria. Radiation is used to sterilise medical equipment and food. Doctors can use radiation to destroy cancer cells during radiotherapy. |

| Starter | Support/Extend | Resources |
|---|---|---|
| **A risky business?** (5 min) Ask students to recap the story of Marie Curie and how she, together with husband Pierre, discovered the radioactive elements radium and polonium. Then tell students about how the Curies became ill. This can be used as an introduction to the risks of radioactive materials. <br><br> **Risk assessments** (5 min) Ask students to recap the difference between risks and hazards before asking them to write one entry on the risk assessment of a simple task (e.g., sharpening a pencil) on a mini-whiteboard. | **Support**: Students may require a reminder of the headers required in a risk assessment table. | |
| **Main** | **Support/Extend** | **Resources** |
| **Uses and risks of radioactive materials** (40 min) Introduce the risks and benefits of using radioactive materials. This should include the effect of radiation on healthy cells, as well as its effect on tumour cells. The use of radioactive material in medical tracers and scans, and the irradiation of food and medical equipment should also be mentioned. <br> Students then carry out an activity where they interpret information given about medical uses of radioactive materials and answer questions that follow. This activity requires students to analyse scientific text and numerical data, forming their own conclusions about why radioactive techniques continue to be used in medicine despite their risks. | **Support**: You may wish to read the information together as a class to help weaker readers access the information provided. | **Activity**: Uses and risks of radioactive materials |
| **Plenary** | **Support/Extend** | **Resources** |
| **The correct treatment?** (10 min) Students categorise statements given on the interactive resource as being true or false. Students should then correct the statements that are false and justify their changes. <br> This activity then leads onto a discussion of ways that the risks of radiation exposure can be minimised. This can be done as a diamond nine if time. | **Extension**: Encourage students to suggest further statements to add to the interactive resource. | **Interactive**: The correct treatment? |
| **Uses of radioactive materials** (10 min) Students are presented with a list of possible uses of radioactive materials on the board. They should correctly identify these uses (using thumbs up/down, coloured cards, or traffic lights) and give further descriptions of each one. | **Extension**: Encourage students to compare the uses of radioactive materials, rather than to give a description. | |
| **Homework** | | |
| Students write a short letter for the opinions column of a newspaper, in response to the article 'Radiation – good or bad?' In this letter students should evaluate the risks and benefits of radioactive materials and present a conclusion. <br><br> An alternative WebQuest homework activity is also available on Kerboodle where students research radioactivity in medicine. | **Extension**: Students write a letter supporting the use of radioactive materials by countering risks with safety precautions that can be taken. | **WebQuest**: Radioactivity and medicine |

# 2.8 Electromagnetism 1

**KS3 Physics NC Link:**
- current electricity
- magnetism.

**KS3 Working Scientifically NC Link:**
- use appropriate techniques, apparatus, and materials during laboratory work, paying attention to health and safety.

**KS4 Physics NC Link:**
- explain the difference between direct and alternating voltages
- explain how to show that a current can create a magnetic effect and describe the directions of the magnetic field around a conducting wire
- recall that a change in the magnetic field around a conductor can give rise to an induced e.m.f. across its ends, which could drive a current, generating a field that would oppose the original change; hence explain how this effect is used in a alternator to generate a.c., and in a dynamo to generate d.c.

| Band | Outcome | Checkpoint | |
|---|---|---|---|
| | | Questions | Activities |
| **Developing** ↓ | Name the process used to generate electricity (Level 3). | A, 1 | Main, Plenary 1, Plenary 2 |
| | Carry out an experiment to induce an electric current (Level 4). | | Main |
| **Secure** ↓ | Describe how to generate electricity using electromagnetic induction (Level 6). | 2, 3 | Main, Plenary 1, Plenary 2, Homework |
| | Carry out an experiment to induce an electric current, describing trends shown by the results (Level 5). | | Main |
| **Extending** ↓ | Suggest how to change the amount of current produced in electromagnetic induction (Level 7). | | Main, Plenary 1, Plenary 2 |
| | Carry out an experiment to induce an electric current, describing trends shown, and use this to predict further results (Level 7). | | Main |

**Maths**
Students identify numerical patterns from experimental results, and use these patterns to predict further ammeter readings.

**Literacy**
Interpret scientific diagrams and instructions to carry out an experimental method.

**APP**
Students collect data from an electromagnetic induction experiment (AF4), present this in a table (AF3), and analyse results to draw a conclusion (AF5).

**Key Words**
electromagnetism, electromagnetic induction, peer review, alternating current

### Answers from the student book

| In-text questions | **A** electromagnetic induction |
|---|---|
| Activity | **Peer review** Students must include the importance of publishing in journals for communication of scientific ideas, and the importance of peer review to verify if results are correct and reproducible. |

● P3 Chapter 2: Turning points in physics

| Summary Questions | 1 moving, stationary (2 marks)<br>2 As you wind up the torch, the coil of wire moves.<br>This means that the coil of wire is moving relative to the stationary magnet inside the torch.<br>A potential difference is produced, causing a current to flow in a complete circuit. (3 marks)<br>3 QWC question (6 marks). Example answers:<br>You need a magnet and a (coil of) wire to generate electricity.<br>A potential difference, and hence current in a complete circuit, is induced when a magnet is moved inside a coil of wire.<br>Alternatively, the (coil of) wire can be moved inside a magnetic field. This is called electromagnetic induction. Electricity is generated in power stations using this method.<br>The direction of magnetic movement determines the direction of the current. If the magnet spins, or is moved in two directions, an alternating current is induced. |
|---|---|

**kerboodle**

| Starter | Support/Extend | Resources |
|---|---|---|
| **Revisiting electromagnets** (5 min) Ask students to describe what electromagnets are. Electromagnets were introduced in P2. This can lead onto ideas about electromagnetic induction later on in the lesson.<br>**Revisiting power stations** (10 min) Recap stages in electricity generation in a power station. This was introduced in P2. You may wish to use an animation or a short video to trigger students' memory. Animations and videos are readily available on the Internet. This activity can then be used to introduce electromagnetic induction in the generator. | **Support**: Provide prompt questions as required.<br>**Extension**: Ask students to explain how electromagnets work. | |

| Main | Support/Extend | Resources |
|---|---|---|
| **Electromagnetic induction** (40 min) Introduce electromagnetic induction as the use of a magnetic field to cause a potential difference, which in turn induces a current in a complete circuit. The concept is simple—move a coil of wire and a magnet relative to each other to generate a potential difference. This can be linked back to what happens in a generator in a power station. Students then carry out an experiment where they investigate the difference in the induced current when using different numbers of turns in the coil of wire.<br>A preliminary investigation of moving an uncoiled copper wire between magnets in a metal yoke is included in the experimental method. Although this is the case, you may wish demonstrate this experiment before asking students to follow the rest of the method to save time. | **Support**: Demonstrate the preliminary experiment. This will help students familiarise themselves with the apparatus required.<br>**Extension**: Students should consider using magnets of different strengths if time. | **Practical:** Electromagnetic induction |

| Plenary | Support/Extend | Resources |
|---|---|---|
| **Generating electricity** (5 min) Students complete the sentences on the interactive resource using the words provided to explain how current is induced in electromagnetic induction.<br>**What's inside a generator?** (10 min) Ask students to answer the following question 'What is inside a generator in a power station that causes electricity to be generated?' Students can then peer mark their answers using a mark scheme. | **Extension**: Students add other ways in which the current induced can be increased.<br>**Extension**: Students should describe how the current induced can be increased. | **Interactive**: Generating electricity |

| Homework |
|---|
| Students pretend they are Faraday, who has recently discovered electromagnetic induction. Students should write a letter/report/journal article to describe his experiment and findings. |

# 2.9 Electromagnetism 2

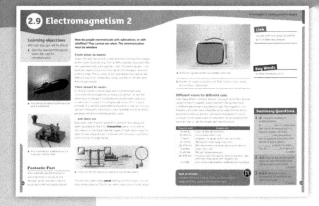

**KS3 Physics NC Link:**
- energy and waves
- light waves.

**KS3 Working Scientifically NC Link:**
- interpret observations and data, including identifying patterns and using observations, measurements, and data to draw conclusions.

**KS4 Physics NC Link:**
- explain the relationship between velocity, frequency, and wavelength
- describe the main groupings of the spectrum; that these range from long to short wavelengths and from low to high frequencies; and that our eyes can only detect a limited range.

| Band | Outcome | Checkpoint | |
|---|---|---|---|
| | | Questions | Activities |
| **Developing** | Name one piece of equipment used to detect electromagnetic waves (Level 4). | A, 1 | Plenary 1, Plenary 2 |
| | Use data provided to state some electromagnetic waves that are used in communication (Level 4). | | Main |
| **Secure** | Describe how electromagnetic waves are used for communication (Level 5). | 2, 3 | Main, Plenary 1, Plenary 2 |
| | Deduce the type of electromagnetic wave used given data on frequency (Level 6). | | Main |
| **Extending** | Compare the frequency of electromagnetic waves with their uses (Level 7). | 3 | Main, Plenary 1 |
| | Interpret frequencies of different waves to compare how they are used in communication (Level 7). | | Main |

**Maths**
In the student-book activity students calculate the time taken to send one verse of 'Happy Birthday' using Morse code.

Students compare frequencies of different waves used in communication, convert between Hz and MHz, and rearrange the wave speed equation to find wavelength.

**Literacy**
Students summarise a range of information from different sources and organise this into well-developed, linked ideas in a poster.

**APP**
Students interpret data provided to draw conclusions (AF5).

**Key Words**
wireless, transmitter, aerial

## Answers from the student book

| In-text questions | **A** aerial |
|---|---|
| Activity | **Just a minute...** <br> There are 16 words in a verse of Happy Birthday. <br> It would take 16 ÷ 8 = 2 minutes to send this verse by Morse code. |

| Summary Questions | 1 carrier, wireless, transmitter, aerial (4 marks) |
|---|---|
| | 2 A transmitter in a circuit with an alternating current produces radio waves. |
| | A detector in the form of a loop of wire (an aerial) can be used to receive the radio signal, feeding this to the electronic device to provide an output. |
| | For example, radio waves are used in radio broadcasting. |
| | Other types of EM waves can also be used, for example, IR in remote controls, or microwaves in satellite communications. (4 marks) |
| | 3 Poster should be informative and eye-catching. It should contain information about how EM waves are used in a selection of the following (6 marks): |
| | submarines       avalanche beacons |
| | mines            television |
| | navigation       microwave ovens |
| | time signals     astronomy |
| | heart rate monitors  mobile phones |
| | radio broadcasting   communication satellites. |

| Starter | Support/Extend | Resources |
|---|---|---|
| **Forms of communication** (10 min) Ask students how methods of communication have evolved over the years, from letters and Morse code to emails and texts. Lead the discussion into wireless communication and uses of the different parts of the electromagnetic (EM) spectrum.<br><br>**The EM spectrum** (10 min) Students have met the EM spectrum before, in P3 Chapter 1. Ask students to share what they remember about the different waves in the spectrum, and how they are used.<br>Students may remember a mnemonic they have made for remembering the order of waves in the EM spectrum. | | |
| **Main** | **Support/Extend** | **Resources** |
| **Communications** (35 min) Introduce the different uses of the EM spectrum in communication and how these waves are transmitted and received. Students then complete an activity where they fill in a partially completed diagram of the EM spectrum, use the information in the diagram to deduce the types of EM waves used in different methods of communication given frequency data, and design a poster to illustrate the variety of uses of EM waves in communication.<br>Students will likely need to complete their posters for homework. | **Support**: Information in the student book may be explored as a class to help weaker readers. | **Activity**: Communications |
| **Plenary** | **Support/Extend** | **Resources** |
| **Electromagnetic communication** (10 min) Students use the clues provided to complete a crossword on the interactive resource that covers key concepts of the lesson. This crossword includes the types of EM waves used in communication and how these EM waves are used.<br><br>**How are EM waves used for communication?** (10 min) Ask students a series of true or false questions to describe how EM waves are used in communication. Questions may also include how EM waves are transmitted and received by different devices. Ask students to show their answers using thumbs up/thumbs down, coloured cards, or a traffic light system. | **Extension**: Students use their activity sheets to compare frequencies for different uses of EM waves.<br><br>**Extension**: Students may suggest their own questions to pose to the rest of the class. | **Interactive**: Electromagnetic communication |
| **Homework** | | |
| Students complete their posters and questions for homework. | | |

# P3 Chapter 2 Checkpoint

## Checkpoint lesson routes

The route through this lesson can be determined using the Checkpoint assessment.
Percentage pass marks are supplied in the Checkpoint teacher notes.

**Route A (revision)**
Resource: P3 Chapter 2 Checkpoint: Revision
Students work through a series of tasks that allows them to revisit and consolidate their understanding of the major turning points in astrophysics, electromagnetism, and radioactivity. Students can keep this as a summary of the topic, and use this when revising for future assessments.

**Route B (extension)**
Resource: P3 Chapter 2 Checkpoint: Extension
Students design a poster for A-Level students starting the topic 'Turning points in physics' that includes a summary of the key concepts covered in this topic.

## Progression to *secure*

| No. | Developing outcome | Secure outcome | Making progress |
|---|---|---|---|
| 1 | State some ideas about the Universe that developed in different cultures. | Describe some ideas about the Universe that developed in different cultures. | In Task 1 students link three ideas about the Universe that developed in ancient cultures with their descriptions. |
| 2 | State what is meant by geocentric. | Describe the geocentric model of the Solar System. | In Task 1 students describe similarities and differences between the geocentric and heliocentric models. |
| 3 | State some observations that led to our present model of the Solar System. | Describe how observations led to a different model of the Solar System. | In Task 1 students identify from a list of possible statements the observations that led to a shift from the geocentric model to the heliocentric model. |
| 4 | Name our present model of the Solar System. | Describe the heliocentric model of the Solar System. | In Task 1 students describe similarities and differences between the geocentric and heliocentric models. |
| 5 | State the age of the Solar System. | Describe the timescale of the Universe. | In Task 2 students label a scaled timeline with some of the major events that occurred since the Big Bang. |
| 6 | Name the theory of how the Universe started. | Describe what is meant by the Big Bang. | In Task 2 students complete a word fill to describe what is meant by the Big Bang. |
| 7 | Name the orbits a satellite can take. | Describe how to get a satellite into orbit. | In Task 3 students describe the conditions necessary to send a satellite into orbit. |
| 8 | State some uses of satellites. | Describe some uses of satellites. | In Task 3 students identify the orbits required by four different satellites, describing how these are used. |
| 9 | State one risk and one benefit of the space programme. | Describe some of the risks and benefits of the space programme. | In Task 3 students complete a table to describe some of the risks and benefits as a result of the space programme. |
| 10 | State the term given to a material that gives out radiation. | Describe what is meant by a radioactive material. | In Task 4 students complete a word fill to describe radioactive materials. |
| 11 | State one risk of using radioactive materials. | Describe the risks of using radioactive materials. | In Task 4 students are given a list of statements about the uses and risks of radioactive materials. They must correct the statements that are false. |
| 12 | State one use of radioactive materials. | Describe some uses of radioactive materials. | In Task 4 students are given a list of statements about the uses and risks of radioactive materials. They must correct the statements that are false. |
| 13 | Name the process used to generate electricity. | Describe how to generate electricity using electromagnetic induction. | In Task 5 students label a diagram of the apparatus required for electromagnetic induction and use this to describe how electricity can be generated. |
| 14 | Name one piece of equipment used to detect electromagnetic waves. | Describe how electromagnetic waves are used for communication. | In Task 5 students reorder statements to describe how electromagnetic waves can be used for communication. |

# P3 Chapter 2: Turning points in physics

## Answers to end-of-chapter questions

1. geocentric model – the Earth is at the centre of the Universe.
   heliocentric model – the Sun is at the centre of the Universe.
   Big Bang theory – the Universe began when all of space and time expanded. (3 marks)
2. 14 billion years (1 mark)
3. alpha, beta, gamma (1 mark)
4. **a** geocentric (1 mark)    **b** polar (1 mark)    **c** low Earth (1 mark)
5. **a** The needle on the ammeter moves to the right. (1 mark)
   **b** The needle on the ammeter will not move. (1 mark)
   **c** Any two from: size of bar magnet, strength of bar magnet, metal used for the coils of wire.
   **d** Bar chart – because the number of turns in a coil is a discrete variable. (2 marks)
6. **a** Radiation can cause mutations in cells of microorganisms that cause them to die. Because of this we can use radiation to kill bacteria and sterilise medical equipment. (2 marks)
   **b** Patients drink a radioactive material as a medical tracer. These must have short half-lives to reduce the risk of cell damage or mutation that can lead to cancer. (2 marks)
7. Communication with submarines underwater can be carried out using waves of frequencies 30–300 Hz. Signals are added to the carrier wave that represent sound or images and an aerial detects the wave, transforming the signals back to sound or images. (2 marks)
8. The Universe is expanding, with the distance between galaxies increasing. This means that the Universe originated from one point billions of years ago.
   Credit alternative evidence, for example, cosmic microwave background radiation, which is radiation left over in the Universe from the time of the Big Bang. (1 mark)
9. The radiation emitted per second will decrease for both samples. This decrease will be much quicker for Sample A than Sample B. After 10 days the radiation emitted per second will be 12.5 waves/particles per second for Sample A, and 100 waves/particles per second for Sample B. (4 marks)
10. This is a QWC question. Students should be marked on the use of good English, organisation of information, spelling and grammar, and correct use of specialist scientific terms. The best answers will fully explain why doctors need to balance risk and benefit when they use a gamma camera (maximum of 6 marks).
    Examples of correct scientific points: For doctors to use this technique, patients are required to swallow radioactive material. The radioactive tracer emits radiation. This is picked up by the gamma camera so an image can be formed on a screen. On the one hand, this technique can be used to diagnose disease, saving many lives. However, radiation can also damage cells. Mutations in cells can lead to cancer. The risks can be reduced by using material that has a short half-life. Risks can also be reduced by using small quantities of radioactive material.

## Answer guide for Big Write

| Developing | Secure | Extending |
|---|---|---|
| 1–2 marks | 3–4 marks | 5–6 marks |
| • Timeline identifies two or three of the discoveries in the 20th century.<br>• Includes descriptions of some of the ways these discoveries changed how people lived, although the description is limited.<br>• Little or no attempt has been made to write an illustrated story. | • Timeline identifies the discovery of the Big Bang, radioactivity, electromagnetic induction, and electromagnetic waves.<br>• Includes descriptions of the ways these discoveries changed how people lived, for example, radiotherapy and electricity generation.<br>• A brief illustrated story has been written. | • Timeline describes in detail the impact of the discoveries of the Big Bang, radioactivity, electromagnetic induction, and electromagnetic waves, and how these discoveries have changed our lives. Examples include the use of electromagnetic waves in communication, the development of new materials as a result of the space programme, and the use of radioactive materials in medicine.<br>• A detailed story has been written with appropriate illustrations to accompany the story. |

### kerboodle

| | |
|---|---|
| P3 Chapter 2 Checkpoint assessment (automarked) | P3 Chapter 2 Checkpoint: Extension |
| P3 Chapter 2 Checkpoint: Revision | P3 Chapter 2 Progress task Handling information |

# 3.1 Detecting planets

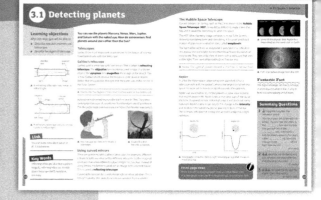

**KS3 Physics NC Link:**
- light waves
- space physics.

**KS3 Working Scientifically NC Link:**
- make and record observations, suggesting possible improvements.

**KS4 Physics NC Link:**
- describe and explain superposition in water waves and the effects of reflection, transmission, and absorption of waves at material interfaces
- use the ray model to show how light travels and to illustrate specular reflection and the apparent position of images in plane mirrors
- use the ray model to illustrate refraction and explain the apparent displacement of an image in a refracting substance (qualitative only)
- recall that electromagnetic waves are transverse
- recall that different substances may absorb, transmit, refract, or reflect electromagnetic waves.

| Band | Outcome | Checkpoint | |
|---|---|---|---|
| | | Questions | Activities |
| **Developing** | State one use of telescopes (Level 3). | 1 | Starter 1, Plenary 1, Plenary 2, Homework |
| | Name the two types of telescope (Level 3). | A | Plenary 2, Homework |
| | Make a simple refracting telescope (Level 4). | | Main |
| **Secure** | Describe how astronomers use telescopes (Level 5). | 1 | Starter 1, Plenary 1, Plenary 2, Homework |
| | Describe two types of telescope (Level 6). | 2 | Main, Plenary 1, Plenary 2, Homework |
| | Make a refracting telescope and describe images formed (Level 5). | | Main |
| **Extending** | Draw a ray diagram to explain how one type of telescope works (Level 8). | | Main, Homework |
| | Compare two types of telescope (Level 8). | 2, 3 | Main, Plenary 1, Homework |
| | Make a refracting telescope and compare it to a reflecting telescope (Level 7). | | Main |

**Literacy**
Students identify meaning in scientific text and summarise information from the student book in order to answer questions about the two types of telescope.

**APP**
Students make connections between abstract ideas when explaining how telescopes work (AF1) and draw conclusions about the different types of telescope based on the advantages and disadvantages for each telescope (AF5).

**Key Words**
refracting telescope, objective, reflecting telescope, eyepiece, magnify, Hubble Space Telescope (HST), exoplanet, intensity

## Answers from the student book

| In-text questions | A reflecting and refracting |
|---|---|
| | B exoplanet |

● P3 Chapter 3: Detection

| Activity | **Front-page news** Credit sensible headline and accompanying text to introduce the discovery of the first exoplanet. For example: Planet X! Astronomers have found evidence of a planet around a star that is not our Sun. This is the first exoplanet they have discovered, and it is too early to know if it is like our planet, or whether there is life on it. |
|---|---|
| Summary Questions | **1** objective, eyepiece, exoplanets, intensity (4 marks) <br> **2** Similarities: both focus light from afar to form an image/both produce images that are upside down/both can be used to observe distant bodies. <br> Differences: one uses reflection, the other refraction/one uses mirrors, the other lenses/refracting telescopes only work with light, whereas reflecting telescopes can focus all types of EM radiation. (2 marks) <br> **3** QWC question (6 marks). Students are required to give at least three similarities and three differences between the two telescopes. Example answers: <br> Both are telescopes. Both have mirrors. Both can be used to look for exoplanets. <br> HST produces images whereas Kepler does not. HST looks at celestial bodies other than exoplanets whereas Kepler's only purpose is to look for exoplanets. HST takes photographs whereas Kepler looks for a change in light intensity as an exoplanet moves in front of a star. |

| Starter | Support/Extend | Resources |
|---|---|---|
| **Looking for exoplanets** (10 min) Ask students to suggest ways they think scientists look for exoplanets. Focus ideas onto using the telescope. Discuss types of telescopes available (from refracting and reflecting telescopes, to the Hubble Space Telescope (HST) and the Kepler space observatory). | | |
| **Reflection versus refraction** (10 min) Review ideas of refraction and reflection, in particular recapping the drawing of ray diagrams. Make curved mirrors and lenses available to students so that they can experiment with how these objects produce an image. Students should compare the processes involved and the type of image produced by each object (virtual or real). | **Support**: Give students partially drawn ray diagrams to complete. <br> **Extension**: Students experiment with two lenses to form an image (like in a refracting telescope). | |
| **Main** | **Support/Extend** | **Resources** |
| **Telescopes** (35 min) Introduce the two different types of telescope (reflecting and refracting), and how scientists have used these when observing the Universe. (To give students an idea of context, you may wish to use the Hubble Space Telescope website for images.) <br> Students carry out a short activity where they make a simple refracting telescope to observe objects around the classroom, before answering questions that follow. | **Support**: Extra time may be required to recap reflection and refraction in detail before starting this activity. | **Activity**: Telescopes |
| **Plenary** | **Support/Extend** | **Resources** |
| **Reflecting and refracting telescopes** (10 min) Students match halves of sentences together to summarise the key points of this lesson using the interactive resource. | **Extension**: Students form further sentences for the rest of the class to complete. | **Interactive**: Reflecting and refracting telescopes |
| **Truth continuum** (10 min) Give statements relating to key points of this lesson, which may be true or false. Students arrange themselves on a truth continuum depending on how confident they are that the answer is true or false. Statements can range from the names of the two types of telescope to images of possible ray diagrams for these telescopes. | **Extension**: Invite students to offer their own statements to test the rest of the class. | |
| **Homework** | | |
| Students design a poster to compare the two types of telescope. The poster should include advantages and disadvantages of each telescope and how scientists can use these telescopes to answer questions about the Universe. Students may wish to include examples of different telescopes, for example, the HST. | **Extension**: Students draw ray diagrams of each type of telescope discussed. | |

# 3.2 Detecting alien life

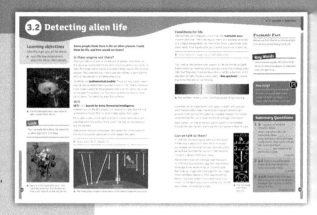

**KS3 Physics NC Link:**
- light waves
- space physics.

**KS4 Physics NC Link:**
- recall that different substances may absorb, transmit, refract, or reflect electromagnetic waves
- give examples of some practical uses of electromagnetic waves.

| Band | Outcome | Checkpoint | |
|---|---|---|---|
| | | Questions | Activities |
| Developing ↓ | State the conditions required for life like that on Earth to exist (Level 4). | B, 1 | Main, Plenary 1, Homework |
| Secure ↓ | Describe how astronomers search for life on other planets (Level 6). | 1 | Main, Plenary 1, Homework |
| Extending ↓ | Explain different techniques astronomers use to search for possible habitable planets (Level 8). | 3 | Main, Plenary 1, Homework |

**Maths**
In the student-book activity students calculate the total time taken for 20 light messages to be relayed from Earth to Proxima Centauri.

Some students also carry out simple calculations to work out the earliest date an extra-terrestrial signal can be sent to Earth for us to receive it successfully.

**Literacy**
Students interpret meaning in scientific text given on the information sheet, summarising this information to answer the questions that follow.

**APP**
Students use appropriate scientific and mathematical conventions to communicate abstract ideas (AF3).

**Key Words**
mathematical models, SETI (Search for Extra-Terrestrial Intelligence), habitable zone, line spectrum

## Answers from the student book

| In-text questions | A Search for Extra Terrestrial Intelligence. |
| | B A region where an exoplanet would be at a suitable temperature (for liquid water to exist on the planet). |
| Activity | **How long?** |
| | Proxima Centaur is 4 light years away from Earth. |
| | Each message will take 4 years to travel from Earth to Proxima Centauri (and vice versa). |
| | Total time taken = 20 × 4 = 80 years |
| Summary Questions | 1 radio, water, oxygen (3 marks) |
| | 2 X-rays are absorbed by the atmosphere. (1 mark) |

# P3 Chapter 3: Detection

> **3** QWC question (6 marks). Example answers:
> Liquid water is essential for life on Earth.
> Astronomers use computers to estimate the habitable zone around other stars. This is the region where an exoplanet would be at a suitable temperature for liquid water to exist.
> Astronomers also use line spectra of light reflected from exoplanets to determine if the unique spectra for water is present for a certain exoplanet. These line spectra work like bar codes. Black lines appear on line spectra when frequencies are missing (absorbed by the substances present in the exoplanet's atmosphere).
> SETI has also been used by astronomers as a way of detecting radio signals from space.
> Astronomers have also put telescopes that detect other waves in the EM spectrum into orbit around the Earth.

| Starter | Support/Extend | Resources |
|---|---|---|
| **Messages for aliens** (10 min) Students work in small groups to decide on a message that they would send to an alien, before suggesting ways this message could be sent. | **Support**: Provide students with prompt questions, for example, 'What can travel through a vacuum?' and 'What language would aliens understand?' | |
| **Introducing light years** (10 min) Introduce relative distances in our Solar System, compared with distances further afield, for example, to Proxima Centauri, our nearest star. This will lead to introducing distances measured in light years. | **Extension**: Ask students the question 'How is it we're looking back in time when we look at the Andromeda galaxy, 2.5 million light years away?' | |

| Main | Support/Extend | Resources |
|---|---|---|
| **Detecting aliens** (35 min) Introduce students to the different techniques astronomers use to detect extra-terrestrial life forms. These should include looking for radio signals (SETI), line spectra of oxygen and water, and using mathematical models to find habitable zones.<br>Students then read an information sheet about different ways astronomers have tried to communicate with possible extra-terrestrial life forms since 1972, summarise this information in a table, and answer the questions that follow. If extra time is available, you may wish to visit the SETI website for its weekly 10-minute broadcasts, which could be used as discussion material. | **Support**: Students may require a brief recap of the requirements of life on Earth, as covered previously in B2.<br>**Extension**: You may wish to introduce the Drake equation used to calculate the probability of life in the Universe. | **Activity**: Detecting aliens |

| Plenary | Support/Extend | Resources |
|---|---|---|
| **Detecting aliens** (10 min) Students match up key terms from this lesson with their definitions provided on the interactive resource. Students should then use these key terms to write a short paragraph to describe how astronomers search for life on different planets. This can be done by giving students criteria for success so they can mark their answers afterwards against a mark scheme. | **Extension**: Encourage students to write the mark scheme instead. | **Interactive**: Detecting aliens |
| **Messages to space** (10 min) Show students images of the Pioneer Plaque and the Voyager Golden Record Cover. These images are readily available on the Internet. Ask students to suggest what these images show before asking students why they think these pieces of information are seen to be important enough to be conveyed to life on other planets. | **Extension**: Students suggest other pieces of information that they would put on the plaque/cover instead, justifying their suggestions. | |

| Homework | | |
|---|---|---|
| Students design a section of a lesson in a textbook to describe how astronomers search for life on other planets. The material in this text book should be aimed at KS3 students. | **Extension**: Students should explain at least three of these techniques. | |
| An alternative WebQuest homework activity is also available on Kerboodle where students research the search for extra-terrestrial life. | | **WebQuest**: Searching for aliens |

# 3.3 Detecting position

**KS3 Physics NC Link:**
- light waves
- space physics.

**KS3 Working Scientifically NC Link:**
- make and record observations and measurements using a range of methods for different investigations; and evaluate the reliability of methods and suggest possible improvements.

**KS4 Physics NC Link:**
- describe the main groupings of the spectrum – radio, microwave, infra-red, visible, ultra-violet, X-rays, and gamma-rays
- recall that different substances may absorb, transmit, refract, or reflect electromagnetic waves
- give examples of some practical uses of electromagnetic waves in each of the main groups of wavelength.

| Band | Outcome | Checkpoint | |
|---|---|---|---|
| | | Questions | Activities |
| **Developing** | State what GPS stands for and give examples of its uses (Level 3). | A | Starter 1, Plenary 1, Homework |
| | State one method to find distances in space (Level 3). | 1 | Starter 2, Main, Plenary 1, Plenary 2, Homework |
| | Record measurements of distances from one place to another using the map provided (Level 4). | | Main |
| **Secure** | Describe how GPS works (Level 6). | 2 | Main, Plenary 1, Homework |
| | Describe how you can find the distance to planets and stars (Level 6). | 1–3 | Main, Plenary 2, Homework |
| | Interpret distances recorded to find a mystery location using trilateration (Level 5). | | Main |
| **Extending** | Evaluate advantages and disadvantages of GPS (Level 7). | | Main, Homework |
| | Compare different ways to find distances in space (Level 8). | 3 | Main, Plenary 2, Homework |
| | Explain how the method of finding a particular location on a map is a model of how GPS works (Level 8). | | Main |

**Maths**
In the student-book activity students calculate the uncertainty in distances given an uncertainty in time.
Students use geometry to pinpoint exact locations on a map using trilateration.

**Literacy**
Students describe how three methods of finding distances work, organising ideas into well-developed paragraphs that include scientific terminology.

**APP**
Students collect measurements of distance on a map (AF4), present these in a table (AF3), and explain how this activity models the technique of GPS (AF1).

**Key Words**
Global Positioning System (GPS), line of sight, radar, parallax

## Answers from the student book

| In-text questions | **A** Global Positioning System |
| | **B** Radio |

# P3 Chapter 3: Detection

| | |
|---|---|
| Activity | **How close?**<br>distance = speed x time<br>uncertainty in distance = speed of EM wave × uncertainty in time = $(3 \times 10^8) \times (3 \times 10^{-8}) = 9$ m |
| Summary Questions | 1 time, position, radar, parallax (4 marks)<br>2 Satellites that orbit the Earth use time to work out distance/position of an object. For example, a mobile phone detects radio waves sent from three satellites. The time taken for the device to receive each signal can be used to calculate the distance from each satellite. This triangulates the mobile phone's position and a fourth satellite can be used to confirm it (trilateration). (4 marks)<br>3 QWC question (6 marks). Example answers:<br>Radar is used to find distances by measuring the time it takes a radio wave to reflect from an object. This is similar to the use of sonar, except that radar uses radio waves (a part of the EM spectrum) instead of sound. This technique is used by astronomers to find distances within our Solar System. For example, a pulse of radio waves will take 2.5 s to reflect from the Moon, and over 5.5 h to reflect from Pluto. Parallax relies on the (apparently) different locations of distant objects relative to the Earth. This technique uses visible light reflected from distant bodies. Mathematics (knowledge of angles) is required to calculate distances using known distances such as the Earth–Sun distance. Astronomers use parallax to calculate distances beyond our Solar System. |

| Starter | Support/Extend | Resources |
|---|---|---|
| **Using GPS** (10 min) Introduce what is meant by GPS (Global Positioning System) and how it uses signals from satellites to work out accurate locations. Students should then list the devices they use or know of that use GPS (phones, satnavs, and so on). | **Extension**: Encourage students to suggest how they think GPS works. | |
| **Planets and stars** (5 min) Ask students how they measure distances on Earth, from small distances (between one student and another) to larger ones (between different continents). Ask students if these methods will work for measuring distances across space and ask students to suggest other options. | **Support**: Prompt students towards the use of light and EM spectrum using the unit of distance in space, light years. | |
| **Main** | **Support/Extend** | **Resources** |
| **Detecting position** (40 min) Introduce the use of radio waves (GPS and radar) and how scientists and mathematicians use parallax to find distances on Earth and beyond. In particular, students should be introduced to how GPS systems use trilateration to pinpoint one location on Earth using the distances from at least three satellites.<br>Students then carry out an activity based on the London Underground map to model how the GPS system works, before answering questions that follow. | **Support**: A review of the speed equation may be required before starting this activity. The support sheet contains step-by-step instructions for Task 2.<br>**Extension**: Make this activity more challenging by using a map of the UK or a star map instead. | **Activity**: Detecting position |
| **Plenary** | **Support/Extend** | **Resources** |
| **Summarising GPS** (5 min) Students match halves of sentences together using the interactive resource to summarise key points about GPS. Ask further questions for students to answer, using the sentences made to exemplify their points, for example, can GPS be used underwater? | **Extension**: Students should pose further questions about GPS to the rest of the class. | **Interactive**: Summarising GPS |
| **Distances to stars** (10 min) Students pair-share, then discuss as a class, ideas about methods of finding distances in space (radar and parallax). | **Support**: Present a list of key words to explain the methods. | |
| **Homework** | | |
| Students design a poster to describe how GPS, radar, and parallax work. Encourage students to include diagrams where possible. | **Extension**: Students compare advantages and disadvantages of using each method. | |

# 3.4 Detecting messages

**KS3 Physics NC Link:**
- sound waves
- light waves.

**KS3 Working Scientifically NC Link:**
- understand and use SI units and IUPAC (International Union of Pure and Applied Chemistry) chemical nomenclature.

**KS4 Physics NC Link:**
- recall that electromagnetic waves are transverse and are transmitted through space where all have the same velocity
- give examples of some practical uses of electromagnetic waves in each of the main groups of wavelength
- explain the concept of modulation and how information can be transmitted by waves through variations in amplitude or frequency, and that each of these is used in its optimum frequency range.

| Band | Outcome | Checkpoint | |
|---|---|---|---|
| | | Questions | Activities |
| **Developing** ↓ | Name the two types of modulated wave (Level 3). | A | Starter 1, Plenary 2, Homework |
| | Convert numerical data provided into SI units (Level 4). | | Main |
| **Secure** ↓ | Describe how a radio wave carries a signal (Level 6). | | Main, Plenary 1, Plenary 2, Homework |
| | Give answers in SI units when using the wave speed equation (Level 5). | | Main |
| **Extending** ↓ | Explain the difference between AM and FM signals (Level 8). | | Main, Plenary 1, Plenary 2, Homework |
| | Use SI units when using rearrangements of the wave speed equation (Level 7). | | Main |

**Maths**
In the student-book activity, students convert frequencies between Hz, kHz, and MHz.

Students also carry out calculations using the wave speed equation provided. Some students rearrange this equation for further calculations.

**APP**
Students process data, using calculations to identify the relationship between frequency and wavelength (AF5).

**Key Words**
carrier wave, modulation, diffraction

## Answers from the student book

| In-text questions | **A** amplitude modulated (AM) and frequency modulated (FM) |
|---|---|
| Activity | **How many hertz?**<br>Radio 1 has frequency of 99.1 MHz.<br>There are 1 000 000 Hz in 1 MHz. 99.1 MHz = 99.1 × 1 000 000 = 99 100 000 Hz<br>There are 1 000 Hz in 1 kHz. 99 100 000 Hz = 99 100 000 ÷ 1000 = 99 100 kHz |
| Summary Questions | **1** diffraction – the spreading out of waves around an obstacle<br>    carrier wave – the radio, micro-, or infrared wave that carries a signal<br>    modulating – changing the amplitude or frequency of a wave (3 marks) |

# P3 Chapter 3: Detection

> 2 AM is amplitude modulation. It means changing the amplitude to represent 1 s and 0 s.
> FM is frequency modulation. This means changing the frequency of the carrier wave. (2 marks)
> 3 QWC question (6 marks). Example answers:
> A microphone converts sound waves into an electrical signal.
> This signal is converted into a digital sequence of 1s and 0s.
> A radio transmitter adds the digital signal of the sound to the carrier wave.
> The frequency of this carrier wave is 99.1 MHz (for Radio 1).
> The transmitter then changes either the amplitude or the frequency of the carrier wave (modulation).
> Radio 1 is an FM station so it is the frequency that is modulated.
> The carrier wave is broadcast and travels across the country as a radio wave.
> A radio set is tuned to the same frequency as the carrier wave.
> The radio set converts the radio signal back into sound.
> The loudspeaker plays the radio programme.

| Starter | Support/Extend | Resources |
|---|---|---|
| An alternative question-led lesson is also available.<br><br>**Analogue radios** (10 min) Show students an example of an old analogue radio. Information on this radio must show a range of frequencies (kHz and/or MHz) and initials of bands (AM, FM). Ask students to discuss and suggest what these abbreviations may mean.<br><br>**SI units** (10 min) Ask students to list as many SI units as they can remember. Students should match SI units to what they measure. This activity should lead to the SI unit for frequency, Hertz (Hz). | **Support**: Students focus on the prefixes k (kilo) and M (mega).<br>**Extension**: Point out SW/MW/LW (short, medium, and long wave) on the radio for further discussion.<br><br>**Support**: Give students a list of SI units and their measurements to match up.<br>**Extension**: Ask students to suggest why SI units were invented. | **Question-led lesson**: Detecting messages |

| Main | Support/Extend | Resources |
|---|---|---|
| **Radio broadcasts** (35 min) Introduce how radio broadcasts work. This should include a brief description of radio waves as carrier waves, AM and FM modulation, the diffraction of radio waves, and the wave speed equation (wave speed = frequency × wavelength).<br>Students then carry out an activity where they will find frequencies of six radio stations using an analogue radio, find the wavelengths of their signals using the wave speed equation, and answer the questions that follow.<br>It is a common misconception for students to confuse radio waves with sound waves. Radio waves are EM waves that are used as carrier waves containing digitalised conversions of sound waves. Misconceptions should be corrected as appropriate. | **Support**: The support sheet gives students hints for unit conversions between Hz, kHz, and MHz, as well as a step-by-step guide to calculating wavelengths given the frequency and wave speed.<br>**Extension**: Challenge students to use standard form in calculations where possible. | **Activity**: Radio broadcasts |

| Plenary | Support/Extend | Resources |
|---|---|---|
| **Broadcasts** (10 min) Students reorder sentences provided on the interactive resource to describe how a radio programme is broadcast and played on the radio, summarising the key points of this lesson.<br><br>**The chain game** (10 min) Students initially pair-share ideas about how radio broadcasts and transmitted, before combining together into groups of four or six. Pick groups at random to sequentially give the steps to describe how radio shows are broadcast and received. | **Extension**: Encourage students to explain details of selected steps in the sequence, for example, the two types of modulation covered.<br><br>**Extension**: Encourage students to include an explanation of different frequencies and why they are necessary. | **Interactive**: Broadcasts |

| Homework | | |
|---|---|---|
| Students design a cartoon to explain the steps involved in broadcasting a radio show. Students may also be required to complete questions on their activity sheet. | **Extension**: Students draw annotated diagrams of AM and FM to explain the difference between them. | |

# 3.5 Detecting particles

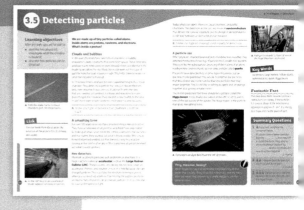

**KS3 Physics NC Link:**
- particle model.

**KS3 Working Scientifically NC Link:**
- understand that scientific methods and theories develop as earlier explanations are modified to take account of new evidence and ideas, together with the importance of publishing results and peer review.

**KS4 Physics NC Link:**
- describe how and why the atomic model has changed over time
- describe the atom as a positively charged nucleus surrounded by negatively charged electrons, with the nuclear radius much smaller than that of the atom and with almost all of the mass in the nucleus.

| Band | Outcome | Checkpoint | |
|---|---|---|---|
| | | Questions | Activities |
| **Developing** | State one method scientists use to investigate what the Universe is made of (Level 3). | A, 1 | Main, Plenary 1, Homework |
| | Name one type of particle detector (Level 3). | B | Main, Plenary 1, Plenary 2, Homework |
| | State Rutherford's hypothesis about the structure of the atom (Level 3). | | Main |
| **Secure** | Describe how physicists investigate what the Universe is made of (Level 6). | 1, 2 | Main, Plenary 1, Homework |
| | Describe how particles can be detected (Level 6). | 2 | Main, Plenary 1, Homework |
| | Describe the stages of developing a new theory (Level 6). | | Main |
| **Extending** | Compare different techniques scientists use to investigate what the Universe is made of (Level 7). | 2 | Main, Plenary 1 |
| | Suggest ways in which scientists use existing knowledge to make further scientific discoveries (Level 7). | | Main |
| | Explain the importance of peer review when developing new theories in science (Level 7). | | Main |

**Literacy**
Students read a piece of scientific text to identify key ideas and summarise information by answering questions that follow.

**APP**
Students describe ideas that refute previous scientific theories (AF1). Students also explain how scientific evidence is peer reviewed and how this may lead to changes in scientific ideas (AF1).

**Key Words**
accelerator, Large Hadron Collider (LHC), semiconductor, quark, Higgs boson

### Answers from the student book

| In-text questions | A bubble or cloud chamber |
| | B semiconductor |

● P3 Chapter 3: Detection

| Summary Questions | 1 tracks, accelerating (2 marks) |
|---|---|
| | 2 In the past, people used detectors like bubble chambers and cloud chambers. When particles pass through these chambers they leave a distinctive trail. Scientists could work out the type of particle from the type of track it made. These days, scientists use particle accelerators with detectors made from semiconductors. A very strong electric field accelerates charged particles inside tunnels, and particles produced from the subsequent high-speed collisions are detected by semiconductors. These detect the mass and charge of the particles produced. (4 marks) |
| | 3 QWC question (6 marks). Example answers: |
| | The muon was discovered in 1936. |
| | The muon did not fit with the existing model that everything was made of protons, neutrons, and electrons. Scientists developed a new model where there were particles smaller than protons, neutrons, and electrons. New families of particles were discovered, one of which was called quarks. Another of the new particles discovered is the Higgs boson, discovered in 2012. This is the particle that gives everything mass. This particle was discovered at the Large Hadron Collider (LHC). This is a particle accelerator that uses very strong electric fields to accelerate charged particles (protons and electrons) so they collide with each other. New particles formed from these collisions are detected using a semiconductor detector. |

**kerboodle**

| Starter | Support/Extend | Resources |
|---|---|---|
| **What's in the tin?** (10 min) Give students food tins without their labels attached. Students should be encouraged to find out what is inside each tin without the need to open them (by shaking, rolling, lifting, and comparing them with similar food tins). Ask students to summarise their findings after five minutes, before linking this with how scientists use existing knowledge and patterns from observations to determine the unknown. | **Support**: Suggest a list of actions or provide a list of possible answers as prompts. **Extension**: Students justify their conclusions using observations. | |
| **What are atoms made of?** (5 min) Ask students to review what atoms are made of. They should give the answer protons, neutrons, and electrons. Introduce how, in 1936, muons were discovered. Ask students to pair-share ideas and suggest how these particles may have been found. | **Extension**: Ask students further questions about the properties of protons, neutrons, and electrons, in particular their charges. | |

| Main | Support/Extend | Resources |
|---|---|---|
| **Rutherford's experiment** (40 min) Ask students to describe the present (Rutherford's) atomic model and how it was developed. Students met this in C3. Introduce students to the fact that other (smaller) particles have since been discovered, for example, the muon, in 1936. Describe how cloud chambers, bubble chambers, and particle accelerators are used to detect the presence of other/new particles, most notably the Higgs boson, discovered at the LHC in 2012. Students then carry out an activity where they read information given about the scientific method used by Rutherford, and how this links to the discovery of other particles, before answering questions that follow. | **Support**: A support sheet is available with shorter, less demanding text. Alternatively, you may wish to read the main text provided as a class to support weaker readers. | **Activity**: Rutherford's experiment |

| Plenary | Support/Extend | Resources |
|---|---|---|
| **What is inside?** (10 min) Split students into three groups (Rutherford's experiment, cloud and bubble chambers, and particle accelerators). You may wish to split these groups further to facilitate discussion and collaboration. Ask students to describe the topic given to their group in one minute. | **Support**: Run this as a set of structured questions – can students answer simple statements about the topic? | |
| **Investigating the Universe** (5 min) Interactive resource where students complete a crossword on the key words from this topic. | **Extension**: Students list several things they have learned about, and at least one thing they would like to find out more about | **Interactive**: Investigating the Universe |

| Homework | | |
|---|---|---|
| Students are given one subatomic particle to research and to write a short paragraph about, summarising their findings. Students should include the date of its discovery, the name(s) of its discoverer(s), and how it was discovered. | **Extension**: Encourage students to explain how this particular method of discovery works. | |

# P3 Chapter 3 Checkpoint

## Checkpoint lesson routes

The route through this lesson can be determined using the Checkpoint assessment.
Percentage pass marks are supplied in the Checkpoint teacher notes.

**Route A (revision)**
Resource: P3 Chapter 3 Checkpoint: Revision
Students work through a series of tasks that allows them to revisit and consolidate their understanding of key concepts in this chapter. Students can keep this as a summary of the topic, and use this when revising for future assessments.

**Route B (extension)**
Resource: P3 Chapter 3 Checkpoint: Extension
Students design a revision poster for a KS3 revision series that includes the key concepts covered in this chapter.

## Progression to *secure*

| No. | Developing outcome | Secure outcome | Making progress |
| --- | --- | --- | --- |
| 1 | State one use of telescopes. | Describe how astronomers use telescopes. | In Task 1 students link three different types of telescopes (Galilean, HST, and Kepler) with a description of how they are used. |
| 2 | Name the two types of telescope. | Describe two types of telescope. | In Task 1 students label diagrams of reflecting and refracting telescopes, using these to describe how these two types of telescopes work. |
| 3 | State the conditions required for life like that on Earth to exist. | Describe how astronomers search for life on other planets. | In Task 2 students complete a word fill using the key terms given to describe how astronomers use mathematical models, line spectra, and powerful telescopes to search for alien life. |
| 4 | State what GPS stands for and give examples of its uses. | Describe how GPS works. | In Task 3 students reorder statements to describe how GPS works. |
| 5 | State one method to find distances in space. | Describe how you can find the distance to planets and stars. | In Task 3 students carry out a simple experiment to test parallax in the classroom, before using this and their own knowledge to decide if a series of statements about parallax, radar, and GPS are true or false. Students then correct the statements that are false. |
| 6 | Name the two types of modulated wave. | Describe how a radio wave carries a signal. | In Task 4 students use a diagram of how signals are changed when transmitting a radio wave to describe how a radio wave carries a signal from a radio station to a household radio. |
| 7 | State one method scientists use to investigate what the Universe is made of. | Describe how physicists investigate what the Universe is made of. | In Task 5 students work through a table of statements to decide if these describe the use of cloud and bubble chambers or particle accelerators. |
| 8 | Name one type of particle detector. | Describe how particles can be detected. | In Task 5 students work through a table of statements to decide if these describe the use of cloud and bubble chambers or particle accelerators. |

## Answers to end-of-chapter questions

1. exoplanet – Kepler Space Telescope
   Higgs boson – Large Hadron Collider
   position of a plane – radar (3 marks)
2. a Y (1 mark)   b amplitude (1 mark)
3. quark, proton, atom, molecule (1 mark)
4. A planet is a body in our Solar System that orbits our Sun but an exoplanet is a body that orbits a star outside our Solar System. (2 marks)
5. a Eyepiece and objective lenses correctly labelled. (The objective lens is the larger of the two.) (1 mark)
   b It is very difficult to make lenses that are very big. They would also be too heavy to send into space. (2 marks)
6. a 93.2 MHz = 93.2 × 1 000 000 = 93 200 000 Hz (1 mark)
   b Sound waves are longitudinal waves that can be converted into an electrical signal and added to a carrier wave. A carrier wave, for example, a radio wave, is a transverse wave and digital signals are added to it by a radio transmitter, changing the amplitude or the frequency of the carrier wave. (2 marks)

## P3 Chapter 3: Detection

**7** Muons were detected using their characteristic tracks made in cloud chambers. The Higgs boson was detected using a detector made from semiconducting material at the Large Hadron Collider (LHC). (4 marks)

**8a** C, D, B, E, A (1 mark)

**b** The larger the exoplanet, the larger the change in intensity of radiation detected by the Kepler observatory. This is because the larger the exoplanet, the more light it can block out from the star, causing a bigger intensity change. (2 marks)

**9** X-rays are absorbed by the atmosphere so the Chandra telescope would be useless on the ground as X-ray readings would be zero. (2 marks)

**10a** speed (m/s) = distance (m) ÷ time (s)

time (s) = distance (m) ÷ speed (m/s) = 6 000 ÷ 300 000 000 = $2 \times 10^{-5}$ s (3 marks)

**b** distance Earth–Moon–Earth (m) = speed (m/s) × time (s) = 300 000 000 × 2.5 = $7.5 \times 10^8$ m

distance between the Earth and the moon = $(7.5 \times 10^8) \div 2 = 3.75 \times 10^8$ m (3 marks)

**c** It is difficult to aim the radio wave correctly so that it hits the object under investigation. The signal would be too feint by the time that it returned to be detectable. (2 marks)

**11** This is a QWC question. Students should be marked on the use of good English, organisation of information, spelling and grammar, and correct use of specialist scientific terms. The best answers will fully explain how an alien astronomer can work out that there is life on Earth (maximum of 6 marks). Examples of correct scientific points:

Computers can be used to estimate the habitable zone around our Sun.

This is the region where a planet would be at a suitable temperature for liquid water to exist.

Line spectra can also be used.

This is light reflected from planets that creates a unique series of lines on a spectrum of light, similar to a bar code.

Black lines appear on the line spectrum when frequencies are missing (because these are absorbed by the substances present in the planet's atmosphere).

This can be compared with known line spectra of substances required for life, for example, water.

Telescopes can also be used to detect radio waves and other EM waves emitted from Earth.

Extremely powerful telescopes may be able to see Earth directly.

## Answer guide for Big Write

| Developing | Secure | Extending |
| --- | --- | --- |
| 1–2 marks | 3–4 marks | 5–6 marks |
| • Design correctly uses telescopes for planets, exoplanets, and stars, and particle accelerators for very small particles.<br>• Language used is appropriate but lacks clarity.<br>• Appropriate key words are used but not explained.<br>• Images are not included. | • Design correctly describes the use of different telescopes for observing planets, exoplanets, and stars.<br>• Design correctly describes what happens in a particle detector during particle collisions.<br>• Language used is appropriate and clear.<br>• Appropriate key words are used and explained.<br>• Illustrations are included but are not appropriate or explained. | • Design correctly describes the use of different telescopes for observing planets, exoplanets, and stars in an imaginative way.<br>• Design correctly describes what happens in a particle detector during particle collisions.<br>• Language used is appropriate, clear, and used in a way that helps understanding.<br>• Appropriate key words are used and explained clearly and concisely.<br>• Annotated/labelled diagrams are used to illustrate ideas discussed in a visual way. |

### kerboodle

P3 Chapter 3 Checkpoint assessment (automarked)
P3 Chapter 3 Checkpoint: Revision
P3 Chapter 3 Checkpoint: Extension
P3 Chapter 3 Progress task (Literacy)

# Index

absorption
　infrared 88, 89
　light 38
acceleration 100, 101
accelerators 156
accuracy 4
additive colours 46
aerials 144
air pressure *see* gas pressure
air resistance 14, 18, 22
alien life detection 150, 151
alpha radiation 139
alternating current 143
AM (amplitude modulation) 154
ammeters 64
amplification, ears 32
amplifiers, microphones 33
amplitude, waves 26, 30
amplitude modulation (AM) 154
amps 64
analogies 133
analogue signals 114
analyses, data 8, 9
Andromeda 51
angle of incidence 40
angle of reflection 40
animals, sound 31
*Apollo* missions 136, 137
Aricebo radio telescope 150
Aristotle 129–131
artificial satellites 50, 134, 135, 152
asteroid belt 52, 53
atmospheric pressure 103
atoms 62, 156, 157
attraction
　electric charge 62
　magnets 72
audible range 31
auditory canal/nerve 32
average speed 99
axis (Earth) 54, 55

balanced forces 22, 23
bar charts 7
batteries 64–67
Baumgartner, Felix 29
Becquerel, Henri 138
beta radiation 139
Bhaskaracharya 129
Big Bang 132, 133
binary, digital signals 114
biomass 91
bits 114, 115
brain, eyes and 44
bubble chamber particle detection 156
bytes 114

cameras 44, 45, 89
cancer 140
carbon dioxide 90
carrier waves, radio 154, 155
categoric data 5
CCD (charge-coupled device) 45
cells, electric charge 64, 65
centre of gravity/mass 109
charge, electricity 62–65
charge-coupled device (CCD) 45
charts 7, 8

chemical stores, energy 82
circuits 64, 65
　potential difference 67
　sensing circuits 117
　series/parallel 68, 69
　symbols 64, 65
climate change 90
cloud chamber particle detection 156
cochlea, ears 32
coils, electromagnets 74, 75
collecting data 2, 6
collision, gas pressure 102
colour 46, 47
comets 50, 51
communication 144, 145, 154, 155
compressed gas 103
compression 16, 27, 103
computers, development 137
conclusions 8–10
conduction 86
conductors 71, 86
cones, retina 44
confidence in conclusions 10
conservation of energy 82
constellations 55
contact force 14
continuous data 5
continuous spectrum 46
control variables 3
convection 86, 87
convection currents 87
converging lens 43
convex lens 43
cores, electromagnets 74, 75
cornea 44
crest of wave 26
critical angle, electromagnetic spectrum 120
Curie, Marie 138–140
current 64, 65
　alternating 143
　convection currents 87
　different components 70
　electromagnets 74
　lightning 63
　series/parallel circuits 68, 69
curved mirrors, telescopes 148, 149

data
　accurate/precise 4
　analysing 8, 9
　collecting 2, 6
　evaluating 10, 11
　recording 6, 7
　types 5
day 54
decibels (dB) 33
defibrillators 119
deformation, forces 16
density, gas pressure 103
dependent variables 3
depth, liquid pressure 104
detection 148–159
　alien life 150, 151
　light 117
　messages 154, 155
　particles 156, 157
　planets 148, 149

position 152, 153
　sound 32, 33
diaphragm, microphones 33
diffraction 155
diffuse scattering 41
digital signals 114
diodes, LEDs 116, 117
direction change
　light 42, 43
　projectile motion 122
　unbalanced forces 23
discrete data 5
discrete variables 7
dispersion, colour 46
dissipation, energy 83, 116
distances
　measuring with echoes 34
　to stars 153
distance–time graphs 100, 101
drag forces 18, 19
driving force 22
dwarf planets 52, 53

eardrum 32
ears 32
Earth 54, 55
　looking after 137
　magnetic field 73
　satellites 50
echoes 34, 35
eclipses 57
Edison, Thomas 71
efficiency, lightbulbs 116
elastic limit, springs 17
elastic stores, energy 82
electric charge 62–65
electric fields 63
electricity 62–71
　circuits/current 64, 65
　demand increases 124, 125
　magnetism and 74–77, 142–145
　paying for 92, 93
　potential difference 66, 67
　resistance 70, 71
　series/parallel circuits 68, 69
electromagnetic induction 142, 143
electromagnetic spectrum 115, 120, 121
electromagnetism 74–77, 142–145
electrons 62, 71
electrostatic force 20
elliptical orbits 52
emitting infrared 88
emitting light 38
endoscopes 120
energy 80–97
　adding up 82, 83
　balance 81
　conservation law 82
　crisis 124, 125
　food/fuels 80, 81
　power and 92, 93
　resources 90, 91
　stores 82–85
　temperature and 84, 85, 92
　transfer 28, 29, 83, 85–89
　waves 26
　work/machines 94, 95
equilibrium 22, 85, 108, 109

errors 11
evaluations, data 10, 11
evidence, scientific 128
exoplanets 149
extension, stretching 16
eyepiece lens, telescopes 148
eyes 38, 44, 45

falling over 109
Faraday, Michael 142, 143
field, force fields 20
filters, light 47
floating 105
FM (frequency modulation) 154
focal point/focus, lenses 43
food 80, 81
force fields 20
forces 14–25
　at a distance 20, 21
　balanced forces 22, 23
　describing 14
　drag forces 18, 19
　driving force 22
　liquid pressure 105
　magnetic fields 72
　measuring 15, 21
　spacecraft 134
　turning forces 108, 109
　types 14
　unbalanced forces 22, 23
　*see also* pressure
fossil fuels 90, 91
frequency
　audible range 31
　light 46
　ultrasound 35
　waves 26, 145
frequency modulation (FM) 154
friction 14, 18, 19
fuels 80, 81, 90, 91
fusion, nuclear 125

galaxies 51
Galilei, Galileo 131, 148
gamma cameras 141
gamma radiation 139
gamma rays 115, 121
gas giants 52
gas pressure 102, 103
gases
　energy transfer 85–87
　pressure in 102, 103
gears 95
generators, electricity 142
geocentric models 129, 130
geostationary orbits 135
geothermal energy 91
Global Positioning System (GPS) 152, 153
graphs 7, 8, 17, 100, 101
gravitational field strength 21
gravitational potential stores, energy 82
gravity 14, 20, 129
　centre of 109
　Solar System formation 53
greenhouse gases 90

habitable zone, life 151

half-life, radioactive materials 139
hearing see ears
heartbeat monitoring 119
heating, energy 85
heliocentric models 130, 131
helium 151
Henry, Joseph 143
Hertz, Heinrich 144
hertz (Hz), pitch of sound 30
Higgs boson particle 157
Hooke's Law 17
hospitals, new technology 118–121
houses, new technology 116, 117
Hubble Space Telescope (HST) 132, 149
hydroelectric energy 91
Hz see hertz

ideas, developing into questions 2
images
    inverted 44
    real images 45
    reflection 40
incandescent lightbulbs 116
incidence, angle of 40
incident rays 40
incident waves 27
incompressibility, liquids 104
independent variables 3
induction, electromagnetic 142, 143
induction hob cooker 143
information storage 114, 115
infrared radiation 88, 89
infrared waves 115
infrasound 31
inner ear 32
instantaneous speed 99
insulators 71, 86
intensity of light 149
intensive care 118, 119
interaction pairs, forces 15
International Space Station (ISS) 50, 135
inverted images, eyes 44
investigations 2, 4, 5
iris of eye 44
iron 72, 74
ISS see International Space Station

joules (J) 80
Jupiter 50

*Kepler* space observatory 149
kg see kilograms
kHz see kilohertz
kilograms (kg) 21
kilohertz (kHz) 30
kilojoules (kJ) 80, 92
kilowatt hours (kWh) 92, 93
kilowatts (kW) 92
kinetic stores, energy 82
kJ see kilojoules
kW (kilowatts) 92
kWh see kilowatt hours

Large Hadron Collider (LHC) 156, 157
law of conservation of energy 82
law of moments 108
law of reflection 40, 41
LDRs (light-dependent resistors) 117
LEDs see light-emitting diodes

lenses 43, 148
LEO (low Earth orbit) 135
levers 94, 95
LHC see Large Hadron Collider
life detection 150, 151
lifting, electromagnets 76, 77
light 38–49
    colour 46, 47
    intensity of 149
    new technology 116, 117
    refraction 42, 43
    source 38
    speed of 29, 39
    stars 151
    travelling 38, 39, 42
    waves 27, 39, 115, 120
light-dependent resistors (LDRs) 117
light-emitting diodes (LEDs) 116, 117
light gates, reaction time 123
light-time 39
lightbulbs 116, 117
lightning 63
line of best fit 8
line graphs 7, 8, 17
line of sight, GPS 152
line spectrum, stars 151
liquids
    energy transfer 85, 86
    pressure in 104, 105
    see also water
longitudinal waves 26, 27
loudness 30, 31, 33
low Earth orbit (LEO) 135
lubrication 18
luminous objects 38
lunar eclipses 57

m/s (metres per second) 98
machines, energy 94, 95
magnetic field lines 73
magnetic fields 72–74
magnetic force 20
magnetic materials 72
magnetic resonance imaging (MRI) 121
magnets/magnetism 72–77, 121, 142–145
magnification, telescopes 148
Mars 50, 52
mass
    centre of 109
    particle detection 157
    weight difference 21
mathematical models, alien life 150
Maxwell, James Clerk 144
mean (average) 6
measurements
    distances 34
    forces 15, 21
    loudness 33
    potential difference 66, 67
    range of 5, 11
    resistance 70, 71
    spread of 4, 10
    see also data
media
    light travel 42
    sound travel 28
Mercury 50, 52
message detection 154, 155
    see also communication
metal-sorting, electromagnets 77

meteorites 50
meteors 50
metres per second (m/s) 98
microphones 30, 33, 114
microwaves 92, 115
middle ear 32
Milky Way 51
mirrors 40, 41, 148, 149
mobile phones see phones
models
    alien life 150
    electric circuits 65, 67, 69
    Universe 128–131, 133
modulation, radio 154
moments, law of 108
Moon 50, 56, 57
    missions to 134, 136, 137
    phases of 56
motion 98–111
    planets 130
    projectile motion 122
    see also speed
motion graphs 100, 101
motors 64, 77
MRI see magnetic resonance imaging
mutations, radioactive materials 140

N see newtons
N/m2 (newtons per metre squared) 106
natural satellites 50
    see also Moon
negative charge 62
neutral objects, atoms 62
neutrons 62
new technology 114–127
Newton, Isaac 129
newton metres (Nm) 108
newtonmeters 15
newtons (N) 15, 21
newtons per metre squared (N/m2) 106
night 54
night sky 50, 51
Nm (newton metres) 108
non-contact force 14
non-luminous objects 38
non-renewable energy 90
normal line, mirrors 40
north pole, magnets 72
nuclear energy 91, 125
nuclear fusion 125

objective lens, telescopes 148
observations 2
Oersted, Hans Christian 142
ohms, resistance 70, 71
opaque objects 38
optic nerve 44
optical fibres 120
optical illusions 42
orbits
    Earth 54, 55
    planets 52
    satellites 50, 134, 135
oscillation 26, 27
oscilloscopes 30
ossicles, ears 32
outer ear 32
outliers (results) 6
oval window, ears 32
oxygen, monitoring patients 118

pacemakers 119
parallax 153
parallel circuits 68, 69
partial eclipses 57
particles
    detecting 156, 157
    energy transfer 85–87
patients, monitoring 118, 119
peak of wave see crest of wave
peer reviews 143
penumbra, solar eclipses 57
phases of the Moon 56
phones 114, 115
photoreceptors, retina 44
pie charts 7
pinhole cameras 45
pinna of ear 32
pitch 30, 31
pivot, turning forces 108, 109
pixels, cameras 45
plane, mirrors 40
planets 50, 52, 53
    detecting 148, 149
    retrograde motion 130, 131
plans 4, 5
Plato 129
polar orbits 135
poles, magnets 72
polonium 138, 139
position, detecting 152, 153
positive charge 62
potential difference 66, 67, 69
    see also voltage
power, energy and 92, 93
power rating, appliances 92
power stations 90, 92, 143
precision, data 4
predictions 3, 9, 128, 129
pressure
    gases 102, 103
    liquids 104, 105
    solids 106, 107
primary colours 46
prisms 46
projectile motion 122
protons 62, 156, 157
Ptolemy 130
pull force 14, 15
pulse rate monitoring 118
pupil of eye 44
push force 14

quarks 157

radar 152, 153
radiation 86, 88, 89, 138, 139
radio telescopes 150
radio waves 115, 144, 145, 152–155
radioactivity 138–141
radiotherapy 141
radium 138, 141
random errors 11
range, measurements 5, 11
rarefaction, waves 27
rating potential difference 66
reaction force 16
reaction time 122, 123
real images 45
receivers, ultrasound 35
receiving information 115
recording data 6, 7
reflected rays 40
reflected waves 27
reflecting telescopes 148

reflection 38, 40, 41
   angle of 40
   infrared 89
   law of 40, 41
   optical fibres 120
   waves 27
refracting telescopes 148
refraction 42, 43, 120, 148
   dispersion 46
relative motion 99
relays, electromagnets 76
renewable energy 91, 124, 125
repeatability 5, 6
repelling
   electric charge 62
   magnets 72
reproducibility 5
resistance 117
   air 14, 18, 22
   electricity 70, 71
   water 18, 19
retina of eye 44
retrograde motion, planets 130, 131
reverberations 34
risk, spacecraft missions 136, 137
risk assessment 5, 136
rods, retina 44

safety 5, 123
satellites 50, 134, 135, 152
   see also Moon
Saturn 50
scientific questions 2, 3
scientific work 2–11, 128
Search for Extra-Terrestrial Intelligence (SETI) 150
seasons 54
secondary colours 46
see-saws 109
semiconductors, LHC 157
sending information 115
sensing circuits 117
sensors, light detection 117
series circuits 68, 69
SETI (Search for Extra-Terrestrial Intelligence) 150
simple machines 94, 95
sinking 105
smart devices 114, 115

solar eclipses 57
solar energy 91, 125
solar flares 136, 137
Solar System 50, 52, 53
   detecting distances 153
   formation 53, 133
   models 130
solids
   energy transfer 85, 86
   pressure on 106, 107
sonar 35
sound 26–37
   detecting 32, 33
   hospital equipment 121
   speed of 28–39
   transfer 28, 29
   waves 26–28, 30
source of light 38
south pole, magnets 72
space 21, 134–137, 148–151, 153
spacecraft 134–137
spectrum, electromagnetic 115, 120, 121
spectrum of light 46, 151
specular reflection 41
speed 98–101
   calculating 98, 101
   of light 29, 39
   projectile motion 122
   of sound 28–39
   unbalanced forces 23
sports, new technology 122, 123
spread of measurements 4, 10
springs 17
squashing 16, 17
stars 51, 55, 151, 153
   see also galaxies; Sun
static electricity 62
steel 72, 74, 75
sterilisation materials 141
storing information 114, 115
story-telling 128
straight-line graphs 17
streamlining 19
stretching 16, 17
subtractive colours 46, 47
Sun 50, 88, 125, 136, 137
   see also solar...
superposed waves 27

switches 64, 76, 77
symbols, circuits 64, 65
systematic errors 11

telescopes 131, 148–150
television 145
temperature
   energy and 84, 85, 92
   gas pressure 102
   intensive care 118
tension 17
terrestrial planets 52
theories 132
thermal imaging cameras 89
thermal power stations 90
thermal stores, energy 82, 84, 85
thermistors 118
thermometers 84
tidal energy 91
time
   distance–time graphs 100, 101
   Universe and 133
total eclipses 57
total internal reflection, optical fibres 120
trains 76
translucence 38
transmission of light 38
transmitters
   radio waves 144
   ultrasound 35
transparent objects 38
transverse waves 26, 27
trough of wave 26
turbines see wind turbines
turning forces 108, 109
turning points in physics 128–147

ultrasound 31, 35
ultraviolet (UV) waves 115
umbra, solar eclipses 57
unbalanced forces 22, 23
uncertainty 5, 11, 123
undulation 26
Universe 51, 128–133
upthrust 15, 105
uranium 138
UV (ultraviolet) waves 115

vacuums
   light and 39
   sound and 28
variables 2, 3, 7
ventilators 119
Venus 50, 52, 53
vibrations 26, 28, 32
virtual images 40
visible light 115, 120
voltage 66, 67
   see also potential difference
voltmeters 66, 67
volts 66
volume changes, gas pressure 102

W (watts) 92
water
   light refraction 42
   resistance 18, 19
   see also liquid...
watts (W) 92
wavelengths 26
waves 26–28, 30, 39
   communication 144, 145
   crest of wave 26
   diffraction 155
   features 26
   hospital equipment 120
   infrared waves 115
   smart devices 115
   superposed 27
   trough of wave 26
   see also radio waves
weight
   forces 21
   pressure 106, 107
white light splitting 46
wind turbines 91, 124, 125
wireless devices 144, 145
wires
   communication 144
   electrons 71
   magnetic fields 74
work as energy 94, 95

X-rays 76, 115, 120

Great Clarendon Street, Oxford, OX2 6DP, United Kingdom

Oxford University Press is a department of the University of Oxford.
It furthers the University's objective of excellence in research,
scholarship, and education by publishing worldwide. Oxford is a
registered trade mark of Oxford University Press in the UK and in
certain other countries

© Oxford University Press 2014

The moral rights of the authors have been asserted

First published in 2014

All rights reserved. No part of this publication may be reproduced,
stored in a retrieval system, or transmitted, in any form or by any
means, without the prior permission in writing of Oxford University
Press, or as expressly permitted by law, by licence or under terms
agreed with the appropriate reprographics rights organization.
Enquiries concerning reproduction outside the scope of the above
should be sent to the Rights Department, Oxford University Press,
at the address above.

You must not circulate this work in any other form and you must
impose this same condition on any acquirer

British Library Cataloguing in Publication Data
Data available

978-0-19-830720-4

10 9 8 7 6

Paper used in the production of this book is a natural, recyclable
product made from wood grown in sustainable forests.
The manufacturing process conforms to the environmental
regulations of the country of origin.

Printed in Great Britain by CPI Antony Rowe

**Acknowledgements**
The publisher and the authors would like to thank the
following for permissions to use their photographs:

**Cover image**: Ase/Shutterstock

Although we have made every effort to trace and contact all
copyright holders before publication this has not been possible
in all cases. If notified, the publisher will rectify any errors or
omissions at the earliest opportunity.

Links to third party websites are provided by Oxford in good faith
and for information only. Oxford disclaims any responsibility for
the materials contained in any third party website referenced in
this work.